The Complete Book of Perfect Phrases for Managers

Douglas Max, Robert Bacal, Harriet Diamond, and Linda Eve Diamond

New York Chicago San Francisco Lisbon
London Madrid Mexico City Milan New Delhi
San Juan Seoul Singapore Sydney Toronto

1 2 3 4 5 6 7 8 9 0   FGR/FGR   0 1 4 3 2 1 0 9 8

ISBN: 978–0–07–148565–4
MHID: 0–07–148565–1

This is a compilation of previously published McGraw-Hill books:

Douglas Max and Robert Bacal, *Perfect Phrases for Performance Reviews*, (0-07-140838-X) © 2002

Douglas Max and Robert Bacal, *Perfect Phrases for Setting Performance Goals* (0-07-143383-X) © 2004

Harriet Diamond and Linda Eve Diamond, *Perfect Phrases for Motivating and Rewarding Employees*, (0-07-145896-4) © 2005

This publication is designed to provide accurate and authoritative information in regard to the subject matter covered. It is sold with the understanding that neither the author nor the publisher is engaged in rendering legal, accounting, futures/securities trading, or other professional service. If legal advice or other expert assistance is required, the services of a competent professional person should be sought.

—From a Declaration of Principles jointly adopted by
a Committee of the American Bar Association
and a Committee of Publishers

McGraw-Hill books are available at special quantity discounts to use as premiums and sales promotions, or for use in corporate training programs. To contact a representative please visit the Contact Us pages at www.mhprofessional.com

Contents

Section One

Perfect Phrases for Performance Reviews

Hundreds of Ready-to-Use Phrases That Describe Your Employees' Performance (from "Unacceptable" to "Outstanding")

Douglas Max
Robert Bacal

Section Contents

Part III: Perfect Phrases for Performance Reviews 45

Topics Listed Alphabetically

Topics by Job Category

General Job Skills/Traits

The Complete Book of Perfect Phrases for Managers

Management/Leadership/Supervisory

Management Control

Communications/Interpersonal

Personal Qualities/Characteristics

Preface

Performance reviews are a delicate matter. Most managers want to write good, fair, and professional performance appraisals, but it's not always easy to find the "perfect phrase."

This book makes it easy by providing hundreds of "perfect phrases" managers can use on performance appraisal forms, to describe the performance of any employee in 74 skill areas—from "Accuracy" to "Initiative" to "Productivity" to "Time Management Skills." Managers can choose phrases from five performance levels that are used on many performance appraisal forms:

1. Outstanding
2. Exceeds Expectations
3. Meets Expectations
4. Needs Improvement
5. Unacceptable

The phrases include general descriptions of employee performance, such as "shows strong initiative," as well as specific behavioral recommendations, such as "needs repeated instruction when learning a new task."

Part I of this book includes some general tips on planning and conducting a performance appraisal. Part II shows some examples of performance appraisal forms, using the phrases in this book. Part III, the core of the book, contains hundreds of "perfect phrases" to describe performance and provide direction for improvement on a performance appraisal form.

Using this book will make it easier to appraise direct reports quickly and fairly. It will give you the phrases you need to accurately describe their performance and help you help them improve their skills and guide their career development.

Acknowledgments

This book is the result of a collaboration. John Woods of CWL Publishing Enterprises asked us to take this project on. We agreed, seeing the value of this for anyone who administers performance appraisals. Richard Narramore of McGraw-Hill, who initiated the project, has been helpful and supportive throughout its development. Bob Magnan and Nancy Woods, also of CWL, edited the manuscript and have a lot to do with the final product you now hold. We thank them all.

Douglas Max
Robert Bacal

Part I

Background for Conducting Performance Reviews

How to Plan, Conduct, and Write a Performance Review

Undertaking formal performance appraisals is not usually an activity most managers relish, but it's an important part of the job of a manager. And it gives you an opportunity, when done correctly, to positively affect the future of your employees. Conducting an effective appraisal means more than just filling out the form your company uses, however. What goes on before you fill out the form is critical to getting the results you're looking for.

However, if you want to simply fill out the form, skip ahead to Part II. But if you need some help in thinking about and preparing for the appraisals you have to conduct, continue reading.

As part of the appraisal process in many organizations, the manager and employee have a meeting where the manager explains the appraisal process and the criteria for judging performance. If the process involves goals, the manager and employee discuss and agree on what both of them would like to see achieved over a certain time period (usually a year) and, perhaps, the kind of resources the employee will need to succeed. If you are responsible for defining employee goals, then use the initial meeting to explain these goals (and how you will work together to achieve those goals, if appropriate).

Throughout the year, document significant behaviors that are worthy of discussing during a performance review. Just keep notes as you observe the performance of your employees. It's simple and easy to do—far easier than waiting until the end of the year and then trying to recollect what happened.

Setting Performance Goals

What is a goal? It's an agreed-upon statement of what an employee will achieve in a specified period of time. A goals statement should also explain the resources necessary to achieve the goals and how you and your employee will measure success.

Each goal should be measurable, attainable, moderately difficult, and accepted by the employee. Here are some examples:

- Number of rejected items from manufacturing line will not exceed .3% per week.
- Sales per quarter will increase by 5%.
- Expense account will not exceed budget.
- Sign up five new customers per month.

In other words, goals should be measurable and aimed at improving the performance of the employee.

Why do we write goals? Written goals allow you to both measure and recognize achievement. They also let you identify and correct performance problems, and they enable you to identify and focus on your top priorities. Aim to limit the number of long-term goals to no more than five. You can also write additional short-term goals for projects that can be completed in a few weeks or months.

How do you write goals? To write goals, you'll first need to collect information from your own records and those of your employees. The next section will explain the kind of information you might use.

What kind of information will you need? This question is best answered by you and your employees, because it depends on the specific situation and each job. Some guidelines:

Most goals will relate to productivity that is generally expressed in terms that include

- Volume of work
- Accuracy of work
- Time to produce X
- Cost per unit of X

Volume measures the amount of work performed, for example, the number of

- orders entered
- cartons packed
- requisitions written
- documents filed

Accuracy measures the degree to which the work is performed free of error, or the quality of the work, for example, the percentage of

- orders entered accurately vs. inaccurately
- cartons packed correctly vs. incorrectly
- requisitions written correctly vs. incorrectly
- documents filed accurately vs. inaccurately

Time measures the duration of the work performed, per hour, per day, per week, per month, per year. Examples include

- claims processed per hour/day/week
- requisitions received and written on the 1st day/2nd day/3rd day
- documents received and filed on the 1st day/2nd day/3rd day

Cost measures the dollars spent for work performed, for example,

$$\frac{\text{Average number of orders per day by the department}}{\text{Average daily wage for department}} = y$$

$$\frac{\text{Average number of claims processed per day by employee}}{\text{Average hourly wage for department}} = y$$

$$\text{Number of requisition errors resulting in rewrites} \times$$
$$\text{Cost per rewrite} = y$$

What if goal achievement is difficult to measure? There may be times when an employee has goals that you *cannot* easily measure. This does not mean that you should not have such goals. Just be certain to have some criteria for evaluating the level of achievement. Here are some examples:

- **Monthly reports.** "Performance is acceptable when I turn in completed monthly reports no more than two times late in any four-month period, without more than one incident of it being more than one week late in any six-month period, and when it is accepted by my boss in all cases with no more than two revisions that are completed in no more than one week."
- **Forecasting.** "I will not fail to bring to my boss's attention adverse trends in my performance before the failure point is reached, no more than two times in any 12-month period."

■ **Employee development.** "Performance is acceptable when training, motivation, and appraisal are discussed during at least two meetings annually between me and each of my direct reports."

Documenting Critical Incidents and Significant Behaviors

An important part of the appraisal process involves recording incidents and behaviors that are out of the ordinary. These are referred to as "critical incidents" and "significant behaviors." A critical incident is behavior that is usually extreme (either good or bad) and that should be recorded for legal reasons, for disciplinary measures, or for purposes of recognizing exemplary actions "above and beyond the call of duty." A significant behavior is one that can make a real difference in an employee's performance.

There are many reasons you should keep record of employees' significant behaviors:

■ It increases the accuracy of the performance appraisal, because it's based on documentation rather than memory.
■ It provides evidence to support ratings.
■ It helps guarantee that you'll consider the performance during the entire appraisal period.
■ It reduces bias that occurs when you rate only the most recent behavior.

To be as accurate as possible, write significant behaviors down *as soon as possible* after you have observed the behavior. Record only the specific behavioral facts of the case. Do not include opinions. Do not rely on hearsay! To ensure that the documentation is a representative record of an individual's performance, document performance during the entire appraisal period.

In documenting behaviors, be consistent in how you do it. Use the same format and the same level of detail with each individual. Document both productive and unproductive behaviors. Documenting significant behaviors helps to make the performance evaluation interview more productive. You'll be more confident going into the interview if you have a record of behaviors to back up your ratings because you'll be more confident you're rating your employee accurately.

Documenting significant behavior helps improve communication in the interview. There is less likelihood to be disagreement about whether an event occurred or not when you have documented behaviors and incidents. It helps keep the tone of the entire appraisal constructive rather than judgmental. Instead of dealing with impressions, you're dealing with *specific examples* of performance. The discussion can focus on how the performance can be improved in the future. Employees are better able to see their deficiencies. They know what they must do in order to improve.

The feedback to employees, both positive and critical, from significant behaviors can enhance employee motivation to improve. When an employee sees that specific behaviors are noted and appreciated, he or she will feel good and work harder to generate such feedback. In the case of behaviors that undermine performance, the employee may not have been aware of the problems. Here are some examples of significant behaviors you might note:

- Customer called after hours with urgent need for a replacement part to deal with an emergency situation. Employee personally delivered part, substantially reinforcing the loyalty of an important customer.

- Made specific suggestion on manufacturing process that resulted in $50,000 in savings over a six-month period.
- Angrily reacted to an incident on the shop floor that intimidated other employees and made it more difficult to investigate what happened.

Accurate documentation of specific behavior and incidents allows an employee to understand which on-the-job behaviors are productive and which are not. Such information gives employees what they need to improve.

Writing the Appraisal

If you've collected significant behaviors during this appraisal period, then the first step in writing an appraisal that will result in improved or continued good performance is to review these notes. Review also any results or other metrics you have to judge how well the employee has met his or her goals.

Even if your appraisal form only calls for you to "check a box," you generally can add additional comments to justify or explain the rating. In fact, if the appraisal process is to have any value to the employee, you must provide more information than a numeric rating. If you aren't required to make comments, you may want to consider including them on the appraisal form anyway.

Combined with the significant behavior statements and actual work results, you're most of the way to completing a form and documenting an effective appraisal.

Common Performance Review Errors

Another thing you'll want to do is to review the common errors made during the appraisal process. It's a wee bit more complicated than you think—the business of providing fair and objective feedback to employees—because … well, you're human. You can easily avoid or reduce errors by understanding what errors are common and following the suggestions below for dealing with them.

Contrast Error. The tendency to evaluate a person relative to other individuals, rather than on the requirements of the job. An example would be rating someone low, even though he or she was above average, because everyone else in the department is superior. A review should be based on comparing performance with established criteria.

First-Impression Error. The tendency to make an initial favorable or unfavorable judgment, which judgment serves as the basis for appraising future performance. All subsequent information is ignored or perceptually distorted. By considering behavior throughout the rating period, you'll reduce this error.

Recency Effect. The tendency to give extra weight to what you have seen recently and diminish the importance of observations you may have made earlier in the review period. In some cases it may be appropriate to weight recent behavior more than old behavior, particularly if it shows improvement. Otherwise, be sure to consider the entire period of appraisal.

Halo Effect. Generalizing from one aspect of performance to all aspects of performance. People have strengths and weaknesses. It is important to evaluate all aspects of performance throughout the period of the review.

Devil Effect. The opposite of the halo effect, generalizing from one or two negative aspects of performance and becoming blind to the positive aspects of the performance.

Similar-to-Me Effect. The tendency to judge more favorably those people whose background is similar to yours. The more similar the attitudes and background, the greater the tendency to judge that individual favorably. Appraise performance and behaviors, not personality or background.

Central Tendency. Occurs when an employee is consistently rated at or near the midpoint of the scale, regardless of the actual level of performance. This is a problem for several reasons. Such evaluations don't differentiate between good and bad performers. And they're particularly damaging to the motivation of high achievers, and they don't provide a realistic basis for discussing actual performance and improvements during the appraisal discussion.

Negative or Positive Leniency. Occurs when an employee is rated too hard (negative leniency) or too easy (positive leniency). Again, it creates a problem because the appraisal doesn't reflect true performance. With negative leniency, good performers may get tired of trying to perform well; no matter what they do, they'll be rated lower. With positive leniency, employees may have unrealistic expectations about raises, promotions, or other career gains.

To reduce rating errors:

- Ensure that the criteria being used are job related.
- Rate employees in relation to the job responsibilities.
- Put other people's input into proper perspective and don't weigh it too heavily. If you feel that this additional input warrants any changes in the appraisal, discuss it with your boss.
- Consider all performance dimensions and realize that they are not always related. A person can do very well on one dimension and perform poorly on another.

- Don't rate people in any particular order. Do not rate all the best or worst performers first.
- Do not compare the ratings of employees until after all employee evaluations are complete.

Legal Issues

When an employment situation becomes a legal situation, there's no substitute for proof—you must have records or other evidence proving that an employee did or did not do something ... whether it's stealing, lying, or being late too many times.

What may be more important is that you document the communication you have with employees, particularly when it involves discussion of performance problems. Generally, if you have not notified or discussed problems with the employee and documented those discussions, you have less backup if the employee accuses you of discrimination or similar charges. That means ensuring that the employee signs any documents you keep about communication with the employee.

Be on the alert for performance that's out of the ordinary, either good or bad, and make a note of it. That way, when it comes time to do the appraisal review, you'll be prepared, and you'll be similarly prepared for court, should it ever come to that.

The best way to deal with legal issues is to prevent them by conducting a competent, fair appraisal; demonstrating that you've invested a lot of time analyzing this employee's performance. Then conduct the review as we suggest and you'll substantially minimize the chances that your conduct would lead to a suit or other legal action. Here are some specifics to remember:

- Keep copies of HR records even if the HR department also has these records.

- Maintain accurate performance data.
- Meet regularly with employees to provide the feedback and information they need to perform well, also reducing any surprises and the motivation to sue.
- Document, document, document.

Conducting the Review

How to talk about your employees' performance. The first thing you can do to conduct an effective performance appraisal is to make sure that there are no surprises in store for the employee. This means that you should have communicated with your employees on a regular basis about how they are doing with their particular assignments and how they are collaborating with others.

The formal appraisal session should be mainly a way to summarize and continue the informal interaction that has previously taken place between you and your employees. It should also be a time to look at how you and the employee can continue to work well together in the future. Your job in this session is not to tell the employee all the things you think he or she did wrong over the past year. One reason performance appraisal sessions are often dreaded is that managers and employees feel the managers have to find something to criticize about the person being appraised. What can happen in that situation is that the manager might mention a negative comment the employee made or the fact that the employee was late to work two times over the past six months or similar trivial points. This causes the employee to feel resentful and become defensive.

Approach the person you're appraising as a partner rather than a judge. This will minimize hostility. Also, by focusing on your employee's development rather than on fault-finding, you'll set a positive tone and the discussion will become more productive and easier for both of you.

You may be conducting a performance review because it's required, but it's also a great opportunity to help your employees achieve job goals. Talk with your employees one on one about your expectations for them. Talk about goals, resources to help them achieve these goals, and what you're planning on doing to help. With some, you'll set goals to meet certain performance results; with others, you might set target levels for different "ratings"; for others, the goals might be relating to on-the-job behavior; for others still, the goals might target both behaviors and results.

Set goals, work toward them with your employees, and discuss what happened at the next review—easier said than done! Nevertheless, employees want to know where they stand. They want to receive feedback on their performance. Both ongoing discussions and periodic performance appraisals enable you to provide employees with this information.

Tell them the purpose. Since performance helps determine salary, job assignments, transfers, promotions, demotions, and termination, it is important to tell the employee that you're rating his or her performance based on responsibilities and goals.

The appraisal discussion is also a time to discuss the employee's job expectations and the organization's expectation of the employee. You should also encourage the employee to talk about any other job-related issues or concerns.

Minimize reluctance. Many employees are not enthusiastic about performance appraisals because previous ones seemed "a waste of time" or unpleasant. Your skill will determine whether employees regard the discussion with enthusiasm or dread. You can change their attitudes by listening to their concerns and by explaining how you plan to handle the meeting and that the main purpose is to help you both improve.

Gain the employee's commitment. You want the employee to actively participate in the entire appraisal process. This can happen if the employee understands that it will be a two-way discussion of performance. The employee should also understand that the purpose of the appraisal is to recognize success and plan improvement where necessary.

To ensure your appraisal meeting is successful, review the recommendations below and then follow the steps outlined later to help guide you through the meeting.

- Discuss actual performance data/significant behaviors.
- Compare data with responsibilities/goals.
- Rate performance (if appropriate in your appraisal system).
- Maintain positive focus.
- Focus on solving problems, not finding fault.
- Solicit and use input from employees.
- Evaluate objectively.
- Provide recognition.
- Discuss specific actions for you and the employee to take.
- Express confidence.

Discuss actual performance data/significant behaviors. If the performance appraisal discussion is to be effective, you should have performance data and significant behaviors for each area of measurement. The employee should have access to this same data before the appraisal session. Both you and the employee must feel that the data is objective and accurate. If the employee reviews the data prior to the appraisal, you can handle any question about its objectivity and accuracy before the appraisal discussion.

Compare data with responsibilities/goals. This way both you and the employee know whether he or she has met, exceeded, or missed the goals for the job. Before the session in some organizations, it is the employee's responsibility to also prepare data on goal achievement.

Rate performance. Rate the employee's performance in each area of measurement, based upon actual data. The ratings should take into account any factors outside the employee's control that contributed to achieving or failing to achieve his or her goals. It's a good idea to discuss your ratings with your immediate supervisor so that both of you are confident that your ratings are justifiable.

Maintain positive focus. If the employee's overall performance rating is satisfactory, the emphasis of feedback should be that he or she is doing well. Allow sufficient time to discuss and recognize those areas where performance met or exceeded goals. Exploring the factors that led to success will help you and the employee build on strengths to increase productivity in the future.

Focus on solving problems, not finding fault. In those areas where the employee is not meeting expectations with regard to responsibilities or goals, the emphasis should be on identifying the causes, focusing on solutions, and outlining specific actions that will enable the employee to meet those expectations. The discussion should be future-oriented, focusing on plans for improvement. Expression of concern with past poor performance should be balanced with recognition of achievements, if overall performance is satisfactory.

Solicit and use input from employees. You should actively involve the employee in the performance appraisal discussion. In addition to sharing performance data and participating in the problem-solving discussion, the employee may also have additional items or concerns to discuss. Be prepared to discuss these items openly and work toward solutions. The employee may want to discuss salary, career opportunities, or barriers to satisfactory performance, such as insufficient resources, lack of management support, etc. If you cannot adequately address such issues during the appraisal discussion, you should set a follow-up date to discuss these items at length.

Evaluate objectively. This means that you're focusing on performance and the factors that led to success or the obstacles that got in the way of success. You are not evaluating the person but his or her performance in a fair and dispassionate way. If the employee knows this is what you are doing and that both of you are there to help each other succeed, the session will be much more productive.

Provide recognition. Praise the employee for those things done well. When you praise, you're helping the person know what he or she is doing well in order to continue to do those things. It also creates a positive tone for the session.

Discuss specific actions for you and the employee to take. At the conclusion of the session, list specific actions the employee will take to finish old business, take on new goals, and improve his or her skills. Also list the actions you will take to support the employee in these activities.

Express confidence. Let the employee know that you feel good about his or her abilities and that you're there to help the employee succeed and that you're confident that, working together, this will happen and that you are glad to be working with him or her.

Making the Session Go Smoothly

As you undertake appraisal, here are some ways you can make the actual session go smoothly:

■ Put the employee at ease at the start of the session. Do this by acknowledging that these sessions can be a little nerve-wracking, but that the purpose is to help everyone in the work group improve and to gather information on how to help these improvement efforts.

■ Ask the employee what he or she thinks of his or her total performance—not just strong or weak areas. In this way, you get an overall sense of how the employee thinks he or she is doing.

■ Question the employee about what he or she thinks his or her personal strengths are. This chance to describe what he or she does best helps the employee feel positive about the appraisal.

■ Tell the employee what you believe his or her strengths are. This demonstrates that you are paying attention to performance.

■ Describe those areas where you think the employee might improve; use documentation to demonstrate why you are making these observations. Then ask the employee what he or she thinks of this and listen silently to the response. His or her reasons for poor performance or problems on the job might include lack of training, personality conflicts with other employees, misunderstandings about expectations or responsibilities, lack of knowledge about how to use new equipment, and physical obstacles, such as poor lighting or poorly maintained equipment.

- Assuming that you can identify the cause of poor performance, ask the employee what you two can do together to take care of it.
- Set new goals for performance for the next appraisal period.
- Keep a record of the meeting, including a timetable for performance improvement and what each of you will do to ensure that happens.
- Be open and honest, yet considerate of the employee's feelings. The goal is to facilitate improvement for the individual, the team, and the organization.

After the appraisal session, it's vital to follow up on what you and the employee have agreed on during the session. It indicates that you and the organization are serious about improvement.

- Mark your calendar to meet with individual employees to review their progress.
- Set up training as needed to address skill deficiencies.
- If a personal problem is involved, arrange for the employee to get counseling, if it is available.
- If an employee continues to perform poorly, make him or her aware of the consequences (discipline, demotion, or termination).
- Provide positive feedback when you see improvements in performance.

How to Talk About Salary

Performance reviews are often held as separate meetings from discussions about salary. If it's this way in your company, then you should explain that to the employee as well as the reasons for doing it this way.

Presumably it's because the focus of the discussion is performance and not money, which will be considered at another time.

You may, though, be able to tell employees more, such as that their performance was superior and that it will bring them nearer the higher bonuses or that their overall performance was below par, and so that's approximately what they might expect with their bonus.

If an employee is adamant about discussing salary and it's against the policy in your company, then you should schedule a meeting to discuss that topic.

Perfect Phrases for Performance Reviews

When documenting performance or justifying the rating you've given an employee, try to focus on behaviors and results. Work on finding a phrase that best describes how you judge the person's performance in a particular area. Helping you do that is the purpose of this book, but you should, of course, modify these phrases to fit your particular situation. Since there are many related categories in the phrases in Part III, be sure to check all appropriate categories to find phrases that will work best for you in a particular situation.

For example, take a phrase like "exceedingly competent," delete "exceedingly," and you're left with "competent." Substitute "not very," "sometimes," etc. and you've got an entirely different meaning—something that may more accurately reflect the shade of meaning you're looking for.

There are two types of phrases or items in each category. One type describes that characteristic in general terms; the other type includes some more behavioral or results-oriented phrases you might use in the appraisal. For these behavioral items, you should, of course, include your own terms, numbers, etc. and place them under the appropriate rating on the form you're using.

You might also use these concrete items to establish goals or as the basis for creating a rating scale. For example, you'll give an employee an "outstanding" or a "5" rating if she makes 1% or fewer errors, an "exceeds expectations" or "4" for 2 to 5% errors, and so on.

Part II

Examples of Forms for Performance Reviews

Performance Appraisal Review Forms

The purpose of this book is to provide you with hundreds of phrases to facilitate the performance appraisal process. In keeping with that goal, this part of the book includes a few examples of appraisal forms used in three organizations. All of these are different from one another, yet all require the person doing the appraising to include descriptive phrases such as those found in Part III.

We have edited and reformatted these forms to fit in this book. The parts of the forms that would use phrases like those included in this book are filled in. The other parts are included so you can see the entire form, including instructions on one of them that define levels of performance and the parts that require the manager and employee to put down their thoughts and goals for the next review period. You can use these examples for models as you use this book to undertake your appraisals.

Performance Expectations/Review		
Key Results Expected:		
10% reduction in waste 5 suggestions for improvement from all employees and so on		

Key Job Competencies:

Competency Group	Competency	Examples/Comments
Communication	Facilitate Communication	Effectively builds interactivity with others
	Oral Communication	Articulate and well-organized
	Written Communication	Writes quickly, clearly, and correctly
Continuous Improvement	Initiative and Innovation	Is above the norm in showing initiative
	Flexibility	Will reset priorities as required
	Technical Expertise	Has mastered SPC techniques
Leadership	Leadership	Led group to exceed sales targets in 14 of 15 regions
	Empowering Others	Turns on the motivation for excellece among employees
	Use of Influence	Demeanor sets an example for others
	Coaching	Delivers feedback directly and constructively
Teamwork	Professional Conduct	Manages the team process with great skill
	Responsiveness	Keeps others informed of status of projects affecting them

We have discussed and agreed upon the above performance competencies.

_____   _____
Employee Signature   **Manager Signature**

Example 1. A form with the focus on competencies

Performance Planning and Review Document	
Employee's Name: _____	**Postition Title:** _____
Hire Date: _____	**Review Date:** _____
Department: _____	**Supervisor's Name:** _____

Items for Discussion	Supervisor's Comments (Required)
Professionalism	
Attitude	Direct, straightforward, and honest. Always focuses on getting things done.
Acceptance of Responsibility	Williingly accepts responsibility for new projects.
Dependability	Always delivers on promises.
Professional/Personal Growth	Demonstrates continuous learning.
Work	
Job Knowledge	Maintains knowledge through training and seminars.
Work Quality	Quality of outputs meets standards.
Customer Service	Solves customer problems with speed and accuracy.
Communication	Articulate and well-organized speaker.
Teamwork	Mostly an optimistic team player.
Flexibility	Able to shift focus rapidly.
Safe/Unsafe Work Practices	Has violated a safety rule only once.
Optional Factors	
Employee-Input Form	
Attached and discussed	

Example 2. A form that focuses on job characteristics (p. 1)

Performance Planning and Review Document
Additional comments by supervisor:
Comments by employee:
Other performance issues discussed during this review period: ____ **Yes, please indicate if other documentation exists ...** ____ **No**
Supervisor and employee are required to sign the form. Signatures indicate that supervisor and employee have discussed performance and the comments written on this document. Signatures do not necessarily indicate agreement. **Supervisor's Signature:**   **Date:** **Employee's Signature:**   **Date:** **Next-Level Supervisor's Signature:**   **Date:**

Example 2. A form that focuses on job characteristics (p. 2)

Performance Appraisal	
Employee's Name	**Title**
Review Period __/__/__ to __/__/__	**Employee SSN**
Work Location	**Supervisor's Name**
Type of Review ___ 90 day ___Performance	

INSTRUCTIONS

1. Rating: Rate the employee in each job area, unless it is not applicable, by placing the rating in the box that best indicates where the employee stands in relation to the accountability. Every factor must be either rated or marked "NA/NO" (Not applicable/ Not observed). Indicate the overall rating at the end of the job areas.

2. Remarks: Use the "Remarks" space after each job area to explain in more detail or to give examples of that area. All except level 3 require comments.

3. Summary: Complete the Major Accomplishments, Job-Related Strengths, Areas for Improvement/Development, Action Plan sections. Have the employee complete the Employee Comments section. Use additional sheets if needed.

4. Human Resources Review: Human Resources must review and sign the evaluation before the actual review is conducted.

5. Signatures: Sign the review and have the employee sign before submitting the original form to Human Resources for filing in the employee's personnel file.

Ratings and Meanings:

5   Performance consistently exceeds job requirements. Demonstrates unusually high level of performance relative to all assignments and objectives. Distinguished performance overall.

4   Performance meets and often exceeds job requirements. Demonstrates successful performance on all major assignments and objectives and consistently exceeds position requirements in some areas.

3   Performance consistently meets job requirements. Demonstrates successful performance on all or most major assignments and objectives.

2   Performance is inconsistent; meets some job requirements but not consistently. Overall performance is below the acceptable level and must improve to meet minimum position requirements.

1   Performance is consistently below job requirements. Fails to meet position requirements in most areas. A corrective action plan and performance improvement are mandatory.

NA/NO   This accountability is not applicable or has not been observed by the reviewer.

Example 3. A form that uses numerical ratings (p. 1)

Job Area	Remarks	Rating
1. *Professional Knowledge/Work Knowledge/Skills:* Possesses and applies knowledge or skills necessary for task completion. Keeps current on new developments in area of work.	Knowledge exceeds what is required to perform well.	4
2. *Quality of Work:* Assignments are accurate, complete, and comply with objectives.	Performs efficiently and well.	3
3. *Quantity of Work:* Produces significant volume of work to support goals within specified time frames.	Work is regularly completed on time and error-free.	3
4. *Communication:* Maintains open, effective communications with all employees and clients. Written and verbal communications are clear, concise, and understandable.	Can explain complicated procedures well. Can express herself clearly in written communication.	4
5. *Teamwork:* Willingly cooperates, shares information, assists, and is tolerant of others in daily interaction with all employees, vendors, and clients.	Gets along well with fellow team members.	3
6. *Reliability:* Can be relied upon to complete tasks and follow up as needed.	Does not disappoint when deadlines are tight.	4
7. *Adaptability/Flexibility:* Easily adjusts to changes in routine, assignments, and company/client needs and continues to be productive.	Willingly assumes others' tasks in case of absences.	5
8. *Initiative:* Voluntarily recommends resourceful, alternative, or original ideas/procedures for work improvement or problem solution.	Will take risks to accommodate customers. Instituted extranet connection for vendor X to improve project coordination.	4
9. *Planning/Scheduling:* Prioritizes tasks, anticipates needs, and makes adjustments.	Others regularly rely on her scheduling abilities.	5
10. *Problem Solving:* Identifies problems within own area, develops resourceful solutions, and makes recommendations for corrective action.	Thorough in analyzing and developing solutions.	4

Example 3. Part of page 2 of the same form, laying out specific characteristics, with definitions of each area, places for comments, and a space for numerical ratings

Summary
Sections 1, 2, 3, and 4 should be completed by the supervisor. Section 5 should be completed by the employee.
1. Major accomplishments since last review
2. Job-related strengths
3. Areas for improvement/development
4. Action plan
5. Employee comments

Signatures
I acknowledge that this review has been discussed with me. My signature does not imply agreement or disagreement.
Employee: Date:
Supervisor: Date:
Human Resources: Date:

Example 3. A form that shows numerical ratings (p. 3)

Part III

**Perfect Phrases for
Performance Reviews**

Part III Contents (Alphabetical)

Topics by Job Category

General Job Skills/Traits

Technical Skills

Productivity

Management/Leadership/Supervisory

Accuracy

Outstanding
- Maintains high accuracy under tight deadlines
- Mistakes don't slip through
- Achieves zero errors when required
- Trusted to do tasks demanding high accuracy
- Less than 1% error rate

Exceeds Expectations
- Takes pride in accuracy and makes effort to improve
- Maintains accuracy even under pressure
- Managers have commented on high level of accuracy
- Identifies own errors early on

Meets Expectations
- Checks finished product before forwarding
- Uses technical tools to improve accuracy (e.g., spellchecker)
- Does not require constant supervision
- Balances accuracy with speed

Needs Improvement
- Sometimes makes small errors
- Less than 5% errors but more than 2%
- Excessively concerned about being perfect
- Does not check work before submitting
- Tends to miss small mistakes

Unacceptable
- Errors have caused money loss
- Mistakes have caused customer loss
- Error rate over ___%
- ___ customers have complained about errors
- Misses small and large mistakes

Administrative Skills

Outstanding
- Has improved many departmental procedures
- Effectively tracks the status of projects
- Handles many tasks simultaneously
- Documents are always ready when needed
- Created important new record-keeping systems
- Uses advanced PowerPoint functions

Exceeds Expectations
- Streamlined many procedures
- Administers accounts payable and receivable without error
- Administers many functions without error
- Thorough, reliable, and accurate
- Maintains vital information
- Sets priorities well

Meets Expectations
- Files and finds documents with ease
- Has all the administrative skills required
- Maintains important records
- Writes clear memos
- Sets priorities to ensure documents are ready when needed
- Uses software effectively
- Knows enough PowerPoint to create effective presentations

Needs Improvement
- Loses essential data occasionally
- Some records can't be found or are inaccurate
- Sometimes does not maintain records

➡

- Reports are lost on occasion
- Administration is a weakness
- Cannot create graphs
- Rarely relies on the computer to simplify tasks
- Makes grammatical and punctuation errors in memos

Unacceptable
- Administrative skills are negligible
- Memos are often unclear
- Uses condescending tone in staff memos
- Formatting errors make documents unusable
- Reports are often misfiled and lost
- Has missed a number of important deadlines

Analytic Skills

Outstanding
- Has outstanding analytic skills
- Can zero in on the cause of a problem and develop solutions
- Can perceive relationships in a mass of data
- Excellent analyst
- Translates analysis into actions that fit
- Communicates analysis results clearly and concisely

Exceeds Expectations
- Possesses good analytic skills
- Analysis shows insight
- Methodical analyst
- In six production failures, made a diagnosis and repair within two hours
- Communicates analysis results clearly to others

Meets Expectations
- Detail oriented
- Possesses the skills to solve basic on-the-job problems
- Analyzes data and makes appropriate recommendations
- Summarizes reports from five supervisors in time for Monday managers' meetings

Needs Improvement
- Needs to develop skills to analyze situations
- Frequently draws wrong conclusions from data
- Doesn't do detailed analysis
- Analysis sometimes focuses on the unimportant
- Delegates research

- Analytic results are questioned by others
- Makes analytic errors regularly
- Makes mathematical errors
- Errors caused problems in 3 out of 10 instances

Unacceptable
- Analysis is limited
- Does not have the analytic skills required
- Analytic skills are below what's necessary
- Frequently comes to the wrong conclusions
- Was unable to solve problems for 7 out of 10 customers on helpline

Appraisal and Evaluation Skills

Outstanding
- Conscientiously gathers information to fairly appraise
- Exceptionally fair
- Involves staff in appraisals
- Uses appraisal to build commitment and motivation
- Provides substantial documentation of performance
- Conducts appraisals on time
- Bases appraisal on pre-agreed goals
- Negotiates fair and appropriate goals
- Negotiates stretch goals to help employees improve

Exceeds Expectations
- Puts employees at ease
- Gains employees' motivation to perform better in the future
- Gets staff involved in the appraisal process
- Evaluations free from bias
- Performance focused
- Creates positive, developmental-focused tone
- Explains appraisal process clearly
- Prepares documents prior to each appraisal
- Negotiates goals

Meets Expectations
- Unbiased
- Handles appraisal responsibilities well
- Believes in the importance of appraisal
- Appraises job performance fairly
- Uses appraisals to achieve departmental goals
- Develops employees with appraisal process
- Involves employees in setting goals

- Records employees' reactions
- Documents significant behaviors

Needs Improvement
- Uncomfortable with appraisals
- Doesn't listen
- Rarely gets staff involved
- Critical, not developmental
- Gives goals, doesn't negotiate
- Appraisal discussions are one-sided
- Employees regularly disagree with appraisals

Unacceptable
- Biased ratings
- Does not set goals at beginning of appraisal period
- Appraisal documents are frequently late
- Does not involve staff in appraisal process
- Dictates, never negotiates goals with staff members
- Makes many rater errors
- Spends only __ minutes on appraisal

Attendance

Outstanding
- Always at work and on time
- Great attendance record
- Makes it to work unless seriously ill
- Never misses work without prior and appropriate notification
- Arrives at work at least __ minutes early every day
- Has missed only one day due to sickness in last three years

Exceeds Expectations
- Consistently arrives at work early
- Good attendance
- Has rarely missed work due to illness
- Clocks in at least five minutes early every day
- Has missed only two days because of illness

Meets Expectations
- Consistently arrives at work on time
- Attendance satisfactory
- Only misses work due to verified illness
- Leaves home early on inclement days to arrive on time
- Has not used more than allotted sick days
- Back from lunch on time

Needs Improvement
- Takes longer breaks than appropriate
- Arrives late at least one day a month
- Has missed work without prior notification 10 times this year
- Consistently uses all sick days
- Has arrived __ times late by __ minutes or more ➡

Unacceptable

- Poor attendance
- Not dependable
- Breaks are long and too frequent
- Gets to work late at least once a week
- Has used ___ sick days on Fridays or Mondays
- Has used ___ days over allotted sick days
- Does not come to work when it's raining
- Often is late more than ___ minutes
- Has failed to call in sick ___ times

Attitude or Approach to Work

Outstanding
- Cordial and happy to help
- Looks for ways to help others
- Comes to work 15 minutes early each day
- Always upbeat and optimistic
- Views success in relation to group's success
- Enthusiastic and energetic

Exceeds Expectations
- Positive, contagious spirit
- Direct, straightforward, and honest
- Winning attitude
- Always pleasant to be around
- Team player

Meets Expectations
- Rarely down
- Friendly and outgoing
- Cooperative and cordial
- Always focuses on getting things done
- Volunteered to be a member of the WorkLife Committee
- Has "can do" attitude

Needs Improvement
- Can be quarrelsome
- Can be negative
- Projects "in it for myself" attitude
- Rarely helps others
- Needs to be prompted to stop daydreaming
- Creates tension

➡

Unacceptable

- Aloof
- Can be snobbish
- Projects attitude of superiority that turns off other employees
- Presence often creates tension in group
- Not cooperative
- Frequently criticizes others
- Pessimistic
- Always finding fault with others

Coaching

Outstanding
- Coaches many to excel
- A role model, teacher, and guide
- Identifies weaknesses and solutions
- Inspires others to do better
- Outstanding ability to explain and teach

Exceeds Expectations
- Builds independence
- Very supportive of others' attempts at improvement
- Excellent at demonstrating appropriate procedures
- Delivers feedback directly and constructively
- Applauds effort

Meets Expectations
- Times coaching interventions effectively
- Does not overwhelm other person
- Draws out knowledge and skills from others
- Leads people to discover their own answers
- Available when needed
- Allocates time for the coaching process

Needs Improvement
- Isn't effective with people slow to learn
- Guides and coaches, but doesn't let others have responsibility
- Gets frustrated when others aren't learning
- Assumes too much knowledge on others' part
- Doesn't enable staff to reduce dependency
- Has difficulty integrating coaching with rest of job ➡

Unacceptable

- Dictates to others rather than involving them
- Has failed to develop a successor
- Insensitive to needs of other person
- Has reduced other person to tears
- Staff uncomfortable being coached by him/her
- Believes coaching not part of job

Communication Skills, Verbal

Outstanding
- Superior skills on phone and in meetings
- Speaks persuasively and convincingly
- Thoughtful and responsive to employees at all levels
- Is an articulate spokesperson for the team's views
- Builds interactivity with audience
- Develops clear, concise computer presentations

Exceeds Expectations
- Is convincing and confident when speaking
- Prepares for all communications
- Speaks articulately and concisely
- Adept at technical explanations
- Concludes on an upbeat note
- Answers questions directly

Meets Expectations
- Uses collateral material effectively
- Can explain complicated procedures well
- Rarely fumbles for an answer
- Seems comfortable while presenting
- Articulate and well-organized speaker
- Clear, understandable voice

Needs Improvement
- Speaks in monotone
- Is not confident when presenting
- Reads script and has little contact with audience
- Uncomfortable responding to questions
- Makes grammatical mistakes when speaking
- Positions often not clearly thought out

Unacceptable

- Often makes grammatical errors when speaking
- Does not build rapport when speaking with others
- Does not build audience participation when needed
- Often misunderstands what others are saying, leading to mistakes on the job
- Does not know how to ask questions that will guide work

Communication Skills, Written

Outstanding
- Exceptional communicator
- All writing is free of punctuation or grammatical errors
- Clear, concise, error-free writing
- Excellent at persuasive writing
- Wrote bids that gained business 7 out of 10 times
- Regularly receives positive feedback on clarity of writing

Exceeds Expectations
- Written communications easily understood
- Writes quickly, clearly, and correctly
- Uses resources when unsure of proper spelling, punctuation, or grammar
- Uses formatting effectively to highlight key information
- Documentation is consistently understood
- Translations of documentation were free of confusion
- E-mails and memos are clear and to the point

Meets Expectations
- Can express him/herself clearly in written communication
- Competent writer
- Makes few grammar or punctuation errors
- Spelling usually correct
- Conveys information reasonably clearly
- Writes professional communications, including e-mail

Needs Improvement
- The point of a written communication not always clear
- Hard to understand focus in written communications
- Makes grammatical and punctuation errors
- Takes a long time to get to the point ➥

- Written communications sometimes lead to misunderstandings
- Many people were confused about report X

Unacceptable
- Poor writer
- Numerous errors and lack of organization make understanding difficult
- Writing fails to meet company standards
- Writing represents our company poorly
- Many customers failed to understand the August Bulletin
- Poor written communication resulted in errors costing $_____

Computer Skills

Outstanding
- Expert in the use of Excel
- Easily uses the more difficult features of Word
- Solves all software and hardware problems quickly
- Has championed movement to paperless operations
- Designed, implemented, and manages department's intranet site
- Creates forms that are virtually foolproof
- Produced __ documents with only __ requiring rework
- Conducted __ Internet searches, with only __ requiring additional information

Exceeds Expectations
- Shows great skills in all areas
- Strengths are in many of our regularly used programs
- Helps others with advanced computer functions
- Established many protocols for file keeping
- Can quickly learn new programs
- Finds customer records quickly while on the phone
- Formatted __-page document within __ days from receipt of submissions
- Created database with __ fields (__ relational) in __ days
- Redesigned enterprise system to speed processing without affecting users

Meets Expectations
- Competent with all software used
- Can fix minor hardware problems
- Communicates expectations to IT personnel effectively
- Understands Windows basics

➡

- Handles computer problems without getting frustrated
- With the exception of Program X, keeps up with colleagues
- Entered __ customer delivery requests with __ errors

Needs Improvement
- Has difficulty with essential programs
- Makes repeated formatting errors
- Learning new software is a challenge
- Sometimes forgets to turn off computer
- Can't find saved files
- Loaded personal software against policy
- Caused two major system failures

Unacceptable
- Lacks the computer skills this job requires
- Makes repeated errors after repeated instructions
- Has not learned basics
- After six months still has problems finding customer records
- Asks questions found in help file
- Calls help desk frequently
- Doesn't heed warning messages
- Deleted required software in error

Conflict Management

Outstanding
- Has resolved several difficult conflicts this year
- Avoids escalation
- Received customer compliments for resolving a conflict
- Made partners out of enemies
- Acted as conflict troubleshooter within organization

Exceeds Expectations
- Looks for common ground
- Listens carefully to both sides
- Builds customer loyalty through conflict management
- Diplomatic without sidestepping critical issues
- Peers seek his/her advice in dealing with conflict situations
- Understands when compromise is needed

Meets Expectations
- Uses basic mediation techniques
- Uses outside personnel when necessary
- Handles conflict in calm, unemotional ways
- Remains calm in tough situations
- Effective third party in handling disputes

Needs Improvement
- Sometimes impatient with disagreement
- Becomes defensive in some conflicts
- Has an ongoing conflict with another staff member
- Starts unnecessary conflict when stressed
- Superiors sometimes need to step in

Unacceptable
- Has made several conflicts worse

- Will not yield in conflict
- Rarely makes compromises
- Argues for trivial reasons
- Often focuses on blaming others
- Does not recognize when outside help is needed
- Stubborn
- Attitude can cause conflict

Cooperation

Outstanding
- Does everything asked without objection
- Immediately puts clients' requests above other work
- Works in concert with others
- Unrivaled willingness to help
- Real team player
- Establishes rapport with everyone
- Works on four project teams, while a volunteer on two other teams

Exceeds Expectations
- Always asks others for extra work
- Shares ideas freely
- Will do what it takes to work with others
- Effective representative of department
- Works toward team goals without consideration of personal effect
- Formed team with representatives from departments affected by software program X

Meets Expectations
- Works well with other departments
- Puts good of company above that of department
- Is flexible with priorities
- Willing to cooperate
- Compliant to others' needs
- Received compliments on spirit of cooperation on the XYZ project

Needs Improvement
- Will object to work when it interferes with schedule
- Is often reluctant to help others on the job

- Won't bend on views without coercion
- Shows lack of cooperation on team projects
- Declined an offer to be part of XYZ team

Unacceptable
- Unwilling to cooperate
- Will not change views
- Inflexible and noncompliant
- Refused to follow rules during a spill cleanup
- Consistently neglects to mark hazardous waste according to regulations

Cost Cutting

Outstanding
- Overachieved cost-cutting targets this year
- Invented innovative cost-cutting measures
- Improved profit margin by ___% last year
- Developed company-wide cost-cutting suggestion program

Exceeds Expectations
- Developed methods to identify cost overruns
- Asks for cost-cutting suggestions from staff
- Used techniques (e.g., outsourcing) effectively
- Welcomes and evaluates any cost-cutting ideas

Meets Expectations
- Implemented corporate strategies
- Met cost-cutting goals
- Stays within budgeted guidelines
- Maintained productivity along with modest cost savings
- Treats company money as his/her own

Needs Improvement
- Sacrificed productivity by cutting too deep
- Insists on spending budget even if not needed
- Needs to improve methods for priority spending
- Has taken advantage of perks on travel status

Unacceptable
- Cost-cutting measures backfired
- Unit unable to function properly
- Spends with no reflection
- Supervisors need to scrutinize every expenditure
- Pads expenses

Creativity

Outstanding

- Is one of our most creative designers
- Exceedingly creative
- Changed campaign based on market surveys
- Solved a long-standing software glitch through a creative workaround
- Developed promotional concepts that won five clients
- Contributed workplace improvement ideas that saved the department $__
- Improved name recognition by __% in __ weeks
- Changed a software program to cut processing time by __%

Exceeds Expectations

- Sees things from a unique angle
- Unique perspectives
- Imaginative ideas for difficult problems
- Unique ideas for recurring issues
- Has solved many problems by looking from unique perspective
- Often has the edge our clients want
- Organized motivational field trip for staff
- Comes up with creative ideas often
- Redesigned workflow between departments that cut approval time 10%

Meets Expectations

- Has an appropriate level of creativity
- Imaginative vision
- Developed a number of new ideas for old problems
- Adds a creative flair to projects

- Always experimenting with new approaches
- Generated a pleasing template for customer letters
- Has a good eye for colors
- Has developed a number of creative solutions
- Generated a number of creative solutions for clients

Needs Improvement
- Prefers the tried and true over radically different ideas
- Lacks creativity
- Rarely has new ideas
- Could strengthen ability to see what's not there
- Needs to be more open to others' ideas
- Tends to be staid in thinking outside the box
- Ideas lack sparkle and pizzazz
- Mostly modifies others' ideas, rarely generates them
- Our clients rarely accept his ideas
- Had few suggestions while on the Quick Start Committee

Unacceptable
- Creativity far below what job requires
- Unimaginative
- Formats tend to be unstylish and dull
- Sees only what's there, not what's not
- Lacks the level of creativity required
- Does not suggest creative solutions to problems
- Fearful of the new and different
- Has not solved any old problems
- Locked into tried and true, not new
- Never contributes a creative idea
- Clients have not accepted ideas

Customer Relations

Outstanding

- Relates to customers exceedingly well
- Has developed an incredibly loyal customer base
- Wonderful at customer relations
- Resourceful in finding solutions to problems
- Always delivers on promises
- It's no wonder we have as many happy customers as we do
- Relates well to corporate and individual customers

Exceeds Expectations

- Has won us customer loyalty many times
- Graceful and tactful under pressure from customers
- Customer relations a strength
- Always patient, competent, and professional with customers
- Solves customer problems with speed and accuracy
- Represents our company very well

Meets Expectations

- Usually competent and professional with customers
- An able representative
- Courteous and knowledgeable
- Professional presentation
- Manages all but the most challenging customer situations
- Handles customer relations responsibilities well

Needs Improvement

- Gets annoyed by customers with a lot of questions
- Sometimes gets sarcastic
- Presents a sloppy and uncaring image

- Customer relations skills need improvement
- On several occasions has lost temper with customers
- Conducts personal phone conversations while customers wait

Unacceptable
- Frequently impolite
- Very weak customer relations skills
- Condescends to customers
- Ignores customers
- Chews gum while speaking with customers
- Shouted obscenities at a customer

Data Entry

Outstanding
- Extremely fast and accurate
- In top 5% for data entry
- Always willing to take on complicated projects
- Enters data for long periods while maintaining excellent accuracy

Exceeds Expectations
- Is very fast and accurate
- Always enters in proper fields
- Enters correct data in correct fields
- Has good stamina in working through a large amount of data
- Can enter _____ characters in _____ minutes

Meets Expectations
- Correctly enters data
- Takes and enters data correctly from customers
- Maintains good accuracy and speed
- Proofs while entering
- Completes data entry within expected time limits

Needs Improvement
- Is slower than most, with lower-than-average accuracy
- Slow at keying data
- Can't touch-type numbers
- Enters data incorrectly regularly
- Puts data in incorrect fields

Unacceptable
- Data entries contain an unacceptable amount of errors
- Frequently makes mistakes in data entry

- Doesn't catch entry errors
- Doesn't put data in proper fields
- Takes 2 hours where the standard entry time is 30 minutes

Deadlines, Ability to Meet

Outstanding
- Consistently ahead of schedule
- Volunteers to work with tight deadlines
- Quickly gets and stays on task
- Completed tasks on time when nobody else could

Exceeds Expectations
- Able to block out distractions
- Amazing task focus when needed
- Seems to thrive on pressure deadlines
- Maintains quality with tight timelines

Meets Expectations
- Generally delivers on time
- Meets deadlines well in periods of calm
- Requires little supervision in tough deadline situations
- Informs when delays anticipated

Needs Improvement
- Missed deadlines more than once this year
- Lack of organization skills sometimes causes delays
- Needs to be more independent to meet deadlines
- Hesitant to take on tough deadlines
- Flustered when deadlines changed

Unacceptable
- Often misses standard deadlines
- Cannot handle any short-deadline tasks or assignments
- Job may be too pressure-packed
- Not suited to any short-deadline work
- Doesn't admit to being behind schedule

Decision Making

Outstanding
- Clearly understands the implications of situations and uses sound judgment when deciding what to do
- Makes tough decisions
- Decisions always appropriate
- Weighs options carefully and thoroughly
- Can decide in the most challenging situations
- Will make decisions about major issues
- Can always be counted on to make good decisions when faced with a dilemma
- Decisions take into account the needs of all stakeholders

Exceeds Expectations
- Will make decision when others are afraid to commit to a course of action
- Analytic and decisive
- Decisions are well thought out
- Considers "human cost" in decisions
- Decisions always result of detailed analysis
- Makes decisions quickly and appropriately
- Involves others in decision making

Meets Expectations
- Usually makes appropriate decisions
- Gathers ample information to make reasoned decision
- Considers many alternatives
- Involves others appropriately when making decisions
- Bases decisions on facts not personalities
- Communicates decisions clearly and directly

Needs Improvement
- Delays making necessary decisions

- Often comes to management for help with a decision
- Sticks with status quo rather than make a decision
- Uses gut rather than facts for decision making
- Always accepts others' decisions

Unacceptable
- Extremely fearful of making a mistake
- Logic fails in decision making
- Often fails to see problems that require decisions
- Fails to gather necessary information for decision making
- Frequently makes bad decisions
- Never makes a decision
- Avoids decision-making situations

Dedication to Job/Work

Outstanding
- Is a "go-getter" in the best sense of the term
- Completes extensive research on potential clients before making a sales call
- Is focused on all projects
- Exceptionally dedicated
- Works overtime whenever asked
- Extremely dedicated and committed
- Follows directions precisely
- Questions unclear instructions
- Three days out of five, works until 8:00 P.M. to complete tasks

Exceeds Expectations
- Assumes personal responsibility
- Very committed
- Does whatever's necessary to satisfy customers
- Always shows a "can do" attitude
- Routinely works late
- Learns about new technologies affecting work
- Often skips breaks in order to minimize backlogs
- Came in on two Saturdays for extra practice
- Studies user manuals to gain greater skills in our database program

Meets Expectations
- Keeps promises
- Dedicated to goals
- Obeys policies
- Requested training to advance computer skills
- Shows pride in work

- Works regularly scheduled hours
- Completes work well enough to pass minimum standards

Needs Improvement
- Doesn't adhere to team goals
- Lacks commitment
- Rarely manifests real dedication
- Does the least required
- Leaves rework for next shift
- Often fails to follow directions
- Frequently engages in personal phone calls

Unacceptable
- Doesn't keep current on projects
- Apathetic about performance improvement
- His/Her work is very slow and inaccurate
- Works only when given a warning
- Leaves work for client undone at end of day
- Recommended a competitor's product during a customer service call
- Missed __ out of __ team meetings

Delegation

Outstanding
- Direct reports gained considerable skill through delegated responsibilities
- Delegates appropriate and challenging responsibilities
- Has strengthened department considerably through effective delegation
- Gives employees energizing and challenging assignments
- Always follows up on results of delegated projects
- Has divided the department's work among five task forces

Exceeds Expectations
- Frequently passes assignments from upper management to able staff members
- Uses delegation to develop staff
- Allows staff to take authority to fulfill responsibilities
- Keeps staff energized with new projects
- Rarely delegates menial tasks
- Creates challenging projects to delegate

Meets Expectations
- Usually keeps workload manageable by enlisting help
- Delegates responsibility with required authority
- Considers staff's capabilities before delegating
- Mixes the mundane and challenging
- Delegates fairly

Needs Improvement
- Fails to check on progress of delegated assignments
- Needs to delegate more challenging assignments

➡

- Fails to give clear directions or goals when delegating
- Stockpiles projects, waiting for time to complete them
- Makes many needless changes in others' work

Unacceptable
- Never delegates and is far behind schedule
- Doesn't consider employees' capabilities when assigning work
- Delegates without direction or support
- Does all complex, challenging projects
- Has failed to meet goals because of lack of delegation

Dependability

Outstanding
- Willingly takes accountability for all departmental activities
- Can always be counted on to complete assignments
- Always delivers on promises
- Highest level of dependability
- Achieves results with minimal resources
- Always achieves stated goals and more
- Assumes personal responsibility for his/her work
- Performs work independently and accurately
- Takes action and makes decisions quickly
- Always delivers on time
- Followed up personally with over __ customers

Exceeds Expectations
- Delivers on promises far more than not
- High level of accountability for projects
- Does not disappoint when deadlines are tight
- Almost always adheres to instructions/directions
- Performs most work independently
- Delivered __ of __ completed reports on time
- Missed only __ days of work in last year

Meets Expectations
- Appropriate level of accountability
- Delivers on promises
- Adheres to policies and guidelines
- Conscientious worker
- Accountable for projects
- Follows directions and instructions
- Needs little oversight on projects

➡

Needs Improvement

- Fails to accept accountability for missed deadlines
- Does not accept accountability for project failures
- Frequently fails to achieve goals
- Does not follow directions or instructions
- Needs oversight
- Doesn't take action or make decisions without direction
- Has missed deadlines __ times
- Returned late from breaks __ times in the year

Unacceptable

- Fails to ever accept accountability for own behavior or results
- Always attributes failure to others or circumstances
- Rarely delivers a project on time
- Does not achieve agreed upon goals
- Frequently does not follow directions or instructions
- Needs constant oversight
- Rarely takes action or makes decisions without guidance or direction
- Needs frequent reminders to keep projects on track
- Arrived late __ out of __ days in __ weeks
- Uses the phone for personal conversations

Development of Subordinates

Outstanding
- Exceedingly devoted to staff development
- Creative and dedicated to developing others
- Training and delegation combine to develop an excellent staff
- Always registers new employees for appropriate training
- Inspires staff to learn
- Always shares relevant company information with subordinates

Exceeds Expectations
- Invests time during all appraisals on personal development
- Has an "open door" to new employees who have questions about the job
- Reinforces and supports new employee orientation
- Uses delegation well to develop staff
- Excellent role model for continuous learning

Meets Expectations
- Gives employees advanced training and additional responsibilities
- Develops employees appropriately
- Regularly shares management information during staff meetings
- Every employee in the department received training in Excel

Needs Improvement
- Insufficient training has led to poor productivity
- Fails to develop staff in needed areas

- Does not appropriately develop staff to perform needed duties
- Her department suffered a 10% error rate due to inadequate training

Unacceptable
- Staff is poorly trained
- Delegates only menial tasks
- Error rate in department is unacceptable
- Received numerous customer complaints about staff's capability and courtesy
- Has repeatedly delayed giving new employees orientation to the department

Equal Opportunity/Diversity

Outstanding
- An excellent model of EEO practices
- Invites diverse ideas
- Ensures staff represents percentage of protected classes in population
- Sensitive to and respectful of all individuals
- Formed a task force to attract minority achievers

Exceeds Expectations
- Provides equal opportunities to members of protected classes
- Is free of bias in personnel evaluations
- Maintains pay equity for all staff in similar positions
- Ensures that staff from disadvantaged backgrounds receive appropriate training

Meets Expectations
- Bases all personnel decisions on performance
- Supports EEO and diversity values
- Shows no indication of bias
- Makes decisions based on performance, not personal characteristics
- Has hired from diverse ethnic backgrounds

Needs Improvement
- Needs to strengthen EEO/diversity orientation
- Has only white males in supervisory positions
- Members of protected classes and women are paid less
- Minorities enrolled in fewer training sessions
- Department lacks ethnic diversity

Unacceptable
- Has blatantly discriminated

- Will not interview minority candidates
- Has told off-color jokes in staff meetings
- Minorities consistently receive lower performance ratings
- Several lawsuits cite his failure to promote Hispanic workers despite their merit

Ethical Behavior

Outstanding
- Exceptionally scrupulous and honest in all activities
- Does what's right regardless of consequences
- Always demonstrates integrity and honesty
- Is exceptionally conscientious in potential conflict of interest situations
- Has received high praise for swift and generous remedies for product defects
- Has retained or gained new customers due to honesty

Exceeds Expectations
- Never lies or bends the truth
- Argues vigorously for fair dealing
- Created a clear values statement for staff about ethics
- Knows and follows applicable laws
- Customers have been happily surprised by honesty

Meets Expectations
- Deals with customers fairly
- Will not exploit loopholes in laws for benefit
- Staff understands and follows ethical guidelines
- Is noted for honesty and fairness

Needs Improvement
- Sometimes sees ethics as an inconvenience
- Has been known to stretch the law for gain
- Has behaved unethically in dealings with clients
- Complaints have been lodged about this store's bait-and-switch tactics

Unacceptable
- Does not behave ethically

- Has lied to others in department
- Violates our ethical guidelines
- The state's attorney general has initiated legal action
- Actions have resulted in customers refusing to do business with us

Feedback, Receiving and Giving

Outstanding
- Always offers criticism in a constructive manner
- Consistently receives feedback constructively
- Involves staff in deciding how to improve work output and quality
- Initiates changes based on all feedback appropriately
- Welcomes feedback, especially negative

Exceeds Expectations
- Delivers feedback in a sensitive and caring way
- Translates criticism into positive changes
- Seeks to understand rather than defend against negative feedback
- Explains feedback to institute behavioral changes
- Accepts all negative feedback positively

Meets Expectations
- Usually is receptive to feedback and appreciative
- Provides feedback to subordinates as necessary
- Works to learn from feedback received
- Delivers negative comments to staff while maintaining positive relations
- Can turn most criticism into appropriate action

Needs Improvement
- Is often silent when constructive criticism is called for
- Will criticize the person and not his or her actions
- Delivers negative feedback in a personally hurtful manner
- Tends to deliver feedback in an insensitive way
- Disagrees with constructive criticism, rather than accepting

Unacceptable

- Never offers criticism in a constructive manner
- Consistently receives feedback defensively and argumentatively
- Consistently shies away from providing necessary feedback
- Does not speak with staff about how to improve work output and quality
- Consistently takes feedback with negativity and disagreement

Financial Management

Outstanding
- Anticipates financial problems before they occur
- Provided meaningful information to decision makers
- Involves staff in financial improvement initiatives
- Implements prudent risk analysis

Exceeds Expectations
- Gets the most from scarce resources
- Implemented measures for financial accountability
- Uses accounting information to make decisions
- Actual expenditures within 10% of budget projections

Meets Expectations
- Understands and uses standard accounting practices
- Prepares budget projections on time
- Translates raw financial data into information for others
- Follows standard financial practices
- Stays current on financial issues during year
- Prepares appropriate year-end statements
- Accurately reports financial status

Needs Improvement
- Exceeded budget by 20% last year
- Loses financial big picture
- Could control expenditures better
- Difficult to understand "the books"
- Financial reports tend to gloss over bad news

Unacceptable
- Often runs in deficit mode
- Uncooperative with company auditors
- Does not inform superiors of potential problems

➡

- Has ignored serious accounting errors
- Financial reports are intentionally misleading
- Does not accept responsibility for financial problems

Flexibility

Outstanding

- When asked to work unusual hours, always complies
- Is among the most flexible members of our team
- Drops current work to promptly address emergencies
- Shifted from the 8-to-4 shift to the midnight-to-8 shift when requested without complaint

Exceeds Expectations

- Has mastered different approaches to situations and can flexibly respond when it's required
- Able to shift focus rapidly
- Willingly assumes others' tasks in case of absences
- Accommodates others' needs first

Meets Expectations

- Gracefully accepts changes to work
- Will reset priorities as required
- Adjusts to changes in procedure fairly well
- Often changes schedule to meet production deadlines

Needs Improvement

- Resists changes
- Argues against resetting priorities
- Becomes agitated when asked to work outside the daily routine
- Frequently will not change mind, despite new evidence

Unacceptable

- Lacks flexibility in most situations
- Won't make changes in priorities until disciplined
- Failure to shift priorities has lost us two clients
- Refused to follow new procedure

General Job Skills

Outstanding
- Mastered every aspect of job
- Exceptional in every skill required on this job
- Rapidly created folders and subfolders for extremely complex document database
- Exceptional organizational ability
- Learned and applied new software within two weeks

Exceeds Expectations
- Has natural ability to quickly comprehend instruction and apply new skills
- Performs efficiently and well
- Quickly adapted to new software
- Created a database comprising over 500 separate documents

Meets Expectations
- Performs tasks competently
- Usually meets deadlines
- Needs strengthening in just a few areas
- Is skilled in most aspects of job

Needs Improvement
- Needs repeated instruction when learning new tasks
- Needs to improve a few fundamental skills
- Has the ability to learn, but seems disinterested in gaining proficiency
- Needed to repeat training for intermediate applications

Unacceptable
- Must improve job skills for satisfactory performance

- Unable to perform a number of functions within standards
- Errors in work often exceed standards
- Time to complete tasks often exceeds standards
- His work contains three times as many errors as the average

Goal Achievement

Outstanding
- The larger the challenge, the more effort
- Achieved goals that others have failed
- In an emergency the person to rely on
- Achieves goals, then looks for more

Exceeds Expectations
- Overcomes frustrating circumstances to achieve goals
- Juggles various goals and achieves most of them
- Doesn't get thrown by tough situations
- Removes barriers to goal achievement
- Does not let everyday problems deflect focus from goals

Meets Expectations
- Meets goals on time
- Takes responsibility for goal achievement
- Comfortable being held accountable for achievement
- Informs others when problems occur
- Helps teammates achieve goals

Needs Improvement
- Goal achievement suffers under pressure
- Lack of confidence sometimes interferes with achievement
- Needs to work on achieving several goals at once

Unacceptable
- Consistently unable to achieve even basic goals
- Doesn't seem to care about reaching goals
- Denies failure to achieve goals
- Makes excuses when goals not attained
- Blames others

Goal and Objective Setting

Outstanding
- Basically self-directing
- Goals she/he sets are always relevant to organization big picture
- Seems to automatically know what must be achieved
- Always seems clear about what to do
- Often asks questions that help the group clarify goals

Exceeds Expectations
- Coaches others in setting sensible goals
- Good at phrasing objectives
- Communicates objectives and goals effectively
- Understands link between goals and planning tasks
- Skilled at mapping out goals and plans of action

Meets Expectations
- Accepts goals set out by supervisor
- Goals chosen are realistic
- Achieves most goals assigned
- Alters goal priorities as needed
- Is guided by goals and objectives

Needs Improvement
- Could show more initiative in setting own goals
- Often asks others what to do next
- Hesitant to work with manager to set goals
- Sets vague or unmeasurable objectives
- Goals and objectives need to be examined by supervisor

Unacceptable
- Sets goals impossible to achieve
- Unaware of organization goals and objectives

➡

- Has no interest in setting goals
- Pays no attention to objectives
- Doesn't make the link between goals and job success
- Just wants to do his/her own thing
- Sets goals way under capabilities

Grooming and Appearance

Outstanding
- Impeccable dress and grooming
- By appearance, represents our company extremely well
- Immaculate appearance
- Immediately conveys positive impression
- Fashionable, yet understated appearance
- Projects a very positive image for company

Exceeds Expectations
- A polished appearance
- Appears composed and professional
- Appears, and is, knowledgeable and confident
- Dresses properly for all business occasions

Meets Expectations
- Comes to work properly attired
- Meets all our guidelines for grooming and appearance
- Carries himself/herself with confidence
- Clothes are clean and pressed
- Shows a professional image

Needs Improvement
- Grooming and appearance need to be improved
- Lacks expression and enthusiasm
- Often has a sloppy appearance
- Pants and shirt are often mismatched
- Others have asked to be seated far away from him/her

Unacceptable
- Ignored requests to deal with appearance
- Will often underdress for important meetings
- Disheveled and unclean appearance

➡

- Shows a poor image of our company
- Clothes are often dirty and wrinkled
- Some have reported unpleasant body odor

Initiative

Outstanding
- Always seeking ways to show initiative
- Knows when and how to take action
- Shows strong initiative in every situation
- Worked an extra __ hours to eliminate error messages in database
- Developed a new work process for communications between accounting and marketing
- Foresaw crisis with client X and express-shipped part to ensure they had no work stoppage—client praised her
- Called together representatives from three departments and solved problem with client X

Exceeds Expectations
- Takes initiative frequently and appropriately
- Is above the norm in showing initiative
- Does not shy away from taking risks
- Without instruction, negotiated lower rates with ___ of ___ vendors
- Redesigned existing software to solve serious customer problem

Meets Expectations
- Takes initiative when appropriate
- Comfortable making decisions to solve customers' problems
- Likes limits specifically spelled out, but goes to them willingly
- Will take risks to accommodate customers
- Created a project oversight committee and its mission statement with minimal direction

- Instituted extranet connection for vendor X to improve project coordination
- Can take initiative when called for

Needs Improvement
- Does only what's asked
- Slow to act
- Rarely shows initiative
- Doesn't make decisions without approval
- Failed to solve customer X's problem
- Not yet confident enough to make decisions
- Shows initiative at a level below what the job requires

Unacceptable
- Shows initiative at a level far below that which is required by the job
- Displays no initiative
- No independent action
- Waits until directed to act
- Delays decisions until it's too late
- Lost a large customer because of lack of initiative
- Takes no initiative to solve customers' problems

Interpersonal Skills

Outstanding
- Often requested as a work partner
- Excellent conflict management skills
- Managers call this person a breeze to work with
- Effective interacting with people no matter the status
- Relates to everyone well regardless of their background
- Genuinely interested

Exceeds Expectations
- Seeks first to understand
- Corrects others without being offensive
- Assertive but doesn't offend
- Open to improving interpersonal skills
- Accepts people from other cultures
- Is accepted by people from other cultures

Meets Expectations
- Does not make sexist or racist comments
- Sense of humor appropriate
- Gets along well in most situations
- Communicates with others well
- A little awkward in some social situations
- Manages own anger well

Needs Improvement
- Doesn't always listen carefully
- Quick to lose patience
- Sometimes tells inappropriate jokes
- Doesn't use skills in emotionally charged situations
- Body language and words don't always match
- Some believe tone is arrogant

➡

Unacceptable

- Often makes insensitive criticisms of others
- Talks behind people's backs
- Received justified complaints from coworkers
- Has not benefited from coaching
- Consistently passive-aggressive
- Tries to look good by attacking others

Judgment

Outstanding
- Shows strong judgment in the most difficult situations
- Excels at balancing risk and reward
- A thorough, thoughtful analyst of complicated scenarios
- Helped company avert a costly strike through skillful negotiation
- Has clear understanding of the implications of decisions

Exceeds Expectations
- Demonstrates mature, seasoned judgment
- Made good decisions in a number of difficult cases
- Interceded effectively in a number of "political" clashes
- Makes decisions based on facts and interests of the organization

Meets Expectations
- Examines different sides of situations prior to making a decision
- Shows clear judgment in resolving conflict
- Elevated customers' concerns to executive-level contact, appropriately
- Strengthened relationship with accounting by authorizing overtime to complete project X on time

Needs Improvement
- Sometimes shows poor judgment in dealing with his/her staff
- Needs to "consider the source" more when judging situations
- Finds it difficult to be nonjudgmental when judgment dictates it
- Needs to strengthen situational awareness

Unacceptable

- Has lacked sound judgment on a number of critical occasions
- Doesn't verify information before forming judgments
- Has shown poor judgment in a number of client interactions
- Got into a shouting match with a VP at a board meeting
- Poor decisions resulted in lowered group performance

Knowledge of Company Processes

Outstanding
- His/her knowledge is unsurpassed
- Knows the organization inside out
- Has been nominated to three cross-functional teams
- Excellent person to answer questions about company
- Applied knowledge to improve company-wide processes
- Has identified process problems others have missed

Exceeds Expectations
- Understands the influences on decision making very well
- Serves as liaison to marketing, sales, and manufacturing
- Uses knowledge of big picture to guide action

Meets Expectations
- Sufficiently understands processes
- Knows interactions between his/her function and others in department
- Understands finance and marketing well, but needs more background on manufacturing
- Changed label location so shipping could find it easier

Needs Improvement
- Is still learning our workflow
- Unfamiliar with a few basic processes
- Still learning his/her way around
- Needs to learn about our clients' expectations of us

Unacceptable
- Is unfamiliar with how his/her function affects others
- Makes changes without checking with those they affect
- Doesn't understand the link between sales and development
- Repeated two past failures because of lack of research

Knowledge of Job

Outstanding

- Has complete mastery of his/her job
- Has a great wealth of knowledge about all job facets
- Her level of knowledge is outstanding
- Is an expert in the functioning of system X
- Has authoritative understanding of job responsibilities
- Is source of information for others in department
- Has kept XYZ certification current for 10 years in a row
- Gained certification in XYZ-2.0 this year

Exceeds Expectations

- Understands all aspects of job
- Strong level of job knowledge
- Knowledge exceeds what is required to perform well

Meets Expectations

- Level of job knowledge appropriate to perform tasks required
- Understands X and Y very well
- Maintains knowledge through seminars and courses
- Knows most of the systems necessary to succeed
- Keeps up to date through reading industry periodicals

Needs Improvement

- Needs to learn more to perform job satisfactorily
- Often runs into situations where he doesn't know what to do
- Is out of date with knowledge
- Needs to improve job knowledge
- Infrequently has the job knowledge to know what to do
- Needs to ask for help on many projects
- Makes more errors than average

Unacceptable

- Needs to learn much more to perform job satisfactorily
- Is many years out of date with knowledge
- Rarely has the job knowledge to know what to do
- Needs to ask for help on every project
- Makes many more errors than average

Leadership Skills

Outstanding

- Uses participative approach whenever called for
- Clearly understands leading as facilitating the success of team and company
- Has employees fired up and committed to organizational goals and vision
- Turns on the motivation for excellence among employees
- Persevered through many leadership challenges
- Excellent at training, motivating, and guiding staff
- Builds excellent team spirit and direction
- Takes all blame, shares all successes
- Employees show great loyalty
- Ranked as superior leader by __ of __ subordinates
- Led group to exceed sales targets in __ of __ regions
- Championed movement to ERP system-migration, completed __ months ahead of target

Exceeds Expectations

- Has the confidence of employees and peers
- Has a participative approach
- Organizes teams with insight into talents and capabilities
- Demeanor sets an example for others
- Considers staff's personal and professional welfare
- Assertive and firm, while fair
- Has authority but leads without dictating
- Dedicates the time and effort necessary to achieve results
- Willing to make tough decisions
- Exhibits traits that generate confidence
- Headed numerous successful projects

Meets Expectations

- Effectively motivates and directs
- Leads staff
- Holds and displays company values
- Satisfactorily overcame some leadership challenges
- Shows strengths in leading, motivating, coaching
- Sits as equal team member on many committees
- Puts worker safety above productivity
- Encourages others to share ideas and approaches
- Could become an excellent leader someday
- Is a developing leader; strong in some areas already

Needs Improvement

- Isn't secure about being in front
- Needs to develop leadership characteristics
- Sometimes fails to inform staff of changes
- Will sometimes put productivity ahead of staff welfare and safety
- Rarely gets involved to resolve disputes among employees
- Needs to ask what others think more often
- Led well, but not in the right direction
- Sets unrealistic goals
- Rarely involves staff in decision making

Unacceptable

- Dictates rather than leads
- Appears totally unable to build teams and direct others' activities
- Doesn't command authority
- Fails to train, motivate, or direct staff
- Will not solicit opinions from others
- Takes over all meetings attended

- Has minimized safety concerns to meet production goals
- Sets goals contrary to company mission
- Fails to act in complex situations
- Never involves others in making decisions
- Is usually late in giving staff vital information
- Behavior generates frequent employee complaints
- Has lost respect of employees

Listening Skills

Outstanding
- Listens and understands even when upset
- Creates a climate where staff listens to each other
- Able to empathize with others' situations
- Manages to appear attentive even in difficult situations

Exceeds Expectations
- Accurately interprets what is said
- Makes frequent use of active or reflective listening
- Only needs to be told once
- Honestly interested in what others say

Meets Expectations
- Understands and can use active/reflective listening
- Follows directions accurately
- Questions when unsure of understanding
- Remembers what others have said over time

Needs Improvement
- Doesn't use listening skills in "tough" situations
- Sometimes so anxious to speak that he/she stops listening
- Needs things explained several times
- Sometimes distracted by own thoughts

Unacceptable
- Constantly interrupts
- Often misinterprets due to bias
- Poor attention span
- Drifts off during important meetings when not speaking
- Not aware when she/he doesn't understand

Long-Range Planning

Outstanding

- Shows great foresight
- An exceedingly strong strategic planner
- Developed a cost-cutting plan that avoided mandatory layoffs
- Makes use of long-range plans in everyday decision making

Exceeds Expectations

- Always looking three to five years down the road
- Anticipated decline in sector and identified three new markets for our product
- Links long-term planning to shorter-term implementation

Meets Expectations

- Has planned for contingencies well
- A good tactical planner
- Identified need and developed an Internet browsing workshop

Needs Improvement

- Needs to look further down the road
- Good with tactics but needs to strengthen strategic plans

Unacceptable

- Has been caught off guard repeatedly by market changes
- Ten-year plan skips the first three years
- Plans long term then ignores it

Management Control

Outstanding
- Able to track multiple issues and problems
- Identifies problems before they occur
- Shares control with employees
- Views control as a means for improving processes
- Expert in the use of statistical process control
- Takes action to prevent problems early in process

Exceeds Expectations
- Manages changing priorities
- Does not overextend by overinvolvement
- Chooses staff wisely to take control of responsibilities
- Regularly looks for ways to improve the system

Meets Expectations
- Provides an adequate level of management control
- Unit tends to run smoothly
- Attends to details when needed

Needs Improvement
- Seeks to control everything, negatively affecting productivity
- Could exercise greater control
- Staff takes advantage of flexibility
- Sometimes relies on wrong people
- Failed to know that a staff member would be absent from a critical meeting

Unacceptable
- Consistently out of touch with work going on
- Exercises minimal control over staff
- Seen by others as hoarding power

➡

- Unable to make fast decisions
- Allows problems to go on too long
- Crises regularly occur in his/her area of responsibility

Management Skills

Outstanding

- Delegates effectively
- Keeps employees in the loop
- An excellent planner
- Organizes people and resources for efficiency and success
- Stays informed without being intrusive
- Uses time and resources effectively
- Strong at screening and hiring new employees
- Effectively handles employee conflicts
- Helps others take responsibility and action

Exceeds Expectations

- Models desired behavior for staff
- Mastered and uses basic coaching skills
- Rarely needs to use formal disciplinary action
- Processes normally operate well with few problems
- Plans well

Meets Expectations

- Maintains personnel and financial records as required
- Plans normally have few glitches
- Regularly informs superiors of progress/problems
- Usually achieves goals and objectives
- Effective participant in hiring process

Needs Improvement

- Micromanages many employee activities
- Has used threats to move employees
- Employee turnover rate higher than the average
- Employee sick time higher than average without reason
- Does not understand how to plan ➡

- New hires often don't work out

Unacceptable
- Takes credit for staff accomplishments
- Plans poorly and problems often occur as result
- Makes poor use of time
- Processes poorly organized
- Often confronts project crises
- Work often finished late and over budget
- Been subject of more than one successful grievance in last 12 months

Managing Details

Outstanding
- Can communicate details to others
- Translates big picture to impact on details
- Breaks down problems into manageable detail
- Makes sure the small things get done well

Exceeds Expectations
- Does not get overwhelmed by details
- Keeps big picture in mind at all times
- Delegates details to best people

Meets Expectations
- Knows when to tend to detail and when not
- Communicates regularly with others involved in detail work
- Seeks help when overwhelmed
- Documents details so others can track

Needs Improvement
- Sometimes loses track of things or misses steps
- Can't identify details of simple problems
- Stress levels rise as detail complexity increases

Unacceptable
- Easily bored with small details
- Many details fall through cracks
- Short attention span causes problems
- Overwhelmed by more than simple details

Managing Expenses

Outstanding
- Does not inflate budget spending estimates
- Often comes in under budget
- Purchases only what is needed for success
- Sets priorities for spending to increase productivity

Exceeds Expectations
- Does not impede necessary small expenditures
- Provides staff with reasonable spending authority
- Teaches staff to link spending with results
- Has developed new lower-cost methods now used in company

Meets Expectations
- Completes expenditure reports on time
- Stays within budget except for emergency situations
- Timely responses to queries about expenditures
- Seeks out cost-effective options

Needs Improvement
- Many unplanned purchases made unnecessarily
- Chronically inflates expenses during planning
- Takes a competitive attitude during budgeting

Unacceptable
- Return on investment for expenditures is low
- Approves and makes purchases impulsively
- Lobbies for unneeded staff and money
- Has used money for purposes other than allocated

Mechanical Skills

Outstanding
- Superior mechanical skills
- Can fix every piece of machinery in the shop
- Works precisely, quickly, and safely
- Has engineered a number of improvements
- Repairs fine mechanical pieces
- An excellent troubleshooter

Exceeds Expectations
- Has troubleshot many mechanical failures
- Repairs most devices without assistance
- Makes delicate repairs
- Problem solves failures quickly
- Consistently within time standards for jobs

Meets Expectations
- Able to repair most common problems with machinery
- An able and safe mechanic
- Competent at mechanical operations
- Know where to find information if needed
- Meets standards for mechanical procedures
- Shows ample strength and dexterity for the job
- Adequate eye-hand coordination

Needs Improvement
- Slow at troubleshooting
- Shortcuts procedures to save time
- Lacks coordination to operate machine X
- Needs to improve understanding of the internal mechanism
- Mistakes hardware problems for software problems

Unacceptable

- Generally poor mechanical skills
- Works slowly and without regard for safety procedures
- Has sacrificed safety for quantity
- Needs oversight on most mechanical operations
- Hasn't diagnosed root cause for machine X's failure
- Unable to operate machine X after ___ months of training

Multi-Tasking

Outstanding
- Manages many projects at the same time effortlessly
- Has met milestones for all four major projects
- Managed $14.7 million worth of projects across three clients
- Uses project management software very effectively

Exceeds Expectations
- Can separate different aspects of her work very well
- Consistently maintains project management log for 13 projects
- Delegated high-level, challenging responsibilities to subordinates while maintaining oversight

Meets Expectations
- Has ably handled multiple tasks
- Can move from one task to another competently
- Usually completes a variety of tasks within needed timeframes
- Capable of coordinating two project teams' needs simultaneously

Needs Improvement
- Could strengthen concentration when working on many tasks
- Has fumbled one or two assignments requiring a number of tasks
- Forgets to do minor tasks that have cost us time later
- Capably coordinates one meeting, but can't handle two at the same time

Unacceptable

- Things often fall through the cracks when he/she has many responsibilities
- Loses focus when faced with even minor additional assignments
- Has walked out of the office on three occasions, frustrated with an average workload
- Fails to remember or write down essential tasks

Negotiating Skills

Outstanding

- Always negotiates successful win-win agreements
- Negotiated agreements that resulted in ___ new projects for company
- Contractees consistently positive about negotiation process
- Does not make agreements that aren't in the company's interests
- Agreements bring positive results for company
- Legal always signs off on agreements
- Takes into consideration needs of all stakeholders

Exceeds Expectations

- Most negotiations go smoothly
- Legal seldom questions agreements
- Contractees happy with agreements
- Takes into consideration most contingencies
- Agreements usually profitable for company

Meets Expectations

- Can be trusted to negotiate in company's interests
- Makes use of legal advice during negotiation
- Informs superiors of progress on negotiations
- Takes others' views into account
- Agreements usually succeed
- Uses reason rather than emotion in negotiations

Needs Improvement

- Does not adequately understand the give-and-take of negotiation
- Sometimes gets emotional during a negotiation
- Sometimes gives more than received
- Not well prepared in some negotiation sessions

Unacceptable

- Consistently tries to take advantage of others
- Does not prepare for negotiation sessions
- Negotiations often result in loss for company
- Often gets emotional while negotiating
- Is unaware of contingencies in an agreement
- Agreements more often lose-lose than win-win

Organizing Skills

Outstanding
- Completed a major reorganizing project this year
- Others rely on him/her to help stay organized
- Taught others organizating skills last year
- Always on top of things

Exceeds Expectations
- Others can find things she/he organizes
- Has customer information at tip of fingers
- Stays organized under high stress
- Keeps track of multiple things at once

Meets Expectations
- Keeps workspace functional
- Keeps well-organized files
- Can find needed information
- Uses organizing tools to save time (e.g., to-do list)

Needs Improvement
- Requires a long time to find documents
- Filing system not easy for others to use
- Sometimes too concerned with neatness
- Intolerant of organizing approaches of others
- Could be more tolerant of others' disorganization

Unacceptable
- Often loses things
- Has missed meetings due to disorganization
- Offends customers due to losing things
- Often fails to file important documents
- Wastes time because of missing items

Orientation to Work

Outstanding
- Keeps job in proper perspective
- Helps team members be more productive
- Completes the toughest assignments
- Has all skills required for excellent work
- Joy to work with

Exceeds Expectations
- Volunteers more than others
- Quick to learn from mistakes
- Interested in learning new things
- Concerned with team members' success

Meets Expectations
- Takes pride in work
- Balances needs of job and family
- Treats customers well
- Always on time

Needs Improvement
- Avoids leadership opportunities
- Sometimes anxious about new challenges
- Sometimes too cautious
- Easily distracted by nonwork issues

Unacceptable
- Seems uninterested in doing well
- Last to volunteer for work assignments
- Refuses to pitch in during emergencies
- Overly pessimistic
- Lacks skills required to perform acceptably

Participative Management

Outstanding
- Knows when to delegate and not to delegate
- Inspires others to have confidence in themselves
- Identifies and uses employees' strengths and knowledge
- Understands own limitations
- Open to employee criticisms

Exceeds Expectations
- Employees comfortable making suggestions
- Gets staff input for major decisions
- Helps staff understand the company's business
- Provides open-door access that employees use

Meets Expectations
- Delegates, then does not meddle
- Treats employee input seriously
- Provides needed information to staff
- Rewards staff for good ideas

Needs Improvement
- Pretends to delegate but stays too involved
- Sometimes defensive
- Prefers autocratic style
- Staff hesitant to approach with ideas

Unacceptable
- Employees afraid to become involved
- Intimidates staff
- Asks for suggestions, then ignores
- Takes credit for employees' ideas
- Negative attitude undermines cooperation among staff

Personal Growth

Outstanding
- Balances work and family/outside interests
- Independently pursues opportunities to learn
- Demonstrates continuous learning
- Has pursued mentor relationship

Exceeds Expectations
- Dramatic improvement in maturity over last two years
- Improved stress management ability this year
- Seeks to improve understanding of diverse people
- Helps others with personal growth

Meets Expectations
- Seeks help as needed
- Assumes responsibility for own successes/failures
- Regularly asks for feedback and responds by making an effort to improve
- Sees problems as opportunity to learn

Needs Improvement
- Overly sensitive to negative feedback
- Seems to have reached a "growth plateau"
- Goes into denial when faced with personal problems
- Work negatively impacted by personal issues

Unacceptable
- Denies existence of personal difficulties
- Refuses needed help
- Has unresolved substance abuse problems
- Prone to self-deception
- Work suffers because of inability to balance work, family, and outside interests

Persuasiveness

Outstanding

- Captures minds and hearts
- Understands and believes in the problem-solving approach in convincing others
- Makes excellent use of "shared benefits" to influence
- Makes sales others cannot
- When she/he speaks, others want to listen
- Other leaves believing idea was own

Exceeds Expectations

- Anticipates others' needs and wants
- Modifies communication to reach different audiences
- Excellent timing of persuasive messages
- Effective in responding to objections
- Speaks with power
- Confident speaking to large groups

Meets Expectations

- Justifies position logically
- References supporting information
- Can adequately answer questions
- Does not "oversell"
- Writes coherent, persuasive documents as needed
- Seen as helpful during persuasion efforts

Needs Improvement

- Sometimes timid
- Doesn't realize merit of own ideas
- Not always aware of how she/he comes across
- Lacks some large-group speaking skills
- Starts strong but gets thrown by resistance

➡

Unacceptable

- Uses threats and coercion
- Received complaints about being heavy-handed
- Has been described as a bully
- Perceived as wanting "own way"
- Gives up much too easily

Phone Skills

Outstanding

- Effectively calms down angry callers
- Smooth under pressure
- Volume of calls handled consistently exceeds standards
- Handles high volume of calls with ease
- Advises staff on handling tough calls
- Callers call back and request him/her

Exceeds Expectations

- Has received compliments from clients
- Puts angry phone calls behind him/her
- Takes outstanding phone messages
- Transfers calls smoothly and accurately
- Sounds cheery even when busy

Meets Expectations

- Checks back with callers on hold every few minutes
- Answers all calls within four rings
- Returns calls within time promised
- Consistently meets call volume standard
- Keeps promises regarding returning calls
- Updates voice mail message at least daily

Needs Improvement

- Sometimes sounds rushed to customers
- Lacks understanding of phone equipment
- Frequently handles fewer calls than expected
- Leaves poor telephone messages for others
- Uncomfortable using voice mail
- Sometimes impatient or flustered

Unacceptable

- Customers often hang up due to wait
- Complaints received about phone manners
- Lost sales due to phone interactions
- Often does not return calls
- Hangs up abruptly
- Frequently becomes too informal with callers
- Many requests to speak to supervisor

Physical Abilities

Outstanding
- Seems never to become fatigued
- Performs all physical aspects of job flawlessly
- Exceedingly agile
- Makes sure actions are always performed safely
- Can lift ___ pounds above job requirement

Exceeds Expectations
- Rarely misses work due to illness
- Takes care of self
- Excellent depth perception
- Moves quickly without sacrificing safety
- Performs well even when under the weather

Meets Expectations
- Strong enough to meet job requirements
- Sufficient stamina to meet job requirements
- Can lift 40 pounds as per job requirement
- Moves safely around equipment
- Understands and respects own limitations

Needs Improvement
- Becomes uncoordinated under stress
- Lacks some fine motor skills
- Sometimes drops tools
- Bumps into things

Unacceptable
- Safety risk due to clumsiness
- Prone to injury on the job
- Physically unfit for job demands
- Dangerous to self and others
- Comes to work physically unready (e.g., hung over)

Planning and Scheduling

Outstanding
- Overcomes delays caused by others
- Copes well with problems beyond his/her control
- Helps others stay organized and on time
- Others regularly rely on his/her scheduling abilities
- Excellent contingency planner

Exceeds Expectations
- Does not overcommit self
- Has never created scheduling conflicts
- Plans practical and doable
- Anticipates where plans can go wrong

Meets Expectations
- Develops both long- and short-term plans
- Anticipates needs of project
- Uses planning tools effectively
- Makes use of automated scheduling tools

Needs Improvement
- Can't see big picture in planning
- Doesn't consult others when required
- Avoids planning responsibilities
- Leaves planning until last minute

Unacceptable
- Cannot schedule for others
- Fails to plan for any contingencies
- Creates unworkable schedules
- Neglects to tell others of schedule changes

Political Skills

Outstanding
- Understands big picture
- Politically astute
- Uses power with discretion
- Exceptionally skilled at dealing with people at all levels of the organization
- Exceptionally skilled at choosing when to follow and when to lead

Exceeds Expectations
- Influences others without offending
- Accepts superiors' use of power
- Gets along well with people in different situations
- Seen as "peacemaker" by peers
- Can be trusted to handle politically sensitive situations
- Unintimidated by titles or others' power

Meets Expectations
- Compromises effectively
- Respects others' positions in organization
- Sensitive to office politics
- Seeks to minimize politics when possible
- Works well with subordinates
- Accepts prerogative of executive to decide issues

Needs Improvement
- Requires reining in
- Argues trivial points
- Seen as difficult by others
- Wields power unnecessarily
- Sometimes unaware of politically sensitive situations
- Often in conflict with peers

Unacceptable

- Often offends others
- Speaks without regard for others' reactions
- Argues for sake of argument
- Questions authority without valid reasons
- Doesn't work well with superiors
- Unaware of political implications of most situations

Potential for Advancement

Outstanding
- Effective leader without formal power
- Has stood in for supervisor without problems
- Eager for new challenges
- Has undertaken formal study for advancement
- Learns quickly and in depth
- Has potential to advance to high levels in the organization

Exceeds Expectations
- Quickly mastered current job
- Often helps solve others' problems
- Developed skills and abilities without prompting
- Pursues independent self-development

Meets Expectations
- Learns effectively over time
- Does current job acceptably
- Willing to go extra mile

Needs Improvement
- Learns slowly
- Repeats past solutions even when inappropriate
- Unaware of areas that need improvement
- Would require coaching in supervisory skills

Unacceptable
- Does not seem to have the capabilities to rise above current position
- Has not generated the confidence of others required for promotion
- Cannot see this employee in higher levels
- Cannot cope with complex decision making

Problem Solving

Outstanding
- Highly proficient and creative at solving problems
- Identifies problems in own area and develops resourceful solutions
- Weighs cost/benefit of many solutions to a problem
- Always addresses root causes in solutions
- Anticipates problems and solves before they develop
- Analyzes problems thoroughly and takes appropriate action

Exceeds Expectations
- Recognizes similarities among situations and appropriately addresses them
- Thorough in analyzing and developing solutions
- Knows when a problem warrants solving
- Always makes recommendations when a problem surfaces
- Develops alternative solutions to problems

Meets Expectations
- Satisfactory problem-solving skills
- Can analyze facts, information, and evidence logically
- Solutions to problems go beyond surface causes
- Recommends solutions to problems
- Sometimes will anticipate problems
- Uses good judgment and information in solving problems

Needs Improvement
- Generates solutions that don't always solve problems
- Knows solutions but doesn't recommend them
- Fails to identify underlying or systemic problems

- Fails to completely analyze problems
- Doesn't recognize trends in recurring problems

Unacceptable

- Has insufficient problem-solving skills
- Weak problem-analysis skills
- Solutions address only surface problems
- Finds problems but doesn't solve them
- Doesn't generate solutions for problems
- Lets others find and fix problems

Productivity

Outstanding

- A star producer
- High productivity, high safety
- Produces more than anyone else in the department
- Wastes no time on small talk; she/he is all work
- Produced 3,432 units with a .03% reject rate
- Sold four units, surpassing goal by 50%
- Closed 98% of customer issues in first contact

Exceeds Expectations

- Above-average productivity
- Has helped others improve productivity
- Frequently above standards in production
- Maintains safety and quality
- Completed all four projects at a cost 12% below budget
- Installed three new systems on time with one callback

Meets Expectations

- Produces within standards
- Accurate and diligent producer
- Meets production goals while keeping quality high
- Handled 140 calls on average, per month
- Conducted five training days a month with reps in the Northeast region
- Does not sacrifice quality for quantity
- Tracks down problems that interfere with productivity

Needs Improvement

- Quantity is acceptable, but quality is low
- Distracted by trivial, unessential issues
- Speed is good, but accuracy is hurting overall rates

- Needs to increase his/her productivity rates
- Missed production goals _____ times last year
- Generally produces well, but needs to maintain his/her machines better for fewer breakdowns

Unacceptable

- One of the lowest producers in the department
- Hasn't increased productivity despite coaching
- Work needs to be checked by others
- Production rate and quality are consistently low
- Productivity has been below standards for _____ of 12 months
- Average call length was 5.5 minutes, when the target is 2.0
- His/Her department responded to only 75% of customer inquiries within one day

Product Knowledge

Outstanding
- In-depth knowledge of all products
- Can explain product benefits to customers in ways that always address their problems
- Consistently recommends best product for customer
- Often praised by customers for expertise
- Makes it a point to keep up to date on competitors' products
- Knows all technical specifications of all our products
- Translates features to benefits for customer with confidence

Exceeds Expectations
- Partial knowledge of all or most products
- Customers request advice about products
- Has received positive comments from customers
- Makes suggestions to improve product line
- Familiar with competitors' products

Meets Expectations
- Familiar with product line
- Gives credible product descriptions to most customers
- Demonstrates proper use of product
- Effectively troubleshoots product problems

Needs Improvement
- Superficial knowledge of most products
- Often needs help explaining some products
- Customers sometimes ask to speak to someone more expert
- Ineffective teacher on use of product
- Often relies on customer's expertise

➥

Unacceptable

- Lacks critical product knowledge
- Presents incorrect product information to customers
- Loses sales as a result of lack of knowledge
- Almost never matches customer need with proper product

Professionalism

Outstanding
- Balances formality and friendliness
- Others ask for guidance
- Coaches other staff on professionalism
- Known by customers as honest and ethical
- Excellent spokesperson for company

Exceeds Expectations
- Almost never offends others
- Coworkers respect and listen to
- Regularly updates self on professional ethics
- Treats people equally despite their differences

Meets Expectations
- No valid complaints about conduct in last year
- Dresses according to function and expectations
- Rarely makes judgment errors in department
- Follows professional standards for job

Needs Improvement
- Sometimes cuts corners under pressure
- Tends to be difficult under pressure
- Has some gaps in understanding of professional conduct
- Rejects ideas of others in offhand way

Unacceptable
- Has made serious errors of judgment in past year
- Has offended several people during last year
- Does not follow through on commitments
- Sacrifices honesty for sales

Programming Skills

Outstanding
- Others can easily understand and alter code written
- Instructs and helps other programmers
- Has developed innovative ways to reduce computer load
- Solicits feedback on own work

Exceeds Expectations
- Creates excellently documented code
- Creates tight, efficient code
- Works well with minimum supervision
- Provides suggestions to analysts when needed
- Can work long hours when required to finish project

Meets Expectations
- Follows company procedures for coding
- Formats code well
- Debugs own code well before sending it on
- Competent in needed programming languages
- Follows system analyst's specification
- Clarifies specifications when needed

Needs Improvement
- Documentation sparse or difficult to understand
- Confused programming with system analysis
- Programs accurately but slowly
- Lacks depth of understanding of programming language
- Needs upgrading in program testing

Unacceptable
- Changes code without telling anyone

- Alters program specifications without consulting with client
- Code has many bugs
- Consistently misses deadlines
- Has caused project delays in past year
- Has difficulty working with [programming language]
- Has not improved in last two years

Project Management

Outstanding

- Understands the nuances of project planning
- Has complete mastery of Microsoft Project
- Brings projects in
- Knows how to select the best team to undertake a project
- Superior at coordinating resources needed to complete a project
- Communicates well with all project team members so problems don't occur
- Successfully dealt with five difficult problems that could have stalled project
- Interacts effectively with all stakeholders in project

Exceeds Expectations

- Makes effective use of Gantt and PERT charts
- Meets project budgets and timeframes
- Has communication system for keeping all project team members informed
- Accurately estimates project budgets
- Developed systems for keeping projects on track
- Effectively brings projects to closure

Meets Expectations

- Works well with project team members
- Effectively deals with problems when they arise
- Effectively uses project planning tools
- Projects usually come in no more than 5% over budget

Needs Improvement

- Does not fully understand project planning tools

- Materials arrive at project either too early or too late
- Team members sometimes complain they are not fully informed
- Three projects came in ___% over budget
- Needs of external stakeholders not considered

Unacceptable
- Project timeframes frequently are not meant
- Steps in project poorly planned resulting in wasted resources and time
- Cannot understand how to use Microsoft Project
- Did not select the right people for the project team
- Two projects came in more than 25% over budget

Quality Management

Outstanding
- Conscious of customer requirements and makes sure defect-free products are always delivered
- Processes operate to deliver only 99.9% defect-free outputs
- Has all processes documented
- Conscientiously practices continuous improvement of processes
- Developed training course that resulted in all line personnel using SPC to improve processes
- Rework and scrap costs reduced by ___%

Exceeds Expectations
- Rarely loses focus on quality
- Continuous improvement a constant focus
- Consistently meets goals for costs and quality of outputs
- Uses SPC to measure and improve processes
- Shares information and resources to help others improve
- An effective advocate of SPC
- Had only a ___% defect rate
- Has delivered accurately and on time to 23 clients requesting samples

Meets Expectations
- Quality of outputs meets standards
- Practices quality control techniques
- Has mastered SPC techniques
- Understands how to analyze and improve processes
- Defect rates meet company standards

- Understands how to analyze and improve processes
- Takes customer needs into consideration in work
- Makes wise use of resources

Needs Improvement
- Does not have adequate understanding of SPC techniques
- Defect rate in some processes unacceptable
- XYZ project ___% over budget because of errors
- Scrap and rework costs exceeded budget by ___%
- On three occasions, colleague had to redo work
- Customers returned ___% of packages with parts missing

Unacceptable
- Defects greatly exceed standards
- Does not understand or practice SPC
- Makes errors frequently in his/her work
- Production runs averaged 70% acceptance rate
- Wastes resources
- Doesn't proof work or get it proofed before it goes to client

Quality of Work

Outstanding

- Work is consistently without error
- Takes special cautions to prevent errors
- Consistently receives praise for work quality
- Other employees use his/her work as model
- Customers regularly send commendations about work

Exceeds Expectations

- Leads group in reducing errors in work
- Has received commendations from five customers
- Work is regularly completed on time and error free
- Output quality makes it easy for others to do their jobs
- Focuses on continuously improving quality

Meets Expectations

- Work is regularly error free
- Quality of work meets standards
- Seeks training to learn how to improve quality
- Works well with customers to assure quality
- Makes use of quality improvement techniques
- Works well with other employees to ensure quality

Needs Improvement

- Employees complain about quality of his/her work
- Mistakes caused work stoppage on two occasions
- Does not pay enough attention to quality issues
- Needs to focus on reducing error rate
- Needs to apply training received to improve quality of outputs

Unacceptable

- On five occasions, errors caused work stoppage

- Defects in outputs caused one customer to choose another vendor
- Does not understand how to improve quality of outputs
- Quality is not a priority

Quantity of Work

Outstanding
- Overcomes obstacles to hitting targets
- Helps others achieve their targets
- Diagnoses barriers to producing desired quantities
- Fixes problems and barriers to hitting targets
- In top 5% in sales each month

Exceeds Expectations
- Exceeded target by __% last year
- Effective at dealing with obstacles
- Suggested ways for everyone to increase quantity of output
- Contributes to profit margin

Meets Expectations
- Ordinarily achieves targets
- Produces well without slowing others down
- Takes on challenge of difficult quotas
- Produces __ items per month

Needs Improvement
- 10% below target last two years
- Lacks a few skills needed to increase production
- Hasn't volunteered for skill upgrades
- Output sometimes affected when under stress

Unacceptable
- Interferes with coworkers' production
- Unwilling to learn how to improve
- Seriously below targets for one year
- Doesn't show concern for missing targets

Research Abilities

Outstanding
- Zeros in on essential information
- Consistently prepared with information before needed
- Excellent at reconciling conflicting information
- Accurately interprets complex statistical data

Exceeds Expectations
- Finds needed information quickly
- Evaluates contradictory information
- Determines relative importance of information
- Ferrets out difficult-to-find information

Meets Expectations
- Completes assigned research projects
- Prepares research reports on time
- Understands technical research papers in own field
- Sets realistic deadlines for gathering information

Needs Improvement
- Doesn't use all research tools available
- Sometimes suffers information overload
- Reports research findings in confusing way
- Cannot research outside of specialized field

Unacceptable
- Mistakes trivial information for important
- Does not distinguish between wheat and chaff
- Conclusions often muddy the waters
- Consistently misinterprets data

Resource Use

Outstanding
- Creates excellent return on investment
- Excellent resource forecaster
- Has introduced cost-saving measures
- Uses innovative ways to save

Exceeds Expectations
- Works within budget and allocated personnel
- Required more resources only due to emergency
- Suggests ways to save money and resources
- Considers various ways to complete job at less cost

Meets Expectations
- Coordinates resource use with others
- Rarely needs overtime to get job done
- Returns resources so others can use
- Treats resources carefully

Needs Improvement
- Takes resources without informing others
- Uses resources designated for others
- Consistently underanticipates resources needed
- Sometimes forgets others may need same resources

Unacceptable
- Rarely comes in on budget
- Negatively impacts others' work
- Received complaints about hoarding resources
- Has damaged resources needed by others

Safety

Outstanding

- Always adheres to safety rules and procedures
- Consistently safe
- Has had no safety infractions
- Wears appropriate safety gear on shop floor at all times
- Tolerates no safety violations
- Monitors employees' safety practices at least one hour every day
- Always reminds staff of safety issues in morning meeting

Exceeds Expectations

- Has excellent safety record
- Encourages safe practices often
- Very safety conscious
- Team had only one minor accident in hazardous work
- Enforces safety very strictly

Meets Expectations

- Performs all work within safety guidelines
- Had good safety record
- A safe worker
- Values safe working procedures
- Maintains vehicle strictly according to maintenance manual

Needs Improvement

- Uses safety equipment only when told
- Failed to wear safety goggles twice in last quarter
- Missed work three times owing to unsafe practices
- Does not enforce safety practices among employees
- Fails to adhere to safe work practices
- Sacrifices safety for productivity

Unacceptable

- Has violated safety guidelines many times
- Failed to adhere to safety rules ___ times in one month
- Ignores safety rules
- Tolerates unsafe or hazardous conditions
- Repeatedly ignores "no smoking" signs
- Frequently does not wear safety equipment

Sales Ability

Outstanding
- Is among our finest sales representatives
- Has closed all our large sales
- A role model for other salespeople
- Always makes the sales target
- Closed 33% of sales where employee was called in as a product specialist
- Exceeded sales target by 23%
- Successfully leveraged our success with company X to have it try our latest version of product Z
- Powerful openings and closings
- Clearly understands clients' needs

Exceeds Expectations
- Maintains excellent relations with clients
- Very good openings
- Always closes with some action for prospect to take
- Represents our company very well
- Comes across as an educator more than a sales representative—and this works well!
- Introduced product X to three new markets—auto, computer, and appliance
- Employee's clients referred three other companies to us, citing the individual's good service
- Great closer!
- Sends birthday, anniversary, holiday cards to clients and their staff

Meets Expectations
- A dedicated salesperson
- Consistently makes sales quota

➡

- Rarely misses sales quota
- Could become a very good salesperson soon
- Persuades more often than not
- Stocks car with appropriate samples on a weekly basis for all upcoming calls
- Successfully had our product specifications included in prospect X's RFP
- Maintains folders with newspaper articles and clippings for each account and delivers them on the sales call
- Good product knowledge, but weak on closing

Needs Improvement
- Is almost making his/her quota
- Needs to learn a lot more about our products
- Needs to learn more about sales techniques
- Is uncomfortable presenting to large client groups
- Maintains good relations with prospects, but doesn't close

Unacceptable
- Met only 80% of quota
- Knows few sales techniques
- Has weak relationships with clients
- Sales ability is very poor
- Needs to improve sales in area of responsibility immediately

Stress, Ability to Work Under

Outstanding
- Shows an outstanding ability to manage her/his own stress
- Demonstrates calm when most others are panicking
- Never raises his/her voice no matter what the circumstances
- Is relaxed and calm in the face of major problems
- Always responds to provocation with calm and grace
- Always helps others deal with stress

Exceeds Expectations
- Does a very good job of managing stress from the job
- Is mostly calm in stressful situations
- Frequently helps others deal with stress
- Rarely raises his/her voice in stressful situations

Meets Expectations
- Manages the stress from the job satisfactorily
- Generally shows calm when faced with stressful situations
- Occasionally helps others manage the stress from the job
- Will raise his/her voice occasionally in stressful situations

Needs Improvement
- Must improve his/her ability to manage stress
- Often can't manage the stress from his/her job
- Often raises his/her voice in stressful situations
- Gets nervous and avoids making decisions in stressful situations
- Rarely helps others deal with a stressful situation

Unacceptable

- Is frequently nervous and on edge
- Never handles project changes calmly
- Frequently yells and screams in stressful situations
- Rarely is relaxed and speaks quietly
- Spreads increased stress to others
- Hardly ever manages his/her stress
- Is insensitive to others' stress
- Never helps others deal with stressful situations

Supervisory Skills

Outstanding
- Exceptionally dedicated and sensitive to employee needs
- Actions have resulted in strong staff loyalty
- Excellent mentor to employees
- Provides excellent and regular feedback to employees
- Has mastery of all staff jobs
- Excellent team leader
- Successfully removes obstacles that get in staff's way
- Has the affection and support of staff

Exceeds Expectations
- Supervises staff with skill
- Excellent staff motivator
- Lays out projects clearly for staff
- Assigns job responsibilities to stretch staff
- Provides opportunities for staff to develop
- Understands workflow and technologies used

Meets Expectations
- Appropriately trains staff
- Explains new projects clearly to reduce errors
- Delegates when appropriate
- Keeps management informed
- Acknowledges and rewards good performances
- Sets goals with staff

Needs Improvement
- Occasionally heavy-handed
- Overdelegates
- Poor planning results in staff overload
- Tends to restrict learning opportunities
- Could listen more to staff

Unacceptable
- Frequently critical of staff
- Avoids communicting with staff
- Staff shows little respect for person or position
- Hoards information
- Has had more than one legitimate grievance filed
- Does not respect confidentiality issues
- Always uses command-and-control approach

Teamwork

Outstanding
- Shows exceptional teamwork
- Drives others to exceed goals
- Works within and between teams knowledgeably and capably
- Manages the team process with great skill
- Serves as the head of _____ teams

Exceeds Expectations
- Gets along well with fellow team members
- Works well on teams
- Performs team-assigned work on time and effectively
- Keeps others informed of status of projects affecting them, when responsible for doing so
- Creates strong teams

Meets Expectations
- Serves as an effective team member
- Communicates well with other teams
- Mostly an optimistic team player
- Dedicated to team goals
- Heads _____ teams and serves on _____ teams

Needs Improvement
- Motivated more for his/her own goals than those of team
- Not seen as a team player
- Has worked against team goals on occasion
- Fails to coordinate work of his/her teams
- Was reassigned from the Safety team earlier this year

➡

Unacceptable

- Does not work on teams well
- Has consistently failed to achieve goals as team member
- Doesn't contribute to team mission
- Does not communicate project status to affected groups when responsible for doing so
- Has been taken off _____ teams

Technical Skills

Outstanding

- Understands all work procedures and methods
- Shows technical excellence in all areas of her/his position
- Adapts well to technological developments relevant in his/her area
- Shows outstanding technical skills
- Has learned new tools to teach to others
- Uses own time to update skills
- Maintains all certifications
- Anticipates and acquires skills before they are needed
- Creates or fixes job tools as necessary

Exceeds Expectations

- Able to learn new job-relevant skills when needed
- Demonstrates both skill and understanding of job tools
- Seen as expert helper by peers
- Takes leadership role in acquiring new technology

Meets Expectations

- Mastered skills needed for job
- Operates job machinery effectively
- Has trouble dealing with computerized machinery
- Able to acquire and use new skills as job requires
- Consistently follows safety and security procedures

Needs Improvement

- Retraining needed in one or two skills
- Does not have skills in problem prevention
- New technology has outstripped existing understanding
- Lack of use has eroded a few skills

Unacceptable

- Understands very few work procedures or methods
- Demonstrates few technical skills
- Needs improvement in level of knowledge in many areas
- Has allowed certifications to lapse
- Does not alter methods to keep current with technological changes
- Lacks majority of skills needed
- Hasn't benefited from technical skill training
- Unaware of lack of crucial skills

Time Management Skills

Outstanding
- Rarely any wasted effort or time
- Paces self to avoid burnout
- Makes effective use of time management tools
- Excellent at prioritizing of tasks
- Able to deal with emergencies

Exceeds Expectations
- Never procrastinates
- Creates atmosphere for good concentration
- Works to tight deadlines
- Delegates when appropriate

Meets Expectations
- Prioritizes effectively
- Usually meets deadlines
- Does not promise what can't be delivered in specific timeframe
- Manages interruptions well
- Effectively uses time management tools (e.g., planners, computers)
- Does not overextend self
- Accurately estimates how long work takes
- Outlines tasks with timeline to finish overall assignment
- Breaks down task or project into workable parts

Needs Improvement
- Occasionally procrastinates
- Allows people and events to interrupt when not necessary
- Needs to use a daily planner
- Tries to do everything herself/himself

- Is easily distracted from task on hand
- Does not deal well with time crises
- Loses track of what the job involves

Unacceptable
- Often does not meet deadlines
- Easily distracted
- Does not understand how to use time management tools
- Does not prioritize tasks
- Unable to distinguish important from trivial activities
- Spends too much time socializing

Appendix A

Ten Mistakes Managers Make When Conducting Performance Appraisals

Robert Bacal

Performance appraisals aren't fun. But a lot of the time they are agonizing because many managers have some misconceptions about the process and why they do it, and the mistakes they make in light of this end up destroying a process that is important to everyone (or should be).

Mistake #1: Spending more time on performance appraisal than performance planning or ongoing performance communication. Performance appraisal is the end of a process that goes on all the time—a process that is based on good communication between manager and employee. So, more time should be spent preventing performance problems than evaluating at the end of the year. When managers do good things during the year, the appraisal is easy to do and comfortable, because there won't be any surprises.

Mistake #2: Comparing employees with each other. Want to create bad feelings, damage morale, get staff to compete so badly they will not work as a team? Then rank staff or compare staff. A guaranteed technique. And heck, not only can a manager create friction among staff, but the manager can become a great target for that hostility too. A bonus!

Mistake #3: Forgetting appraisal is about improvement, not blame. We do appraisal to improve performance, not find a donkey to pin a tail on or blame. Managers who forget this end up developing staff who don't trust them, or even can't stand them. That's because the blaming process is pointless and doesn't help anyone. If there is to be a point to performance appraisal, it should be getting manager and employee working together to have everyone get better.

Mistake #4: Thinking a rating form is an objective, impartial tool. Many companies use rating forms to evaluate employees (you know, the 1-5 ratings?). They do that because it's faster than doing it right. The problem comes when managers believe that those ratings are in some way "real," or anything but subjective, often vague judgments that are bound to be subjective and inaccurate. By the way, if you have two people rate the same employee, the chances of them agreeing are very small. *That's* subjective. Say it to yourself over and over. Ratings are subjective. Rating forms are subjective. Rating forms are not behavioral.

Mitake #5: Stopping performance appraisal when a person's salary is no longer tied to the appraisals. Lots of managers do this. They conduct appraisals so long as they have to do so to justify or withhold a pay increase. When staff hit their salary ceiling, or pay is not connected to appraisal and performance, managers don't bother. Dumb. Performance appraisal is *for* improving performance. It isn't just about pay (although some think it is *only* about pay). If nothing else, everyone needs feedback on their jobs, whether there is money involved or not.

Mistake #6: Believing they are in a position to accurately assess staff. Managers delude themselves into believing they can assess staff performance, even if they hardly ever see their staff actually doing their jobs, or the results of their jobs. Not possible. Most managers aren't in a position to monitor staff consistently enough to be able to assess well. And, besides what manager wants to do that or has the time? And, what employee wants their manager perched, watching their every mood? That's why appraisal is a partnership between employee and manager.

Mistake #7: Cancelling or postponing appraisal meetings. Happens a whole lot. I guess because nobody likes to do them, so managers will postpone them at the drop of a hat. Why is this bad? It says to employees that the process is unimportant or phony. If managers aren't willing to commit to the process, then they shouldn't do it at all. Employees are too smart not to notice the low priority placed on appraisals.

Mistake #8: Measuring or appraising the trivial. Fact of life: The easiest things to measure or evaluate are the least important things with respect to doing a job. Managers are quick to define customer service as "answering the phone within three rings" or some such thing. That's easy to measure if you want to. What's *not* easy to measure is the overall quality of service that will get and keep customers. Measuring overall customer service is hard, so many managers don't do it. But they will measure the trivial.

Mistake #9: Surprising employees during appraisal. Want to really waste your time and create bad performance? This is a guaranteed technique. Don't talk to staff during the year. When they mess up, don't deal with it at the time but *save* it up. Then, at the appraisal meeting, truck out everything saved up in the bank and dump it in the employee's lap. That'll show 'em who is boss!

Mistake #10: Thinking all employees and all jobs should be assessed in exactly the same way using the same procedures. Do all employees need the same things to improve their performance? Of course not. Some need specific feedback. Some don't. Some need more communication than others. And of course jobs are all different Do you think we can evaluate the CEO of Ford using the same approach as we use for the person who cleans the factory floor? Of course not. So, why do managers insist on evaluating the receptionist using the same tools and criteria as the civil engineers in the office? It's not smart. One size does not fit all. Actually why do managers do this? Mostly because the personnel or human resource office leans on them to do so. It's almost understandable, but that doesn't make it any less excusable.

This article is based on the books *Performance Management: Why Doesn't It Work?* and *Performance Management*, a title in the Briefcase Books series published by McGraw-Hill. Copyright © 1999 by Robert Bacal. This article may not be reproduced without permission.

Appendix B

Seven Mistakes Employees Make During Performance Appraisals

Robert Bacal

G enerally, when performance appraisal goes awry, the primary cause has little to do with employees. For the most part, employees take their cues from management and human resources. However, when individual employees perceive the process in negative ways, they can damage even the best of appraisal processes.

Mistake #1: Focusing on the appraisal forms. Performance appraisal isn't about the forms (although, often managers and HR treat it as such). The ultimate purpose of performance appraisal is to allow employees and managers to improve continuously and to remove barriers to job success. In other words, to make everyone better. Forms don't make people better, and are simply a way of recording basic information for later reference. If the focus is getting the forms "done," without thought and effort, the whole process becomes at best a waste of time, and at worst, insulting.

Mistake #2: Not preparing beforehand. Preparing for performance appraisal helps the employee focus on the key issue—performance improvement—and examine his or her performance in a more objective way (see "Defensiveness" below). Unfor-tunately, many employees walk into the appraisal meeting not having thought about the review period, and so are unprepared to present their points of view. Being unprepared means being a reactive participant, or being a passive participant. Neither are going to help manager or employee. Employees can prepare by reviewing their work beforehand, identifying any barriers they faced in doing their jobs, and refamiliarizing themselves with their job descriptions, job responsibilities, and any job performance expectations set with the manager.

Mistake #3: Defensiveness. We tend to take our jobs seriously and personally, making it more difficult to hear others' comments about our work, particularly when they are critical. Even constructive criticism is often hard to hear. If employees enter into the discussion with an attitude of "defending," then it's almost impossible to create the dialogue necessary for performance improvement. That doesn't mean employees can't present their own opinions and perceptions, but it does mean that they should be presented in a calm, factual manner, rather than a defensive, emotional way. Of course, if managers are inept in the appraisal process, it makes it very difficult to avoid this defensiveness.

Mistake #4: Not communicating during the year. Employees need to know how they are doing all year round, not just at appraisal time. Generally it is primarily management's responsibility to ensure that there are no surprises at appraisal time. Often managers discuss both positives and negatives of employee performance throughout the year, but this is unfortunately not a universal practice. It's in the employee's interests to open up discussion about performance during the year, even if the manager does not initiate it. The sooner employees know where they are and what they need to change (or keep doing), the sooner problems can be fixed. In fact many problems can be prevented if they are caught early enough. Even if managers aren't creating that communication, employees can and should. It's a shared responsibility.

Mistake #5: Not clarifying enough. Life would be much easier if managers were perfect, but they aren't. Some communicate and explain well. Some don't. Some are aggravating and some not. At times employees won't be clear about their manager's reasoning or comments, or what a manager is suggesting. That could be because the manager isn't clear himself/herself, or simply isn't good at explaining. However, unless employees clarify when they aren't sure about the reasoning or explanations, they won't know what they need to do to improve their future job performance. It's important to leave the appraisal meeting having a good understanding of what's been said. If that's not possible, clarification can occur after the meeting, or down the road, if that's more appropriate.

Mistake #6: Allowing one-sidedness. Performance appraisals work best when both participants are active and expressing their positions and ideas. Some employees are uncomfortable doing that, and while managers should be creating a climate where employees are comfortable, some managers aren't good at it. Performance appraisal time is an excellent time for employees to make suggestions about things that could be changed to improve performance, about how to remove barriers to job success, and about ways to increase productivity. Remember also that managers can't read minds. The better managers will work with employees to help them do their jobs more effectively, but they can't know how they can help unless employees provide them with good, factual information or, even better, concrete ideas.

Mistake #7: Focusing on appraisal as a way of getting more money. Unfortunately, many organizations tie employee pay to appraisal results, which puts employee and manager on opposite sides. Employees in such systems tend to focus too much on the money component, although that focus is certainly understandable. It's also understandable when employees in such systems become hesitant to reveal shortcomings or mistakes. But it's still dumb. If employees' main purpose is to squeeze as much of an increase out of the company, and the managers try to keep increases as small as possible, it becomes totally impossible to focus on what ultimately matters over the long term, which is continuous performance improvement and success for everyone.

Pay *is* important, but it is not the only issue related to the appraisal focus. If employees enter into the process willing to defend their own positions in factual and fair ways and to work with managers, the process can become much more pleasant. If not, it can become a war.

Conclusion

The major responsibilities for setting performance appraisal tone and climate rest with managers and the human resources department. However, even when managers and human resources do their jobs well, employees who come at the process with a negative or defensive approach are not likely to gain from the process or to prosper over the long term. The constant key is for employees to participate actively and assertively, but to keep a problem-solving mindset and keep focused on how things can be improved in the future. No matter who initiates it, performance appraisal is about positive open communication between employee and manager.

Section Two

Perfect Phrases for Setting Performance Goals

Hundreds of Ready-to-Use Goals for Any Performance Plan or Review

Douglas Max
Robert Bacal

Section Contents

Preface

There's a popular misconception that performance appraisal starts and ends with the performance appraisal meeting. That's not so. In fact, the many benefits of managing performance are lost when you focus solely on the appraisal process, the end point.

The secret to success—for organizations, managers, and employees—is to put more emphasis on making sure managers and employees know what they must accomplish. When each employee understands what he or she needs to do to succeed, it's much easier for that person to contribute. It's also much easier for managers to do their jobs, to improve productivity, and to manage proactively rather than spending time stomping out small fires later. Clear purpose helps everyone succeed and, bottom line, that's what everyone wants and benefits from.

This book helps you set performance goals—those statements that are used to aim and guide performance throughout the year. These same performance goals are also used to evaluate employee performance and, perhaps more importantly, help identify barriers to performance so they can be removed. Our purpose is to make the goal setting process as easy and painless as possible. When you get the goals in place, it also makes the appraisal process much easier.

The performance goals ("perfect phrases") offered in this book can help you create a common understanding of expectations, improve your ability to track progress all year long, and reduce the stress and anxiety associated with performance reviews when the review criteria are fuzzy or vague.

If you would like more in-depth coverage and explanations of performance management and performance review processes, try the following:

Manager's Guide to Performance Reviews, by Robert Bacal, McGraw-Hill, 2003, ISBN: 0-07-142173-4

Performance Management, by Robert Bacal, McGraw-Hill, 1999, ISBN: 0-07-071866-0

If you need assistance with writing performance reviews, try the first book in the "Perfect Phrases" series:

Perfect Phrases for Performance Reviews, by Douglas Max and Robert Bacal, McGraw-Hill, 2003, ISBN: 0-07-140838-X

We'd also like to invite you to make use of The Performance Management Resource Center on the Internet. You'll find hundreds of articles and tips on the performance management process and be able to interact with others involved in performance management. You can access it at www.performance-appraisals.org.

Acknowledgments

You'd think that writing books like this is easy. It's harder than it looks. We'd like to thank John Woods and Bob Magnan for their patience, perseverance, and contributions to this book. Also, Richard Narramore of McGraw-Hill, who initiated this project and its companion, *Perfect Phrases for Performance Reviews*.

Finally, a special thanks is due to Nancy Moore, who contributed to a number of the sections in this book with both general and specific ideas on goals.

Douglas Max
Robert Bacal

Part I

Background for Developing and Writing Performance Goals

Using This Book to Write Better Performance Goals

Before we start you on the path to writing better performance goals and before we explain how to use this book to help improve both individual work performance and overall performance of your work unit or company, we need to place performance goals within the business and management context and examine why it's important to take the time to establish performance goals for employees.

After all, if you don't see the sense or value in working with employees to set goals, it's not likely you're going to do it. And employees also need to understand what goals are, how they can be used, and, most importantly, what value there is in having them.

What Are Performance Goals Used For?

There's a popular misconception that the way to improve performance, whether on an individual basis or for a work unit, is to appraise and evaluate it after the fact. You're probably familiar with the performance appraisal process that is often used once a year. Manager and employee sit down to discuss and evaluate performance for the past year. Some forms are used to record the conversation. Sometimes the process goes smoothly and sometimes not. More often than not, the appraisal meetings do little to meet the needs of the employee or the manager and neither considers them helpful. Or worse, they dread them.

Performance appraisals can be valuable, but not on their own. In fact, the many benefits of managing and appraising performance are lost when managers focus solely on the appraisal process or the end point. It's like driving while looking in the rearview mirror: you see what's already past and beyond your control. If we want to improve performance, we need a forward-looking process so we *prevent* performance problems. And we need some way of harnessing and coordinating the work of individual employees so we increase the effectiveness of the work unit and the company in general. After all, that's what we really want—for each employee to contribute to the effectiveness of the whole.

The secret of success—for organizations, managers, and employees—is to put more emphasis on making sure every employee and every manager knows what he or she needs to accomplish in the present and future. When an employee understands what he or she needs to do to succeed, it's much easier to contribute. It's also much easier for managers to do their jobs, to improve productivity, and to manage proactively, rather than have to spend time stamping out small fires after the fact. Clear purpose helps everyone succeed and, bottom line, that's what we all want.

Enter performance goals. Like the bull's-eye on an archery target, performance goals specify what the employee needs to aim at. Let's look at how they can help.

For the Organization

To succeed, organizations need to be able to coordinate the work of individual employees and work units, so that everyone is pulling in the same direction. Performance goals provide the foundation to allow this kind of coordination to occur.

The process of setting individual performance goals provides the mechanism for translating the goals of the organization as a whole into smaller chunks that are then assigned or delegated to individual employees. That's necessary because organizations achieve their overall goals to the extent that each employee does his or her part in completing the right job tasks in effective ways.

For the Manager

It's easy to think about performance management and goal setting as "overhead." In a world where many managers are exceedingly busy, there's a tendency to think that performance management and goal setting are simply a paper chase that has little to do with the manager's life.

That's not true. Yes, the process takes time and effort. What's easy to miss is that goal setting is an investment that pays off through higher productivity. Let's look at how properly set goals help managers.

First, most managers want employees to do their jobs with a minimum of direct supervision. Employees who require constant guidance and direction eat up a lot of managerial time. Where do performance goals fit?

When an employee knows what he or she needs to accomplish and what is expected, it's a lot easier for that employee to work without constant supervision. Also, by helping employees understand how their individual work contributes to the overall goals of the organization, we enable them to make their own decisions about how to spend their work time so that their work is consistent with the priorities of the organization. The result? The employees know what they must do, how well they must do it, and why they are doing it. That means there's much less need for ongoing supervision. Also, clear performance goals allow managers to empower their staff to make decisions relevant to their work without having to consult the manager on every little question.

Second, clear goals allow employees to monitor their own progress all year round and correct their efforts as necessary. If employees know what they need to accomplish, they can look at their results as they go and identify barriers to achieving those goals. Once again, this ability to self-monitor and self-correct means less managerial time is needed to supervise and guide employees.

Third, the performance appraisal/review becomes much easier, causes far less anxiety, and goes much faster when there are clear performance goals. In fact, the better the performance goals, the clearer they are and the more measurable they are, the less managers and employees have to venture into the realm of vague opinions about performance during the appraisal process. Combine this with the fact that performance goals allow employees to monitor their efforts and the results throughout the year and we get an appraisal process that is much more effective and yields no surprises for the employee.

Finally, let's consider the value of performance goals in helping to proactively identify barriers to performance. It does little good to identify poor performance after the fact or after it has affected the organization. Clear performance goals make it much easier to monitor performance throughout the year and catch situations where performance may be veering off course. Then what follows is a diagnostic process in which employee and manager can figure out what might be causing performance deficits and take action early. In other words, the goals serve as the basis for an "early warning system," because they are specific enough to allow employee and manager to gauge progress all year long.

For the Employee

Most employees want and need to know four things about their work so they can contribute and feel comfortable about where they are in the organization:

- What do I need to accomplish?
- Why am I doing what I'm doing?
- How well must I do it?
- How am I doing?

Job descriptions are of some help in outlining what an employee needs to accomplish, but usually don't specify the "how well" part. Performance appraisals can provide information about how an employee is doing, but they are usually not done often enough to provide enough information.

Ideally, performance goals specify what accomplishments are necessary and how well the work should be done. They are much more specific than job descriptions. This helps the employee have a better understanding of his or her job. That's always a good thing. The more an employee understands the job, the more likely he or she can contribute.

Of course, employees want to know how they are doing. As we mentioned earlier regarding the organization and the manager, clear performance goals help employees to monitor their efforts and assess their results during the year and provide a basis for performance appraisals and reviews. The goals can also serve as a basis for ongoing discussion between manager and employee or, for that matter, among employees, aimed at improving work contributions. Employees can receive recognition for accomplishments throughout the year, since it's easy to identify when an employee has met or exceeded a performance goal.

The bottom line here is that performance goals help employees know where they need to go and what they need to do to get there and help them determine how they are doing.

Where Do Performance Goals Come From?

Performance goals don't appear out of the blue and they aren't created from nothing. Where do they come from?

Since performance goals are used to coordinate and aim employees so they can contribute to the overall performance of the organizations, they need to link to the goals of the organization. Performance goals can't result in better performance unless they are derived from the goals and priorities of the work unit and the company. We recommend that performance goals be based upon the needs of the organization. That's where they must originate to be most effective. (In the next chapter, we'll map out the sequence that links individual goals to organizational goals.)

It's not uncommon for managers to pull or generate performance goals from job descriptions. That's not a good idea.

Job descriptions are notorious for being out of date and far too general to provide meaningful yearly goals for employees. Also, they do not take into account the individual strengths and weaknesses of any particular employee, since they don't describe people, but positions. Job descriptions may be useful as background material for setting goals, but keep in mind that it's quite possible, and even desirable, for different *people* in the same position, with the same job description, to have somewhat different goals.

Finally, individual performance goals develop from corporate goals through discussion and dialogue between the manager and each employee. The goals are set and negotiated individually and collaboratively. They are not imposed, dictated, or "given" to the employee. Why? Here are the main reasons:

1. Most employees—those who have been in their positions for a while—know how they can best contribute. They know their jobs and how well they need to do them. Employees are in the best positions to set goals for themselves.

2. Since we want employees to buy into the goals and treat them as most important, they need to participate in the specification of the goals that apply to them. When people are active participants in setting goals, they tend to work harder to achieve them, since they have a feeling of ownership.

3. Performance goals, by themselves, are important, but so are the discussions that generate them. As you will see later, the discussion between manager and employee serves many purposes, the least of which involves writing down goals. The discussion helps employees understand where they fit in the organization and provides meaning and context for

their work. It helps employees understand the importance and the larger purpose of their work. We know that when employees feel their work has meaning, they tend to be much more motivated and diligent in their efforts to achieve those goals.

So, to summarize, performance goals are based on the needs of the organization and are generated through discussion and dialogue with employees. If you skip or gloss over the dialogue, the process becomes less meaningful and more a paper chase.

How to Use This Book

Developing performance goals isn't easy. It requires an investment of time and effort by the manager and each employee. The purpose of this book is to make the process a bit shorter, less frustrating, and easier for all parties.

The book is organized into two parts. The first part is this one. READ IT! Don't simply assume that you know what's in the first part, since it's absolutely critical that you understand the details of performance goals and goal setting. We'll provide those to you and map out how to go about setting goals so they work and how to go about using the goals you've set.

Once you've read this first part, you'll be ready to make use of the goal phrases in this book. You can use it in several ways.

First, you can use the statements in this book "as is," to the extent that they fit your situation. We've tried to generate goal phrases that will fit a wide variety of jobs and job responsibilities and we've categorized them to make them easy to find. However, you must make sure that the goals you use reflect *your* situation, *your* company, and the needs of company, management, and employee. So that means you may need to customize extensively.

Second, you may find that one of the strengths of this book is that it can stimulate employee and management thinking about goal setting. These phrases provide good starting points for reflection and discussion. Just keep in mind the point—performance improvement and coordination.

Generally, we suggest that you use this book prior to sitting down with employees to set goals. Before meeting with each employee, take a few minutes to go through the sections you think are relevant to him or her and take note of or jot down any goals you think may be applicable.

Consider sharing the book with employees beforehand. To reduce the time you spend in goal-setting meetings, you can provide a copy of this book to the employee and ask him or her to go through and identify a certain number of goals—let's say, 10 to 15 goals—that might fit his or her job. This will work only if the employee understands the job well and also understands where your work unit and company are going in the next year, so consider spending a few minutes with the employee before the goal-setting meeting to discuss those issues.

What's Next?

Now that we've covered some of the basics, we'll guide you step by step through the goal-setting process and provide you with valuable suggestions for ensuring that everyone benefits from the investment in goal settng.

Setting Performance Goals That Work

What are performance goals? There are many ways to define performance goals and there are a good number of other terms with similar meanings, such as *performance objectives* and *standards of performance*. We can simplify our answer to this question by stripping away the fancy language and saying that performance goals are statements that describe what an employee needs to achieve in order to contribute to the overall success of his or her organization. Usually the statements describe a desired result rather than specify how the result is to be obtained.

Specific and Measurable Goals? A Balancing Act

There is no one "right" format for performance goals. There are formats and ways of writing goals so they tend to be more useful, but wording performance goals so they work is often a balancing act. Ideally, performance goals should be as specific as possible. The more specific a goal is, the more likely the employee and the manager will have a common, shared understanding about what it means. That's important.

An example might help to clarify. Consider this phrasing: "Ensure that all work is done properly." This is an example of an exceedingly vague goal. It's likely it will mean different things to the employee and to the manager and then, when the time comes to discuss or evaluate performance, these differences in understanding can cause conflict. This goal is simply too general. Contrast this with a more specific goal: "Complete monthly financial reports and submit to manager by the end of each month." This one is far more specific and less likely to be interpreted in different ways. When it comes time to determine if the employee has achieved this goal, the process is quite straightforward. All the manager and the employee have to do is answer the question, "Were the monthly reports completed and submitted to the manager by the end of each month?"

So, we want specific goals and we want goals that can also be measured, if possible. With our vague example, there's no measurement criterion we can apply to determine if the goal has been met. The second includes a criterion: We can measure whether the employee achieved the goal if we check whether the report was submitted by the end of each month.

Now, here's the catch—the balancing act, if you want to call it that. The more specific the objective, the narrower it is. Narrow goals don't cover much ground because they are so specific. So, the more specific and narrow the goals, the more goals you need to accurately describe what an employee needs to accomplish. At some point you hit the point of diminishing returns, where setting goals becomes so time-consuming and frustrating that the goal-setting process costs more than it benefits.

Or, in the pursuit of specificity and measurability, we can end up with goal statements that are very long and involved. For example, take a look at this goal statement:

Complete monthly financial statements containing final revenue and cost figures, broken down by capital expenditures and salary categories, accurate and not needing revision after submission, and received by the manager by month end, and to the satisfaction of the manager.

It's specific, right? It can be measured. But can you imagine writing dozens of these for each employee? It's a problem. Most managers try to attain some level of balance, so that the goals set are detailed enough to ensure that employee and manager share a common understanding of the meaning of the goals but not so detailed that the goals take hours and hours to craft.

You need to be aware of another "gotcha" with respect to writing specific and measurable goals. As you write more specific and measurable goals, you may find that the goals are less and less important to the employee's actual contributions to the organization. In the pursuit of the easily measurable, it's possible to end up with a set of goals that are so picky and niggling that they are really useless. That's because it's easy to measure trivial and unimportant things in objective, observable ways, but it's hard to measure important things.

Where does that leave us? We still want to phrase goals so they are as measurable and specific as possible, but we have to balance that desire with practical workplace issues, as we've described above. This balancing act becomes a lot less important if you take the position that one function of setting performance goals is to develop a common understanding between manager and employee. If the dialogue and communication between the parties is effective, then the goals need not be quite as specific as would otherwise be the case. That's one reason why it's so important that the goal-setting process involve both employee and manager as active participants.

In any event, we'll take the position that you are going to use your common sense during goal setting. Make the goals as specific as you need them to be to improve performance.

Parts of a Goal Statement

There are two major parts to a goal statement. The first part describes what the employee must accomplish, the "what." The second part describes the criteria that will be applied to determine if the employee has achieved the "what." Let's look at some examples.

Consider this statement: "Reduce overall spending by 10%." The first part—"reduce overall spending"—describes the "what." The second part—"by 10%"—describes the metric that can be used to determine if the overall goal is achieved. By itself, the first part is too vague. By adding the second part, the criterion, we now have a specific and concrete way of determining success and evaluating progress toward the goal throughout the year.

Not all goals are so easily quantified. Take this example: "Prepare accounting statements that are approved without significant modification by the independent auditors." In this case, the "what" is "prepare accounting statements." The criterion, however, is not something that is counted or measured. If the accounting statements are approved "without significant modification" by the auditors, then the employee has achieved this goal. (Of course, it would be good if you could define or describe what you mean by "significant.") This makes perfect sense. This goal accurately reflects the business importance of having auditors provide the stamp of approval. So criteria can be quantifiable ("by 10%") or simply demonstrable ("approved ... by the independent auditors").

Sometimes, goals may reference criteria that already exist and need not be repeated in the goal itself. Here's an example: "Prepare annual budgets in accordance with the guidelines provided by the Chief Financial Officer." In this case, we don't need to list all the particulars contained in the guidelines. It's enough to refer to them more generally; this can save time.

There's another way to specify the performance criteria. In the examples above, we've focused on what we *want* (10% reduction, approval by auditors, conformance to guidelines). Sometimes it's easier to specify an absence of what we *don't want*. For example, "Receive no more than three validated customer complaints per year" or "Assemble 100 widgets per month with no more than one widget requiring rework."

Goals Without Criteria

The common wisdom about performance goals is that they should *all* be measurable and therefore all have measurement criteria. There's no doubt that performance goals that are clear and specify measurement criteria are generally more useful than those that don't. Does that mean you can specify only goals that have criteria? Also, is it OK to have fuzzy, opinion-based criteria?

There are some situations where it may make sense to set performance goals without criteria *or* with very fuzzy, subjective criteria. Some contributions are simply not easily quantifiable or even observable in the specifics without the task of setting goals becoming more than it's worth.

Consider the issue of contributions to a work team. It's possible to write a number of specific goals for this domain.

For example, "Contribute at least one idea per meeting" or "Communicate well in teams as measured by his or her team members' surveys." In some situations, those specifics strengthen the goals; in other situations, they might be unnecessary.

Let's consider another example, from goals for support staff: "Prioritize phone calls to the satisfaction of the manager." Maybe, depending on your situation, you could set a criterion that is more specific and less subjective, based on the priorities of the manager. That would strengthen the goal, but it might make more sense to make a list of priorities to post for support staff as a guide, rather than to write a goal that is long and complicated.

Perhaps we need to ask ourselves two questions. Is it worthwhile to list a number of specific goals that are measurable and observable? Are we really going to use those criteria anyway?

You have to make your own judgments about what you need, but it may be sufficient in some cases to have a general goal that serves as a reminder to employees that, for example, teamwork is important. When we simply want to point out the importance of something, rather than actually measure that something, general goals can suffice as the "aiming" device.

One final comment about goals and criteria: You get what you measure. Before you develop a measure of performance, think through the consequences of evaluating performance in that way. Make sure that the results are what you want. Some measures may lead to clashes among goals for an employee or to conflicts among employees. In such cases, setting performance goals could hurt performance by undermining collaboration and negatively affecting productivity in the work unit.

The Goal-Setting Process

Here are the basic steps in setting goals with an employee.

1. Preparation and Prework

Several weeks in advance, the manager explains the goal-setting process, its purpose, and its benefits. Prior to the goal-setting meeting, the manager and the employee review the goals of the work unit and the organization and identify what the employee might do to contribute to achieving them. Experienced employees can often generate goals beforehand for discussion at the meeting.

2. The Meeting

The manager explains the purpose of the meeting, reiterating the basic purposes of the process. Then, he or she outlines the work-unit goals. Sometimes the manager and the employee review the job description and update it to reflect any changes in responsibilities or job activities. The manager plays a facilitating role—encouraging the employee to define critical work activities, goals, and criteria, rather than telling the employee what he or she needs to achieve. The two develop a set of goals together. It's also good to discuss the relative priorities of the various goals. Once a list is done, it's also good to discuss whatever the employee needs in order to achieve the goals (help from the manager, new tools, extra resources).

3. Action Planning and Follow-Up

Some goals may be sufficiently complex that they require formal action plans, with progress indicators, timelines, and action steps. If so, the employee should develop action plans and then review them with the manager within a few weeks of the goal-setting meeting.

Follow-up involves ongoing communication about progress made or not made toward achieving the goals. Although it's technically not a part of goal setting, follow-up is an absolute necessity to make the whole process work and justify the time spent creating goals.

10 Tips for Setting Performance Goals

1. Performance goals must be individualized for each employee, even if there are a number of employees with identical job descriptions. Employees with the same job titles and descriptions rarely do *exactly* the same things and can contribute in ways different from their peers, provided their unique needs, skills, and abilities are recognized in their performance goals.

2. The process of setting goals is probably more important than the goals created. It is the dialogue between manager and employee that develops an employee's sense of his or her contributions to the organization as a whole.

3. It's easy to write performance goals that are measurable, but it's hard to write goals that are measurable *and* meaningful or important. Don't shy away from areas that are hard to measure if they are important to the organization.

4. Technically perfect goals are great, but it's more important that the employee and the manager share the same understanding of what each goal means and how it links to the success of the organization.

5. Even goals that are phrased perfectly are useless unless there is communication about those goals throughout the year. Two major reasons for having goals are to allow employees to

monitor themselves during the year and to form the basis for formal and/or informal discussions during the year to identify and remove any barriers to achieving the goals.

6. The process of setting individual performance goals should take place after the employee's work unit has its set of goals for the year. Then each employee's goals can be directly tied to what the work unit needs to accomplish.

7. Performance goals should specify the results the employee is expected to achieve rather than how the results are to be achieved. We don't want to be too rigid about this, since means and ends are not so black and white. In situations where the process to be followed is as important as the result, it should be mentioned (e.g., "File statutory information in accordance with government requirements"). Often process-based goals (means) can be turned into results (ends), but let's focus on common understanding and flexibility.

8. Shift your thinking about performance goals from using goals to *evaluate* performance to using goals to *aim* and *guide* performance. Proper aiming and guiding means you need to evaluate less.

9. It's possible to generate dozens, sometimes hundreds of goals for any one employee. Clearly the cost and effort of doing so can outweigh the benefits. Strive to cover the *important* functions. Try to limit the number of goals for any employee to 10 or so, with those goals covering at least 80% of what the employee actually does.

10. Goals should not be etched in stone. The work world is fast-paced and changes often. It's not uncommon for managers

at any level to modify or even completely remove some goals during the year. Priorities change. Keep in mind that as the goals of the work unit are shuffled, you and your employees may need to modify some individual performance goals or reallocate them to other employees.

Getting the Most from Performance Goals

We've walked you through the basic process of setting performance goals. Keep in mind that performance goals are *tools* to improve and manage performance. Like any tool, they do no good if they're left in the back of the drawer to gather dust. You can buy a hammer, but unless you know how to use it and then you use it effectively, it's not going to be of much good.

The last chapter ended with 10 hints important for setting and using performance goals. In this chapter we're going to provide you with essential tips and guidelines to make sure you get maximum benefit from the goals you set with your employees.

Using the Goals During the Year

Setting goals is only the first step in maximizing performance. You need to use those goals during the year as tools to manage and improve performance. Here are some important tips and guidelines.

1. *Ensure that there is adequate communication about performance goals between you and each employee during the year.*

Performance goals aren't "fire and forget" tools. They bring about maximum productivity when they are coupled with a communication process that goes on all year.

2. *Consider a regular and scheduled way to communicate about progress toward the goals.*

    One way to communicate about goals and progress toward those goals is to have some regular and formalized way to do so. There are a number of ways, including the following:

    a. Set up a regular reporting system in which employees submit a brief statement (let's say monthly or quarterly) outlining "where they are" in terms of hitting their goals. Not only does this help you know what is going on, but it also makes the performance goals more visible to each employee and emphasizes that you take the goals seriously. Perhaps most important, it encourages employees to monitor their *own* progress and measure it when possible. When setting up a reporting system, keep in mind that it should be simple, straightforward, and *not* time-consuming.

    b. Schedule regular, short meetings with employees to discuss progress toward their goals. Believe it or not, these may be as short as five minutes—just long enough to share information about progress. These meetings should have two purposes: first, to provide a forum for basic communication so all parties know the situation, and second, to serve as opportunities to discuss barriers to performance, any things that are slowing progress toward their goals. In other words, use these meetings to identify barriers *and* to develop strategies to remove them. That's one of the prime roles of managers and supervisors, to work with each of their employees to build success.

c. You can also schedule group reporting meetings where information about progress is exchanged, not only between you and the employee, but among employees. This can be particularly effective in team-based work where goals are shared among members of a team. Some managers devote a short segment of each staff meeting to this purpose. Keep in mind that the purpose is to improve performance and to facilitate good communication practices, not to blame people. Focus on improvement and identifying and removing barriers to performance.

3. *Use informal methods for communication about goals.*
Some managers prefer less formal means of communicating about performance goals. Sometimes more formal, scheduled methods aren't necessary. It's quite possible to have occasional, short discussions without scheduling them. Some people refer to this process as "management by walking around" and the process is simple.

Allocate some of your work time to chatting with employees in informal ways. Visit with employees and ask questions: You'll be amazed at how much you can accomplish. Drop by their work stations. Talk at coffee breaks. That kind of thing can provide great results.

What questions can you ask? It's good to start with general ones. Here are some examples:

- How are things going?
- Is there anything I can do to help you on the [XYZ] project?
- Are you noticing anything that's slowing down your work that I can help you with?

■ What do you need from me so things will go more
smoothly for you?

Notice that we've phrased these questions in a "helping
way," not in a way that might be construed as threatening.
That's important. You don't want to give the impression
that you are snooping or conducting some sort of sneaky
inquisition. Take the position that you are there to help.
That will encourage employees to tell you the truth and
give you the information you need to offer help.

It's also important that you avoid "micromanaging" in
these conversations. That means that you should avoid
"looking over the employees' shoulder" and telling them
how they should be doing their work. It's OK to offer occasional suggestions, but if you micromanage in these informal conversations, staff are going to stop being open in
communicating with you.

Using Goals for Evaluation and Appraisal

By the time performance reviews and evaluations roll around,
there should be nothing that you and the employees need to
discuss in those meetings that you haven't been discussing
throughout the year. That brings us to the following suggestions
to help you use performance goals in the evaluation process.

Prepare for Appraisal Meetings

Appraisal meetings work best when both parties are prepared
and know what to expect. Proper preparation means that
appraisal meetings can be shorter and less stressful. There are
several ways of preparing.

First, ensure that employees understand the purpose of the
appraisal meetings. Most employees have had some unpleasant

experiences with performance review meetings and can bring some unpleasant baggage to them that interferes with good communication. So, the first step is to talk to employees prior to the meeting and explain why you are doing it and what to expect. Here are some basic points to cover:

- The meeting is to review performance for the purpose of helping the employee succeed in the future.
- There will be no surprises, since there will be nothing discussed in the review meeting that hasn't already been discussed during the year.
- Both employee and manager get to give input into the process: The opinions and perceptions of both are important to the process.

Describe the process you will be using for the meeting—an agenda, if you like. Here are some possible items.

- Review the employee's major job responsibilities and discuss how they relate to the goals of the organization.
- Go through each of the employee's major goals to determine whether he or she has achieved them.
- Identify any problems or barriers the employee has experienced in achieving the goals.
- Identify strategies and plans to remove any performance barriers.
- Complete any forms and documentation as needed.
- Begin the process of setting goals for the next year.

Once you and the employee understand the purposes and conduct of the performance appraisal meeting, it's time to determine how you and the employee should prepare for it. To reduce the time needed for the meeting, you might ask the employee to review his or her goals for the past year and make notes on how he or she feels the work has gone. You can do the same thing. You might also both review the employee's job description to see if it is still accurate and review the appraisal form you will be using in the meeting. Add preparation elements as you see fit.

Take on a Facilitative Role in Evaluations

During performance appraisals, you want to create a state of affairs that encourages each employee to evaluate his or her performance. One reason we use performance goals is to make it easier for employees to do so, during the year and at appraisal time. So, you need to take on the role of questioner and enabler rather than judge and jury. That's not to say you can't offer opinions, suggestions, and an occasional judgment and it doesn't mean you have to agree with the employee's self-evaluation. It means that your starting point in evaluations is to ask the employee to assess how well he or she has done in achieving his or her goals.

Base Discussions on the Performance Goals

Since you've gone to the trouble of creating performance goals, use them. Most of the discussions during performance appraisal should relate directly to whether the employee has achieved his or her goals and what factors have impeded or helped. That means that you shouldn't introduce extraneous observations about performance during the performance appraisal meeting. It's not fair, for example, to criticize an employee for doing or not doing something, when there is no reference to that thing in his or her performance goals.

Focus on the Discussion, Not the Form

While you may be responsible for completing an evaluation form, don't let that drive the appraisal process. Remember that the ultimate purpose of the whole thing is to improve performance. Forms don't perform. Neither do they improve performance. People do. Focus on identifying whether employees have met their goals. If not, discuss the reasons and ways to ensure they will meet them in the future.

Eliminate Blame

Performance appraisal meetings can focus on the past and on blame or they can focus on the present and future, on solving problems and creating success. It's up to you. Keep in mind that, while employees need to be held accountable for performance, you can't change the past and you won't improve performance by spending your time blaming the employee. The appraisal process is a problem-solving process. Use the past to inform your decisions about engineering success in the future. Focus on diagnosis and fixing things, not blaming, embarrassing, or humiliating employees.

Conclusion

By now you should have a good understanding of what performance goals are for, what they look like, and how to use them to guide and improve the performance of employees and the company in general. If you "keep your eyes on the prize," the positive benefits of having and using performance goals properly, you should be able to harness the power of goal setting to make your own life easier while improving your managerial contributions to the organization.

Part II

Perfect Phrases for Setting Performance Goals

Descriptive Contents

Information Technology: Hardware and Operations Goals

Goals in this section can be used with anyone involved in the selection, purchase, deployment, maintenance, and security of computer hardware, networks, and related job functions.

Information Technology: Software— Management Goals

Goals in this section can be used with anyone involved in leading, managing, or supervising individual staff or teams involved in developing, programming, testing, and deploying software systems and solutions.

Information Technology: Software Goals

Goals in this section can be used with anyone involved in developing, programming, testing, and deploying software systems and solutions and anyone involved with data entry.

Financial Goals

Goals in this section can be used with anyone involved in financial management and processing financial information (e.g., accounts receivable clerks), executives and managers, and anyone directly involved in financial functions (e.g., accountants, auditors). Because financial functions are often distributed throughout different levels of the organization, goals in this section may fit those with management responsibilities and those without.

Creative Communication Goals   311

Goals in this section can be used with employees involved in creating written and graphic material in all forms—advertising copy, corporate image graphics, brochures, newsletters, and Web sites.

Production/Manufacturing Goals   314

Goals in this section can be used for those directly involved in manufacturing or producing physical items.

Food Preparation—Management Goals   317

Goals in this section can be used with anyone who supervises staff involved in the preparation of food.

Food Preparation Goals   319

Goals in this section can be used with any employees who are involved in the preparation of food that is to be directly consumed, such as cooks, chefs, bakers, and those preparing ready-to-eat meals in various contexts.

Human Resources and Personnel—Management Goals

Human Resources and Personnel Goals

Physical Plant Maintenance—Management Goals

Chapter 1

Performance Goals for Any Position

Readiness for Work

Goals in this section can be used with almost any employee. Generally, these kinds of goals are not regularly included in the goal-setting process unless some specific issue has arisen that warrants special attention. For example, most employees don't require an explicit goal to encourage them to arrive at work on time, but employees with a history of arriving late might benefit from setting such a goal.

Punctuality

- Arrive at work on time 98% of the time.
- Arrive at meetings on time so as not to inconvenience other participants.
- Return from breaks on time 98% of the time.
- Notify your supervisor at least one hour before scheduled arrival if you anticipate arriving late.
- Clock in and out in accordance with company procedures 100% of the time.
- Begin working within five minutes of arriving at work.
- Arrive on time for meetings with customers 98% of time.

Attendance and Absenteeism

- Limit less serious health-related absences to seven days per year.
- Use sick days only for health reasons or for other reasons approved by supervisor in advance.
- Provide documentation, as required in company policy, for any absences greater than three consecutive work days.
- Arrange in advance with supervisor for any absences not related to health (e.g., child care).

- Notify supervisor of emergency absences as soon as possible.

Health

- Take care of health and stress issues to reduce impact on productivity.
- Ensure that there are zero instances of arriving at work under the influence of alcohol or drugs.
- Maintain sufficient physical conditioning to carry out work responsibilities.
- Notify manager if on-the-job injuries may impact productivity.
- Cooperate with manager and/or employee assistance programs to rearrange job responsibilities as required by health issues.
- Attend regular alcohol counseling sessions as agreed upon.
- Participate in the drug-testing program as agreed upon.
- Avoid any conduct that might result in infecting others.
- Attend employee assistance meetings as agreed upon with manager.

See also: Self-Management and Work Habits

Conflict Management and Team Contributions

Goals in this section can be used with any employee; they focus on desirable methods of dealing with conflict and how the employee can contribute to better team functioning.

Contributions to Team Health

- Ensure that all participants in group discussions can express themselves without being embarrassed, bullied, or belittled by other participants.
- Play facilitating role in team meetings to encourage other team members to participate.
- Ensure that credit is given to others who contribute to team well-being.
- Role-model desirable team behavior to the satisfaction of the manager.
- Balance task and process so work gets done and positive team climate is maintained.
- Advocate the "celebration" of different talents of team members and capitalize on those talents to make the team more effective.
- Move between leadership role and team member role on various projects, as required.
- Establish solid rapport with each team member, as indicated by team members.
- Refrain from gossip or other discussions about fellow team members behind their backs.
- Redirect group conversation away from gossip.

Contributions to Team Productivity

- Generate at least two ideas per year that help the team improve productivity.

- Initiate group discussion for process improvement.
- Learn and teach the use of control charts to team members.
- Encourage others on the team to identify barriers to team functioning and to suggest remedies.
- Perform team-assigned work on time and to standards.
- Coordinate own responsibilities with those of other team members so no project is delayed due to lack of team coordination.

Handling Customer Conflicts

- Use active listening techniques when customer complaints are directed your way.
- Address problems with customers so manager need not be involved 95% of the time.
- Resolve every customer conflict within 24 hours of the initial conflicted interaction and to the customer's satisfaction.
- Handle customer conflicts in calm, unemotional, and helpful way, to the satisfaction of the manager.
- Refer a customer to the manager in cases where the conflict is not resolvable at your level.
- Ensure that the customer recognizes that the employee is trying to resolve the problem.
- Eliminate customer complaints regarding lack of effort to resolve disagreements.

Handling Internal Conflicts

- Address peers privately when critiquing work at hand.
- Handle provocation in ways that de-escalate conflict situations.
- Deal with differences of opinion in open and respectful ways.

➡

- Ensure that there are zero incidences of losing temper and lashing out at colleagues.
- Accept criticism from peers without becoming defensive.
- Refrain from lobbying other staff members for support in conflicts.
- Receive no valid complaints about conduct during the year from peers.
- Accept help from manager to resolve conflicts, according to manager.
- Refrain from public efforts to humiliate or embarrass colleagues who disagree.

See also: Communications, Communication, Customer Service and Support

Self-Management and Work Habits

Goals in this section can be used with almost any employee. Generally, these kinds of goals are not regularly included in the goal-setting process unless some specific issue has arisen that warrants special attention. For example, most employees don't require an explicit goal to encourage them to behave scrupulously and honestly, but employees with a history of behaving negligently and with little regard for the truth might benefit from setting such a goal.

Appearance and Clothing

- Maintain well-groomed, neat appearance, to the satisfaction of your supervisor.
- Follow corporate dress code at all times.
- Arrive at work with required safety clothing and equipment in good condition.
- Ensure zero validated complaints about appearance from customers.
- Modify clothing worn to reflect the particular work tasks of the day.

Ethical/Personal Conduct

- Behave scrupulously and honestly in all activities.
- Do what's right regardless of personal consequences.
- Demonstrate integrity and honesty while interacting with customers, coworkers, and managers.
- Report any personal conflicts of interest to manager before others identify them.
- Follow all guidelines regarding ethical and proper use of company equipment, including Internet access.
- Provide visible leadership to colleagues regarding the importance of ethical conduct. ➥

- Seek out guidance from others regarding appropriate conduct when ethical conflicts occur.
- Know and follow all applicable laws.
- Receive zero validated complaints from customers regarding dishonesty.

Organization and Use of Time

- Keep personal work space tidy and well organized.
- Spend five minutes or less a day on personal phone calls.
- Develop a plan to complete work before requesting time away from work.
- Schedule vacation time by negotiating with supervisor to mutual satisfaction.
- Adhere to company policy regarding eating and drinking at desk.
- Replace any shared equipment or resources as soon as possible.
- Ensure that others can find things you have organized or moved.
- Ensure that no more than one minute per call is spent finding a customer information file.
- Balance work-space functionality and neatness.
- Manage multiple projects at the same time with no delays resulting from disorganization.
- Meet project milestones at least 90% of time.
- Maintain project time sheets as agreed upon with supervisor.
- Maintain billable hours according to company standards.

Willingness to Help/Volunteer

- Volunteer 75% of the time to "buddy up" with new team members.

- Volunteer 50% of the time to take team meeting minutes and publish them.
- Volunteer 50% of the time to organize after-hours social outings.
- When daily work quota is met, volunteer 100% of the time to help others meet their daily quota.
- Take responsibility for at least one United Way charity activity every three years.

See also: Readiness for Work, Work Outputs and Productivity, Conflict Management and Team Contributions

Work Outputs and Productivity

Goals in this section can be used with any employee; they pertain to maintaining and improving productivity for the individual employee, for colleagues, and for the work unit.

Own Work

- Develop and implement at least one cost-saving idea applicable to your own work each year.
- Redesign the file system to reduce file retrieval time by 10%.
- Increase your processing speed by at least 10% by August 2005.
- Improve the profit margin on items sold by 12% this year.
- Seek out advice from supervisor for ways to improve work quality and quantity.
- Complete all major assigned projects on time and within budget.
- Accept responsibility for quantity and quality of work without blaming others for problems.
- Balance the demands of multiple projects so no project falls behind schedule.
- Ensure that outputs are free of defects by the time they reach the customer.
- Produce outputs that meet agreed-upon standards 98% of time.

Contributing to Work of Others

- Ensure that your actions do not interfere with coworkers or reduce their productivity.
- Help at least one coworker each month improve his or her productivity.

- Inform coworkers if you become aware of issues that may affect their productivity.
- Ensure that resources used (e.g., books, tools, manuals, supplies) are returned to their proper place so others can use them.
- Refrain from interrupting the work of others for social reasons.
- Respond to requests for information from coworkers within one day of request.
- Inform support staff when unavailable for phone calls so they can inform callers of the approximate callback time.
- Refrain from avoiding work and passing it off to coworkers.
- Encourage coworkers and recognize their contributions.
- Provide feedback and suggestions to peers without being intrusive or overbearing.
- Coach others in developing sensible goals.
- Document and communicate about shared work so others have information they need to be productive.

Contributing to Overall Productivity
- Contribute via the suggestion system at least one useable idea for improving productivity every six months.
- Generate at least one cost-cutting idea that is implemented and does not reduce productivity.
- Modify individual work to reflect changes in current work-unit priorities.
- Prioritize your own work according to work-unit priorities.
- Volunteer for tasks outside of job responsibilities to help the work unit achieve its goals.

- Lead the improvement team in reducing errors by 12% this year.
- Play a lead role in helping others understand the basics of statistical process control.
- Assist in diagnosis of root causes of productivity problems.

See also: Self-Management and Work Habits, Conflict Management and Team Contributions, Productivity/Process Improvement/Organizational Results

Personal and Skill Development

Goals in this section can be used with any employee; they relate to the employee improving his or her ability to contribute to the organization through acquiring skills, whether to remedy weak areas as revealed through performance appraisals or to grow in areas that would increase chances of promotion.

Assessment

- Identify the two most important specific skill gaps that might impede work performance.
- Determine at least one means (formal and/or informal) to close each of the skill gaps identified.
- Identify and communicate career goals to manager and develop a career development plan, to be updated each year.
- Choose one area of new skills to acquire that will expand your current abilities to prepare you for other responsibilities and then specify the outcomes you expect.
- Target one aspect of personal development and specify criteria by which coworkers will assess your growth in that area.

Formal Learning

- Research training options to identify the most cost-effective training methods for each of the areas identified for development.
- Attend at least one work-related training seminar per year.
- Attend evening or weekend classes as agreed upon with supervisor and as identified as important for promotion.

- Earn at least a B grade in all company-sponsored college courses.
- Attend one annual professional conference in your field and prepare a report for others in the company.
- Satisfy all conditions required to maintain licensing in your field.
- Report on any formal training attended, within one week of completion, and make recommendations.
- Abide by any agreements made with the company regarding return of service for training.
- Receive zero validated complaints about conduct in seminars and training attended.

Informal Learning

- Seek out coaching from more experienced staff members to build your skills.
- Share new skills with coworkers doing similar jobs.
- Request help from the manager before your productivity is negatively affected by insufficient knowledge.
- Communicate that you are willing to receive feedback from supervisors and coworkers.
- Ask others for suggestions about how to do something more efficiently.
- Take the initiative for learning by researching and reading independently and then submitting a written summary to the manager by the end of each month, listing the main research sources used and the articles and books read and outlining what you learned from each.
- Demonstrate initiative when unable to accomplish a task, by consulting manuals before calling for help.
- Show interest in professional development by using personal time for development activities when appropriate.

- Ensure zero instances of problems resulting from not reading product instructions.

See also: Work Outputs and Productivity

Communication

Goals in this section can be used with any employee; they relate to the processes of written and oral communication within the organization and with outside entities.

Interpersonal/Team

- Communicate with respect with others in the organization, regardless of their status.
- Accept feedback from others without becoming defensive.
- Provide feedback to others that conforms to general feedback rules regarding tone and timing.
- Reduce the need for others to require clarification resulting from unclear communication.
- Eliminate work errors resulting from being unclear in communicating.
- Speak persuasively, using facts and figures, not emotion, to support position.
- Refrain from communication that conveys that others are inferior.
- Draft internal documents free of typographical and spelling errors.
- Refrain from telling jokes based on sex, race, religion, physical characteristics, or profanity.
- Contribute to team communication in meetings by bringing discussions back to the topic when they digress.

Management

- Communicate so that the manager can respond to questions from executives.
- Inform management of problems before they affect productivity.

- Report any anticipated variances from schedules to management at least one month in advance.
- Listen to improvement suggestions offered by management and act upon them.
- Respond to management requests for information within 24 hours.
- Document customer concerns and forward to management promptly.
- Draft required reports for management on time and with no need for revisions.

Customers
- Inform customers of unavoidable delays.
- Explain to the customer's satisfaction why his or her needs cannot be met.
- Project an image of patience and expertise to customers.
- Refrain from using pressure or coercion when communicating with customers.
- Follow up all oral agreements with written summaries to the customer within four days of oral agreement.
- Communicate with customers in plain language, to the satisfaction of the customers, as indicated by feedback.
- Ensure that the customer understands what you are saying so that he or she and you are on the same page at the conclusion of the meeting.
- Interpret the language of contracts into plain language so the customer understands, so there are no contractual disputes involving employee communication.
- Notify customers of any changes to schedules that affect them, to avoid unnecessary inconvenience.

Media Relations

- Direct all media inquiries to the appropriate media relations person, as designated.

- Refrain from any public comment on issues beyond the scope of your communication authority.

- Respond to media requests for information in appropriate fashion within one day.

- Project a positive corporate image even when provoked by media.

- Draft clear, understandable press releases that require no further clarification of the facts.

- Appear on local television shows to discuss the company at least once every three months.

- Respect confidentiality in all dealings with the media.

- Communicate a calm demeanor when under pressure.

See also: Communications, Customer Service and Support

Chapter 2

Performance Goals for General Management Responsibilities

Managing Performance

Goals in this section can be used with managers and supervisors responsible for performance management and appraisal.

Setting Performance Goals

- Meet with all reports to discuss and negotiate annual performance goals.

- Set performance goals with employees in compliance with the company format.

- Prepare employees for the goal-setting process to ensure that they can be equal participants.

- Inform all employees of major work-unit goals prior to the process of setting individual goals.

- Ensure that all reports understand their major job responsibilities, as indicated by favorable survey results.

- Set goals that take into account individual strengths and weaknesses.

- Modify goals throughout the year in response to changes in work-unit priorities.

- Ensure that goals are in place for each employee by January 6th of each year.

- Ensure that goals are directly linked to unit objectives for the year.

Communicating About Performance

- Develop a method for staying informed about progress toward goals and barriers to achieving goals.

- Provide monthly feedback to employees about ways to improve performance.

- Inform human resources of any possible performance problems that may require their involvement, at least one month before intervention is required.

- Identify and implement strategies to remedy performance difficulties.
- Identify with each employee any factors interfering with achieving performance goals.
- Develop with each employee strategies to remove blocks to achieving goals.
- Apply a progressive discipline process as required and in accordance with the organization's policy.
- Ensure that every employee receives at least one interim review during the year.
- Address performance problems early so they do not escalate into major problems.

Observing and Documenting
- Document any significant performance-related discussions.
- File a copy of performance goals so it can be found easily.
- Send a copy of the final performance appraisal to human resources by the deadline.
- Ensure that documentation is sufficiently detailed to explain disciplinary action to a third party.
- Share all documentation with the employee and make sure that the employee signs off on each document.
- For each employee, make recommendations about salary increments to human resources two weeks prior to his or her anniversary date.
- Ensure that no personnel decisions are overturned due to a lack of documentation or inadequate documentation.

Performance Appraisal/Review
- Explain the appraisal process to employees in a way that stresses common benefit.

- Make the review useful to employees, as indicated by employee comments and surveys.
- Use performance goals as a basis for the performance review.
- Identify at least two areas in which employees can improve next year.
- Augment written forms as necessary to ensure a complete performance picture.
- Give and receive feedback and information about how the employee and the work unit can improve performance.
- Ensure that there are no surprises for any employee during the review meeting.
- Use performance appraisal information as a basis for planning performance for next period.
- Identify at least one action the manager can take to help the employee do his or her job.

See also: Leadership and Organizational Climate, Productivity/Process Improvement/Organizational Results

Planning

Goals in this section can be used with managers and supervisors responsible for planning of all kinds—financial, personnel, strategic, projects.

Financial Planning

- Develop a five-year plan every year, projecting income and costs, and present it to the VP Finance each January.
- Provide a work-unit budget for each year that is within 10% of actuals.
- Plan expenditures to minimize financial risk to company.
- Identify and plan for capital expenditures that will return on total investment within two years.
- Provide integrated cost and schedule control systems, thereby providing tools to meet the project financial goals.
- Develop financial plans that superiors consider useful for making decisions.
- Communicate financial plans to staff so they can use them in making decisions.
- Forecast financial expenditures for upcoming year, separating out mandatory and discretionary spending.

Personnel Planning

- Identify at least two employees per year to be groomed for supervisory positions.
- Identify alternatives to hiring new staff to cover increased workload.
- Communicate anticipated personnel needs to human resources three months prior to point at which action is required.

- Identify for layoffs staff members whose loss will affect work-unit production the least.
- Maintain a stable staff complement that is sustainable (no layoffs) in varying economic conditions.
- Promote at least one current employee each year into a supervisory position.
- Assist employees with career-development strategies and use acting status appointments and temporary assignments to other positions to develop employees for increased responsibility.
- Identify reasons for high staff turnover in the work unit and develop a plan for reducing it.

Strategic and Work-Unit Planning

- Prepare work-unit summary and/or environmental scan for use in the company strategic planning meetings.
- With staff, develop work-unit strategic plan that reflects the larger organization's strategic goals.
- Attend the company strategic planning meetings with the material needed.
- Define clear and achievable work-unit goals that will contribute to company success.
- Develop action plans for achieving each work-unit goal that includes timelines and specifies individual accountabilities.
- Revise strategic work-unit plan in the event that major shifts occur in the market, the economy, and/or the environment.
- Attend annual conferences so as to be able to predict future trends in the industry.

Work Planning/Scheduling

- Assign projects to the most qualified and appropriate employees.

➡

- Ensure that all major projects are completed according to planned estimates.
- Plan work to minimize overtime by 5%.
- Ensure that all employees have the skills needed to achieve their work goals, as indicated by the employees.
- Balance staff workloads so that more projects are completed on time this year than last.

See also: Personnel/Hiring/Retention

Goals in this section can be used with managers and supervisors who are involved in workforce planning, hiring candidates, and ensuring that the best employees are retained.

Employee Retention

- Ensure that employees who are not performing to standards either improve within three months of notification by their manager or are terminated.
- Ensure that key, valuable employees are identified by their managers and retained at a rate of at least 90%.
- Research salaries to ensure that offers are attractive enough to retain valuable employees.
- Address organizational issues that may contribute to above-average turnover rates.
- Ensure that your managerial behavior does not contribute to loss of key employees.
- Provide sufficient work challenges for younger, high-potential employees, to rate at least 4 out of 5 for "work challenges" on surveys of employees hired within last three years.
- Develop career development plans with high-value employees to improve retention.
- Ensure that 85% of new hires are retained past the probationary period.
- Maintain employee turnover rate at 10% less than industry average.

Forecasting

- Provide workforce need projections to Human Resources by Dec. 1.

- Ensure that personnel forecasts are accurate enough that no layoffs will be necessary if the quarterly EBITDA does not drop below 90% of estimates.
- Identify skills needed for the upcoming year and ensure that employees have those skills.
- Identify alternate strategies (e.g., outsourcing) to meet forecasted personnel needs within personnel budget.
- Ensure that no projects are delayed due to lack of staff or lack of staff skill.

Interviewing
- Follow the required interview protocol 100% of the time.
- Take relevant notes in interviews so decisions can be justified with specifics.
- Contribute to creating a professional interview environment in which candidates feel comfortable, as indicated on follow-up surveys.
- Use behavioral interviewing techniques as outlined by company procedures.
- Refrain from dominating interviews when there are other interviewers.
- Provide sufficient opportunity for job candidate to demonstrate knowledge and abilities.
- Ensure that zero validated complaints are received regarding illegal interview questions.
- Arrive at interviews on time and ready to be an active and effective interviewer.
- Prepare for all interviews as evident by asking relevant and useful questions.
- Refrain from acting during interviews on any personal biases that are not job-related.

- Refrain from canceling or rescheduling interviews except for valid health reasons.
- Ensure that contributions and questions are consistent across interviews for any one position.
- Assess all candidates using the required point system.

Preparing for Hiring

- Update job descriptions at least once a year so they reflect the actual work done.
- Work with Human Resources to develop ads that attract highly qualified candidates.
- Ensure that all specified job qualifications are legal and do not contravene EEOC regulations.
- Develop a general plan for bringing new hires up to speed quickly.
- Cooperate with Human Resources to develop strategies to expand the pool of minority applicants.
- Create relevant in-basket exercises to be used in interview.
- Ensure that all involved Human Resources staff are clear about work-unit needs for every position to be filled.
- Assist Human Resources staff in classifying each position accurately to reflect skill and responsibility requirements.
- Collaborate with Human Resources staff to establish for each position a fair salary level that will attract desirable candidates.
- Help Human Resources staff set point values for all qualifications for every position to be filled.

See also: Human Resources and Personnel—Management, Planning

Leadership and Organizational Climate

Goals in this section can be used with managers, supervisors, and team leaders who are expected to demonstrate leadership within their organizations and contribute to the development and maintenance of a healthy and productive work climate.

Communication

- Align verbal and nonverbal language in a consistent manner.
- Balance listening and speaking to demonstrate an interest in others' thoughts and feelings.
- Proactively seek out both bad and good news from peers and employees regularly and systematically.
- Speak with and listen to at least eight employees each month, to create person-to-person relationships.

Personal and Staff Development

- Create a "teachable vision"—a vision of the future that everyone in the company can grasp and understand.
- Seek coaching and mentoring from other effective leaders, both within and outside the organization.
- Conduct a leadership self-assessment every year.
- Identify at least one leadership skill gap and develop and implement a plan to remedy the gap.
- Coach and mentor at least one staff member who has leadership potential.

Work Climate

- Make realistic promises and keep them.
- Develop a flexible budgeting system to permit employees to make some financial decisions on their own.

- Provide clear goals to staff and leave it up to them to determine how to attain the goals.
- Sponsor yearly surveys of employee to determine their perceptions of organizational climate.
- Develop and implement an action plan to improve employee perceptions of trust.
- Identify and correct situations where work-unit actions are inconsistent with unit vision or corporate values.
- Hold yourself and the employees accountable for actions and results without blaming.
- Focus on the present and the future and encourage staff to do so.
- Make decisions based on "the big picture" and the demands of the current problems.
- Identify the best and brightest employees and retain their services and loyalty.
- Take personal risks by being authentic, open, and honest.
- Improve employee job satisfaction ratings by 20% next year.
- Recognize employee contributions publicly and privately and share the spotlight for successes.
- Focus on action and timing and avoid "analysis paralysis."
- Show confidence in staff by delegating important work to them.

See also: Productivity/Process Improvement/Organizational Results, Communication

Productivity/Process Improvement/ Organizational Results

Goals in this section can be used for managers and supervisors and are related to responsibilities for improving productivity, becoming more cost-effective, and contributing to the overall results of the company.

Productivity

- Increase total work-unit output by 3% this year.
- Reduce labor costs by 3% in work unit without lowering output.
- Increase profit margin by 3% per year without negatively impacting customer satisfaction.
- Research and identify possible capital investments required to update equipment to improve productivity.
- Ensure that any capital expenditures to increase productivity achieve complete cost recovery within three years.
- Identify and provide for staff training identified as needed to improve productivity.
- Engage staff in identifying and implementing strategies to improve productivity.
- Set yearly productivity improvement goals and communicate them to all staff.
- Ensure that each employee understands his or her role with respect to improving productivity for work unit.
- Ensure that no productivity is lost as a result of employees being unclear about work-unit priorities.
- Delegate authority to employees so they can respond to productivity barriers quickly or immediately without requiring further approvals.
- Reduce by three weeks the time it takes new hires to become fully productive.

- Identify any staff members whose productivity is below average and use performance management procedures to help staff members improve.
- Monitor staff and take action if any employees appear to be lowering the productivity of their colleagues.

Process Improvement

- Educate all staff in the use of process improvement and basic statistical tools.
- Create a climate so employees at all levels feel comfortable enough to offer process improvement suggestions to managers.
- Monitor statistical reports on process problems in order to improve process.
- Implement local suggestion box system that generates at least one process improvement idea per month that is implemented.
- Communicate proactively with employees to help remove barriers to improvement.
- Identify root causes for problems, as demonstrated by productivity improvements resulting from correct diagnosis and remediation strategy.
- Contribute in an active way to the company's process improvement team.
- Request assistance from executive managers when a process improvement requires their approvals.
- Model for employees the importance of a continuous improvement philosophy.
- Use performance management to improve processes rather than assign blame for errors.

Organizational Results

- Ensure that the work unit achieves goals and objectives for critical responsibilities.

➡️

- Proactively provide executive managers with the information they need to prioritize expenditures to improve company results.
- Subordinate the work unit's budgets and needs to the improvement needs of the organization.
- Provide input into any overall downsizing strategy, to minimize the negative impacts on company productivity.
- Coordinate with other managers to reduce duplication of effort or wasted effort.
- Identify and recommend actions that will result in cost savings for the company through outsourcing.
- Become a company resource for teaching other managers about applying process improvement tools.

See also: Work Outputs and Productivity

Communications

Goals in this section are relevant to all personnel who have staff reporting to them; these goals relate to communications within the organization and with clients.

Downwards

- Communicate work-unit goals to staff so they understand the bigger picture.
- Help employees understand their roles in the organization and how they can contribute.
- Share information with staff as soon as possible.
- Operate on "want to know" rather than "need to know" in terms of what is communicated to employees.
- Explain why things are done a certain way, and not only how they should be done.
- Create communication climate so employees are comfortable questioning and challenging decisions.
- Provide feedback that majority of employees feel is fair and constructive.

Customers/Clients

- Make final approvals on any written/promotional material seen by customers.
- Handle 80% of phone calls from angry clients on first call and to the satisfaction of the client.
- Collect customer satisfaction data by contacting at least five customers per month.
- Communicate bad news to clients effectively and respectfully.

Peers

- Refrain from withholding information from other managers that is important for their success.

- Coordinate work with other units to reduce duplication of effort.
- Apply a consultative process when project involves decisions that may affect other work units.
- Participate actively in division management meetings and chair the meetings at least once every six months.
- Maintain effective communication with all division managerial peers regardless of personal feelings.
- Use effective communication techniques to address conflicts with peers.
- Eliminate any need for involvement by the vice president to resolve conflicts with managerial peers.

Upwards
- Communicate so there are no surprises to managers higher in the hierarchy.
- Inform your manager of any events of critical importance, to the satisfaction of your manager.
- Prepare and submit all reports as required, on time.
- Identify and communicate sales shortfalls at least one month before end of quarter.
- Suggest at least two cost-saving initiatives each quarter to your manager.

See also: Communication, Customer Service and Support

Chapter 3

Performance Goals for Common Functions

Customer Service and Support—Management

Goals in this section can be used with anyone who manages or supervises staff having customer service and support responsibilities.

Customer Communication/Satisfaction

- Conduct monthly customer focus groups that yield at least one customer service improvement tactic each.
- Develop and implement customer feedback system by year-end.
- Ensure that customer inquiries and complaints are responded to within one working day.
- Ensure that customer complaints are resolved within five working days.

Customer Service Improvements

- Reduce department complaint level to 3% of transactions.
- Develop strategy to use employee suggestion boxes to improve customer service.

Customer Service Management

- Ensure that all employees can explain various merits of products to customers.
- Train all staff in operation of cash register so each employee can cover in emergencies.
- Orient new floor staff within two days of hiring.
- Schedule shifts so there are no fewer than three floor workers available at any time.
- Contact 10 customers a week to follow up on customer service perceptions.
- Monitor 10% of incoming calls to call center.
- Provide feedback to each employee on his or her customer-handling process at least once a month.

- Ensure that service call scheduling results in no more than an average delay of 10 minutes in arriving.
- Ensure that all staff members understand and apply proper phone etiquette.
- Reduce time that customers spend on hold by 10%.
- Reduce merchandise returns from present level storewide.
- Ensure that all staff can correctly apply returns and refunds policy 100% of the time.
- Accurately plan customer service loads to reduce overtime to less than 2% of total hours worked.
- Implement a system of employee recognition (for superior customer service) that majority of employees endorse.

Customer Service Quality

- Maintain at least 95% of items as "in stock" for any given month.
- Reduce checkout wait time to an average of five minutes.

See also: Communication, Retail/Merchandising—Management, Sales and Business Development—Management

Customer Service and Support

Goals in this section can be used with any employee who has direct contact with customers (both internal and external), who is involved in enhancing customer experience, or who supervises or manages employees who have direct customer contact.

Customer Communication

- Conduct monthly customer focus groups that yield at least one customer service improvement tactic each.
- Develop and implement customer feedback system by year-end.
- Notify customers of changes in service call timing 100% of time.
- Design and write clear and understandable product manuals, as measured by customer feedback.
- Inform other employees in contact with customer of previous conversations with that customer and the history of the situation.
- Ensure that no customer needs to repeat his or her information during ordering/support call.
- Contact each customer at least 30 days before expiration of contract to negotiate renewal.
- Contact product purchasers within 30 days of purchase to discuss service agreement options.

Customer Satisfaction/Retention

- Maintain rating of at least 3 in customer surveys.
- Maintain a minimum of 90% customers returning to store.
- Receive no more than two customer complaints validated by manager per year.
- Receive no more than three customer requests per year to assign different staff member.

- Receive no more than three order cancellations per year resulting from customer service complaints.
- Ensure that 90% of customers choose to renew their contracts.
- Identify reasons why customers are not renewing and report this information to customer service manager each month.

Customer Service Improvements

- Contribute at least two customer service improvement strategies per year.
- Evaluate and report on competitors' customer service procedures.
- Reduce department complaint level to 3% of transactions.
- Develop strategy to use employee suggestion boxes to improve customer service.

Customer Service Management

- Ensure that all employees can explain various merits of products to customers.
- Train all staff members to operate cash register so they can cover in emergencies.
- Orient new floor staff within two days of hiring.
- Schedule shifts so there are no fewer than three floor workers available at any time.
- Contact 10 customers a week to follow up on customer service perceptions.
- Monitor 10% of incoming calls to call center.
- Provide feedback to each employee on his or her customer-handling process at least once a month.
- Ensure that service call scheduling results in no more than an average delay of 10 minutes in arriving.
- Ensure that all staff members understand and apply proper phone etiquette.

- Reduce time that customers spend on hold by 10%.
- Reduce merchandise returns from present level storewide.
- Accurately plan customer service loads to reduce overtime to less than 2% of total hours worked.
- Implement a system of employee recognition (for superior customer service) that majority of employees endorse.

Customer Service Quality

- Maintain at least 95% of items as "in stock" for any given month.
- Reduce checkout wait time to an average of five minutes.
- Price items so every item on shelf has price sticker/UPC.
- Fulfill all orders the same day as received.
- Process refunds without intervention/help of supervisor.
- Route phone calls to proper person 98% of the time.
- Solve customer problems in single phone call 90% of the time.
- Identify and report to superior any slowdowns in providing customer service.
- Provide at least two possible options for purchase to each customer.
- Fulfill promises to customers 100% of time or notify them of changes.
- Provide job quotes that are no more than 10% off final price.
- Answer all calls professionally, using proper phone etiquette.
- Handle customer complaints without supervisor intervention 90% of time.
- Maintain abandoned call levels to 4% of total calls.
- Do not interfere with overall customer service team performance as measured by comments from other team members.

➡

- Provide advice to customers that works the first time in 95% of contacts.

See also: Communication, Retail/Merchandizing, Sales, and Business Development

Goals in this section can be used with anyone involved in managing personnel with responsibilities for the selection, purchase, deployment, maintenance, and/or security of computer hardware, networks, and related job functions.

Project/Staff Management

- Ensure that 90% of projects are completed on time and require no rework.

- Ensure that all emergency calls are responded to within 20 minutes.

- Schedule operations staff to ensure 24-hour coverage in person or via pagers.

- Coordinate hardware and software teams to reduce unnecessary wait time for project implementation.

- Ensure that all hardware purchases delivered to customer are effective as indicated by minimum 85% of clients.

- Ensure that computer resources are available for all high-priority corporate initiatives.

- Identify key operational goals of other work units in conjunction with disaster recovery planning.

- Negotiate computer operations chargeback rates with other department managers that are seen as fair by managers.

- Ensure that reports have skills and knowledge required to complete planned projects.

- Create schedules that anticipate staff absences and assign backup roles to staff on high-priority projects.

Purchasing and Maintenance

- Authorize purchases according to corporate priorities for current year.

➡

- Prepare hardware procurement budgets that are approved without modification by the CFO.
- Ensure that total cost of purchased equipment for the year is within budget.
- Negotiate supplier contracts to balance cost versus quality of equipment.
- Review and approve cost estimates for capital expenditures prepared by direct reports.
- Contact each division manager at least once every two months to determine levels of satisfaction with supplied resources and to project/identify future needs.
- Ensure that other divisions use key suppliers to take advantage of negotiated discounts/cost savings.

Results Management

- Reduce reliance on paper files within total organization by creating document management system by June 2005.
- Contribute to overall "white-collar" productivity improvement by 2% this year.
- Ensure that zero purchases are necessary that result from inadequate equipment maintenance.
- Reduce operations staff overtime by 15% this year.
- Improve job processing throughput by 10% without incurring additional costs.
- Ensure that 85% of users are satisfied that interactive response time is adequate.
- Prepare annual report for senior executives outlining major activities and costs and benefits of each of those activities.
- Eliminate data losses resulting from computer viruses.
- Consult with managers to reduce computer theft by 50% this year.

See also: Information Technology: Software—Management, Information Technology: Hardware and Operations

Information Technology: Hardware and Operations

Goals in this section can be used with anyone involved in the selection, purchase, deployment, maintenance, and security of computer hardware, networks, and related job functions.

Backups/Disaster Recovery

- Run daily backups as set out in backup schedule (no missed backups).
- Coordinate disaster recovery team dry runs at least twice a year.
- Ensure that disaster recovery process can be completed within two days of event with no loss of data.
- Inspect off-site disaster recovery center at least once a month to ensure operability.
- Ensure that all disaster recovery personnel are clear about their roles and functions in the event of a disaster.
- Deposit completed backups in company safe each day by 6 P.M.
- Send backup media to off-site backup center each day and verify receipt by 9 P.M.
- Maintain disaster recovery plan and communicate to all personnel who need to know.
- Ensure that recovery plan reflects corporate and business priorities.
- Ensure that security/recovery procedures do not negatively impact business functions.

Customer Support

- Acknowledge requests for hardware repairs/maintenance within one hour of receipt.
- Inform customers of planned computer outages at least one working day prior to outage.

➡

- Provide basic training to customers on accessing and using computer network.
- Set up accounts for users within three hours of receiving request.
- Notify job/process owners when jobs are going to be delayed more than one hour.
- Collect information from computer users at least once a year on possible enhancements to the network.

Data and Hardware Security

- Monitor networks and report any attempts at unauthorized system access to security within 24 hours of attempt.
- Develop and implement corporate strategy for reducing junk e-mail by 50% by December 2011.
- Reduce incidence of virus infection on corporate computers to no more than one per year.
- Advise users on safe computing practices to prevent virus infections.
- Ensure that all systems passwords for all users are at least nine alphanumeric characters.
- Develop and communicate procedures to ensure that each computer can be accessed by computer owner only.
- Secure network servers so only authorized personnel have physical access.
- Carry out security audits without disrupting regular business processes according to department managers.
- Reduce theft of computer equipment within company to less than $1,000 per year.
- With Human Resources develop policy on acceptable use of computer resources by December 2011.

- Complete monthly computer/Internet access audits to identify any possible violations of acceptable use policy.

Maintenance and Operations

- Ensure that unplanned network downtime is limited to no more than once every two months.
- Schedule all planned downtime to occur after regular work day.
- Maintain existing desktop PCs so no employee is without computer access for more than one working day.
- Notify systems staff within one hour of failure of scheduled computer runs.
- Prioritize requests for computer maintenance to reflect relative business-case priorities.
- Reduce job reruns due to operator error to no more than one per week.
- Monitor and maintain computing environment so zero shutdowns are required per month due to temperature or other environmental issues.
- Participate in and advise energy management group on possible strategies to reduce computer-related energy requirements.
- Maintain network cables and wiring so there is no more than one network problem per two months attributable to cabling.
- Report computer usage statistics to each departmental manager within 10 days of end of each month.
- Reduce user complaints about delays or slowdowns on network to no more than one per month.
- Monitor and report on corporate use of Internet and recommend best strategies to maintain effective high-speed access for users.

New Equipment

- Help managers prepare for purchase of new hardware a cost-benefit analysis that proves to be accurate within 10% of actual results.
- Prioritize requests for new equipment to reflect relative business-case priorities.
- Ensure that new equipment works properly when made available to users.
- Review cost-benefit analyses, make recommendations, and submit to the CFO so it takes no more than one month to complete new equipment request review.
- Anticipate needs for new equipment and budget for it so no business process is negatively impacted by outdated or nonworking equipment.
- Prepare and submit budget for new equipment acquisitions to division manager no later than September 30 of each year.
- Explain reasons why request for new equipment has been postponed or denied, to satisfaction of requesting manager.
- Ensure that all equipment purchased is compatible with existing software and hardware 100% of the time.
- Ensure that all new hardware is operational within seven days of receipt or in accordance with agreed-upon schedule.

See also: Information Technology: Software, Information Technology: Hardware and Operations—Management

Information Technology: Software—Management

Goals in this section can be used with anyone involved in leading, managing, or supervising individual staff or teams involved in developing, programming, testing, and deploying software systems and solutions.

Communication/Training

- Select and groom an individual to perform the supervisory role so that supervisor's absence is "seamless."

- Provide training for new data entry clerks based on individual learning style so that each new clerk is fully functional within one month of hire.

- Coach and mentor junior analysts so that more subject matter experts are available for work assignments.

- Ensure that line managers understand sign-off procedures so no changes need to be made to specs after sign-off date.

- Ensure that complete documentation for all software projects is available to clients.

- Advise line managers so software solutions increase productivity by a minimum of 10%.

- Coordinate training of end users so all staff are trained and productive within two weeks after system goes online.

Productivity

- Develop strategy to improve the data entry process so that overtime is eliminated.

- Coordinate work with other IT managers so no delays result from lack of communication.

- Chair analyst/programmer meetings so that all agenda items are completed each meeting.

- Reduce average system development life cycle by a minimum of 10%.
- Advise the CFO on relative merits of outsourcing versus in-house development, to the satisfaction of the CFO.
- Coordinate project personnel to eliminate duplicate effort.
- Reduce rework by 20%.
- Create data quality standards that reflect client needs by June 20.
- Make sure that systems do what they are expected to do, according to clients.

Project Management
- Assign data entry special assignments to appropriate personnel so that the data is entered accurately and within the specified time.
- Maintain the expected 80-to-20 supervisor ratio by using 20% of the week performing data entry tasks and 80% of the week performing supervisory tasks.
- Inform data entry clerks of possible changes to completion times of assignments so that they can manage their work and home life accordingly.
- Schedule and manage on-call staff so emergency pages are answered within 20 minutes.
- Prioritize incoming line manager requests according to overall company priorities.
- Ensure that 90% of all software development projects are completed no more than two weeks late.
- Ensure that all new systems developed are ISO 9000 compliant.

See also: Information Technology: Hardware and Operations—Management, Information Technology: Software

Information Technology: Software

Goals in this section can be used with anyone involved in developing, programming, testing, and deploying software systems and solutions and anyone involved with data entry.

Data Entry

- Input data with a speed of 8,000-plus keystrokes per hour.
- Input data with an accuracy rate of 98% or better.
- Edit input prior to data entry so that data is accepted into system with a 95% success rate.
- Recognize and resolve data issues within 24 hours of discovery.
- Proofread coworkers' inputted data and identify all errors.
- Work overtime at least two hours per week.
- Inform supervisor of possible changes to completion times of assignments so that client expectations and department work schedules can be managed accordingly.

Business Systems Analysis

- Identify and solve problems using department standard problem-solving process before problems can affect the clients.
- Identify alternative solutions to a business problem or opportunity, then recommend a solution, to allow client to select the best solution.
- Communicate with all groups of people equally well, knowing when to provide management summary information and when to provide detailed information, so that each group has the information required to make its business decisions.

- Document business and systems requirements appropriately for each group of people so that the programmer can code the solution and the clients can understand what is being delivered and an appropriate test strategy can be applied.
- Design and deliver presentations to clients with one week's notice or less and to the satisfaction of the clients.
- Train end users so that they can use new software within an acceptable time, as defined by the end users.
- Work productively with all team members within each phase of the system development life cycle so that the system or solution is delivered accurately and on time.
- Review vendor software to determine its fit for use within the system.

Programming
- Use department standard coding techniques so that code delivered is easily maintained and upgraded as required.
- Identify alternative coding solutions and recommend a solution to more junior programmers to allow them to acquire systems and business knowledge.
- Document coding and systems solutions appropriately so that solutions to future problems or upgrades can be implemented easily and in a timely manner.
- Apply knowledge of clients' needs and priorities so systems changes or upgrades can be proactive rather than reactive, decreasing time to market.
- Provide feedback on team programmers' coding solutions; suggest better coding when appropriate.
- Document coding changes within each program so as to keep a good and updated history of program changes, reducing the time to market when program changes or upgrades are required.

- Design technical tools for department use that reduces the time required to perform the "business as usual" tasks by 10%.
- Review vendor software to determine its fit for use within the system.
- Deliver program code to production at least 98% bug-free.
- Create 100 lines of program code per day.
- Provide programming effort estimates within 10% of actuals to facilitate the scheduling of project tasks.

Testing
- Identify major system components to facilitate the estimation of time required to test system upgrade or single change.
- Analyze software defects to detect patterns that help discern system problems so that system solutions can be implemented in a timely manner.
- Apply the various test types appropriate to each phase of the system development life cycle.
- Input appropriate test data with which to test the system with fewer than five entry errors.
- Test system with sufficient detail so that the system does not have any major problems when it is implemented.
- Attend to detail so that each system defect is recorded and retested until it is resolved.
- Categorize each system defect so that "showstoppers" are addressed before minor problems.
- Document results so that testing progress can be determined in regard to timeliness, number of defects found, number of defects resolved, number of defects retested, etc.

System Deployment

- Contact most appropriate personnel for problem resolution during implementation.
- Analyze implementation problems to detect patterns that help discern solutions so that system can be implemented on time.
- Understand and apply the company's best practices regarding implementation strategies.
- Recognize and point out potential problems when developers develop their implementation plan.
- Schedule the company's various system changes and upgrades.

System Support (Help Desk)

- Respond to each client within 15 minutes of receiving a description of the problem.
- Resolve the problem within 24 hours of client's initial contact.
- Provide department- or company-wide messages providing details of a current problem when required.
- Communicate courteously to clients who are experiencing problems, to the satisfaction of the clients.
- Escalate the problem as required but only when necessary.
- Provide resolution instructions to each client in writing, via voice mail, or over the phone, according to the client's preference.
- Follow up with client 48 hours after resolving the problem.
- Document a history of each problem logged and forward to supervisor each week.

See also: Information Technology: Hardware and Operations, Information Technology: Software—Management

Financial

Goals in this section can be used with anyone involved in financial management and processing financial information (e.g., accounts receivable clerks), executives and managers, and anyone directly involved in financial functions (e.g., accountants, auditors). Because financial functions are often distributed throughout different levels of the organization, goals in this section may fit those with management responsibilities and those without.

Bottom-Line Results

- Increase shareholder dividends by 1%.
- Increase stock market value by $10 million.
- Increase market share by 10% over next three years.
- Increase ratio of profit to sales by 10%.
- Reduce uncollectible debt by 20%.
- Maintain current AAA credit rating.
- Identify five cost-saving initiatives by midyear and implement at least two by year-end.
- Maintain return on equity at a minimum of 10% a year.

Budgeting

- Complete or oversee preparation of final yearly budget on time and with no revisions required.
- Ensure that submitted budget conforms to required format and conditions.
- Analyze and approve yearly budgets of subordinate work units four weeks prior to year-end.
- Reduce operating budget by 10% for next fiscal year.
- Present budget and obtain approval from the board of directors.
- Develop tax-reduction strategy resulting in 8% tax savings.

- Analyze costs and benefits of outsourcing and report them to the CFO, to her satisfaction.
- Budget funds in accordance with program priorities provided by the board of directors.
- Create unit budget that includes 10% cut in operating funds.
- Submit budget that requires no more than one modification cycle.
- Provide summary of budget options that includes effects of those options on overall revenue.
- Prepare budgetary predictions for next five years for use in strategic budgeting.
- Identify how corporate allocation for employee development is to be spent.
- Identify and prioritize expenditures as required, recommended, and discretionary.

Conformance to Financial Practices
- Ensure that accounting practices conform to industry standards.
- Ensure that financial reports pass auditors' inspection without major challenges.
- Ensure that financial decisions meet legal and ethical requirements.
- Provide documents to auditors within one week of request.

Spending and Financial Control
- Implement cost-saving programs to yield 10% cost reduction without reducing output.
- Reduce ratio of cost-to-collect to collected amount to 12 to 100.
- Reduce nonpersonnel operating costs by 6% while maintaining revenue.

➡

- Develop and implement innovative cost-cutting programs for work unit.
- Contribute to cost-control team by developing company-wide cost-control strategies.
- Limit ratio of operating costs to sales to 10%.
- Partnering with auditors, identify possible unnecessary expenditures.
- Partnering with corporate managers, identify areas of redundant or overlapping responsibilities and unnecessary spending.
- With other division managers, identify possible cost savings by using outsourcing and prepare recommendation.
- With other division managers, identify functions that may be grouped together (centralized) to yield cost savings.
- Implement and evaluate cost-control strategies mandated by company and present monthly reports to project head.
- Develop and implement a plan to identify cost overruns before they occur.
- Reduce total project cost overruns to a maximum of 4% of budgeted value.
- Manage employee suggestion system to increase total saving from suggestions to 5% of operational budget or $75,000.
- Reduce overtime payments to no more than 4% of total labor/salary costs.
- Reduce total overtime hours by 25%.
- Stabilize profit levels to limit layoffs to 2% of total workforce per year. ➡

Processing

- Accurately process and generate a minimum of 100 invoices per week with no more than a 1% error rate.
- Run payroll reports weekly, to be completed by 10 P.M. each Friday.
- Cut accounts payable checks within time limit established by vendors.
- Cut checks in a timely fashion so no interest is accrued on accounts.
- Respond to questions from payroll and accounts payable within two working days.
- Process and validate expense claims within 30 days of submission.
- Identify any problems that slow down processing, inform superior, and offer possible solutions.
- Ensure that all reports to government are delivered on time such that no penalties are incurred.
- Conduct credit checks to reduce defaults to no more than .5% of total billed.
- Write contracts to limit contract disputes to 1% of total contracts written.
- Ensure that 90% of accounts are reconciled by the end of the following month.
- Administer petty cash according to corporate spending guidelines.
- Provide accurate payroll data to IT five days prior to each check run.

Reporting and Communicating

- Prepare and submit monthly financial summaries to the satisfaction of the CFO.
- Inform superiors of anticipated revenue shortfalls and surpluses at least one month before final reporting. ➡

- Submit financial reports that are accurate and do not require correction.
- Prepare and deliver oral presentations to the board of directors outlining fiscal health, to the satisfaction of the board.
- Provide financial projections for five-year period to be used in annual strategic planning sessions.
- Provide financial profit/loss projections that differ no more than 15% from actuals.
- Respond to employee payroll inquiries so no more than 5% need to be addressed by supervisor.
- Report anticipated cost overruns to executive for approval.
- Provide monthly profit/loss statements that do not require revision later.
- Provide monthly profit/loss projections for future quarters accurate within 10%.
- Improve financial reporting procedures by working with internal auditor.
- Deliver year-end reports on time and in proper format.

Revenue Enhancement
- Identify two new revenue streams to come online within two years.
- Increase net revenue by 10%.
- Increase gross revenue by 10%.
- Double percent of total revenue contributed by [product or service].

Other
- Reduce foreign exchange risk exposure to 5% of total equity.
- Provide financial advice to the satisfaction of the CFO.

➡

- Negotiate with external suppliers to reduce costs and error rates.
- Implement supplier education program to help suppliers reduce their own costs.
- Implement new streamlined bid system to allow easier, more competitive bidding.
- Develop and implement plan to make the company's bids on projects more competitive.

See also: Sales and Business Development, Customer Service and Support—Management

Creative Communication

Goals in this section can be used with employees involved in creating written and graphic material in all forms—advertising copy, corporate image graphics, brochures, newsletters, and Web sites.

Copywriting

- Produce copy satisfactory to the client within one revision cycle.
- Write ad copy that highlights key product selling points as specified by marketing.
- Produce three publishable articles per month.
- Create copy with no more than one factual error needing correction.
- Meet copy deadlines as specified by the director.
- Produce copy that meets space guidelines as specified by word count.
- Ensure that all material used complies with copyright laws; obtain permission when necessary.
- Modify writing style to suit client needs as indicated by client satisfaction ratings.

Copyediting/Layout

- Ensure that final copy is completely free of errors.
- Provide feedback to writers on style and quality of copy.
- Meet all deadlines for submitting final copy to production.
- Ensure that all copy contains strong lead and graphic elements.
- Work with graphics department to ensure that copy and graphics reinforce message.

- Ensure that final copy reflects desired corporate image.
- Lay out documents so they are attractive and easy to read.

Graphic Design

- Design graphic images that are memorable and reinforce the company brand.
- Create final graphic images in camera-ready form for production.
- Present graphic designs to client or executive for discussion at least one month prior to final deadline.
- Produce graphics that reinforce the message of the text they are to accompany.
- Help the client define the messages to be conveyed by the graphics, to the satisfaction of the client.
- Create a final product that reflects creative standards and the needs and preferences of client/owner.
- Design conference displays that salespeople perceive as useful in increasing sales.
- Maintain an inventory of graphic materials, supplies, and equipment as required for assigned projects.
- Translate thoughts, ideas, and images into pictures and designs to the satisfaction of the client.

Web Site Design

- Document Web site code so others can understand and work on code.
- Create a Web site that portrays the company consistent with corporate image policy.
- Ensure that the Web site can be updated quickly and efficiently.
- Make the Web site visually more appealing, according to feedback surveys of Web site visitors. ➥

- Keep the content of the Web site fresh and up to date.
- Consult with department heads so their sections of the Web site contain accurate information.
- Ensure that costs for Web site hosting remain under $6,000 per year.
- Prepare the annual budget for Web site production and maintenance accurate within 10%.
- Obtain all necessary copyrights and permissions so that all Web site content is legal.
- Meet Web site sales quotas each year.
- Create an intranet site that is easy to navigate, so 80% of employees accessing it indicate they can find what they need quickly.
- Coordinate Web site contributors so Web site is completed on time.

See also: Communications, Communication

Production/Manufacturing

Goals in this section can be used for those directly involved in manufacturing or producing physical items.

Quantity

- Produce at least 12 widgets per shift.
- Ensure that the assembly line is not slowed down or shut down because of your work more than once a month.
- Help others achieve their production quotas.
- Show progressive increases in output over next six months.
- Manage supplies so output is not reduced due to lack of parts.
- Maintain your output per shift within +/-10% of your average output each month.
- Identify barriers to increased output and work with management to eliminate.
- Work with the product design team to develop new products that are easy to assemble quickly.
- Use assembly techniques that do not slow down the work of others.
- Balance quantity and quality of output to maximize cost-effectiveness.
- Work safely so no line shutdown is required due to any unsafe work procedures on your part.
- Ask for help when your processing speed becomes an impediment to output.
- Proactively seek out and learn new practices and procedures to increase your output.
- Maintain your equipment so there are zero instances of loss of output due to improper tool maintenance.

Quality

- Ensure that no more than 2% of the items you produce are rejected for quality reasons.
- Ensure that no more than 4% of the items you produce require rework.
- Contribute to developing an overall strategy to reduce rework.
- Ensure that 98% of the items you produce meet quality standards.
- Contribute to work-unit establishment of quality standards for products.
- Identify all products received that do not meet standards and return them to the previous station.
- Document any quality problems to use in future troubleshooting.
- Apply statistical process control tools to identify the root causes of quality problems.
- Lead the quality improvement team.
- Stop the assembly line quickly whenever poor quality outputs reach your station.

Safety and Environment

- Follow all safety procedures during assembly 100% of the time.
- Leave the work station clean and functional at the end of the shift.
- Maintain the work station free of clutter that may constitute a safety hazard for others.
- Return all tools to their proper places when not in use.
- Report all equipment problems to maintenance as soon as possible, to reduce downtime.
- Wear and use all safety equipment 100% of the time when on the floor.

➡

- Receive zero reprimands for safety violations.
- Encourage coworkers to work safely and abide by safety procedures.

See also: Work Outputs and Productivity

Food Preparation—Management

Goals in this section can be used with anyone who supervises staff involved in the preparation of food.

Cleanliness/Hygiene/Safety

- Maintain for the upcoming year a record of zero instances of salmonella illnesses linked to restaurant.
- Be first to identify any health code violations and rectify before inspectors arrive.
- Respond to and resolve any inspector concerns that fall within your control within three days of receipt or as required by inspector.
- Prepare job aids and reminders for kitchen staff regarding hygiene practices and post them in visible areas.
- Ensure that all members of kitchen staff follow all hygiene practices 100% of the time.
- Ensure zero validated customer complaints about foreign objects in food.
- Maintain zero incidence of kitchen fires.

Cost-Effectiveness/Organization

- Maintain cost of ingredients for each meal to 30% of total retail cost.
- Schedule food preparation staff to reduce overtime by 20%.
- Schedule staff to meet customer demand, so no customer waits more than 15 minutes for a meal.
- Cut total costs for food preparation by 10% in 2011.
- Reduce produce wastage/spoilage by 10%.
- Plan and order ingredients to take advantage of 10% bulk discount from suppliers.

- Ensure a sufficient supply of ingredients, so that no more than 5% of orders need to be refused due to lack of ingredients.
- Schedule produce purchases and deliveries so no produce served is older than two days.

Quality
- Prepare food so that customers rate taste and appearance on feedback forms as "above average" compared with competitors.
- Provide portions that customers perceive as appropriate in size, as indicated by customer feedback forms.
- Ensure that the portions vary no more than 5% by weight from corporate standards.
- Ensure that all completed orders are picked up within one minute.
- Ensure that all food items leave the kitchen at appropriate temperatures.
- Maintain consistency across batches: all donuts to be between 2.5 and 2.6 inches in diameter.
- Ensure that all meals contain proper nutritional value as outlined in the organization's food standards.

See also: Food Services—Management

Food Preparation

Goals in this section can be used with any employees who are involved in the preparation of food that is to be directly consumed, such as cooks, chefs, bakers, and those preparing ready-to-eat meals in various contexts.

Cleanliness/Hygiene/Safety

- Prepare preserves and canned goods on premises in accordance with procedures and standards from inspection board.
- Follow all safety and health guidelines 100% of the time.
- Notify manager immediately when safety and health guidelines are violated.
- Leave cooking area in spotless and hygienic condition at end of shift.
- Rectify safety issues immediately upon observation when possible.

Innovation

- Introduce two new vegetarian dishes to menu each month.
- Introduce two new featured dishes each month.
- Revise current recipes to eliminate MSG without sacrificing customer satisfaction.
- Conduct pre-meal evaluations of new product items with at least three staff members and one manager.
- Provide at least three new product item ideas to manager each quarter.

Inventory Control/Equipment

- Maintain recipe files so they can be used by other kitchen staff and replacements.
- Maintain ovens according to factory specifications.

- Inspect cooking equipment and verify that it is working and safe at start of each shift.
- Anticipate ingredient shortages and notify manager at least 24 hours before an ingredient is exhausted.
- Ensure that no more than 5% of orders need to be refused due to lack of ingredients.
- Ensure that kitchen utensils are replaced in holders at all times immediately after use.
- Sharpen cutting knives weekly.

Quality

- Cook food to customers' specifications to their satisfaction at least 90% of the time.
- Cook vegetables so they are crisp, neither hard nor mushy.
- Prepare food so that customers rate taste and appearance on feedback forms as "above average" compared with competitors.
- Provide portions that customers perceive as appropriate in size, as indicated by customer feedback forms.
- Ensure that the portions vary no more than 5% by weight from corporate standards.
- Ensure that all completed orders are picked up within one minute.
- Ensure that all food items leave the kitchen at appropriate temperatures.
- Maintain consistency across batches: all donuts to be between 2.5 and 2.6 inches in diameter.
- Ensure that all meals contain proper nutritional value as outlined in the organization's food standards.
- Arrange food on serving trays/plates so presentation is attractive and orderly.

See also: Food Services

Food Services—Management

Goals in this section can be used for those who supervise employees involved in the food service industry, most notably those involved in catering, waiting on tables, delivering food, and maintaining eating areas.

Catering

- Follow up on catering leads within one day of receiving them.
- Present food and catering options to customer in a clear, understandable way.
- Increase total catering revenue by 10% in 2011.
- Coordinate food preparation and serving so that all meals are served on time.
- Convert at least 50% of customer inquiries and leads into confirmed contracts.
- Ensure that all visible members of the catering staff at any event are attired properly before taking the floor.
- Ensure no more than 1% of total catering billings are late or uncollectible.
- Verify that food supplies and ingredients are available and sufficient to prepare contracted meals plus 5%.

Customer Service

- Set customer service standards and communicate them to the staff.
- Ensure that there are no more than two instances per month when a customer leaves as a result of serving delays.
- Address customer complaints to the satisfaction of the customers.
- Speak with at least five customers per week to gather information about the service.

- When service is poor, offer restitution to customers to retain their business.
- Ensure that portions are acceptable to the customers without resulting in wastage.

Employee Supervision and Training

- Ensure that all staff members are properly attired for their shifts.
- Supervise staff to ensure that they follow all health procedures.
- Train all new serving staff in "our way" of serving.
- Provide feedback on service quality to each server at least once a month.
- Train all staff in the use of cash so there are no more than three errors per week that require manager involvement.
- Coach serving staff members so they do not sound wooden or over-rehearsed.

Facilities Management

- Schedule serving staff so there are always enough employees to meet customer demand.
- Ensure that no customer waits more than five minutes in the restaurant before being attended.
- Develop strategies to increase business from families to 20% of total sales.
- Order sufficient copies of menus so there is never a shortage.
- Forward marketing suggestions to the head office at least once a month.
- Supervise the menu design so it reflects the desired image.

- Monitor cooking equipment to ensure that no meals are delayed as a result of preventable equipment failures.
- Develop a staffing plan that takes into account possible staff absences and illness.
- Ensure that staff absences do not have a significant effect on the ability to serve customers promptly.
- Keep payroll records in accordance with company procedures or government filing requirements.
- Deposit daily receipts so there is no more than $200 cash on the premises at any one time.
- Secure premises at closing.

See also: Food Preparation—Management

Food Services

Goals in this section can be used for employees directly involved in the food service industry, most notably those who cater, wait on tables, deliver food, and maintain eating areas.

Environment

- Keep all table condiments fully stocked.
- Clear away dishes within three minutes of patrons leaving.
- Wear required attire and keep it clean and presentable.
- End the shift leaving the eating areas as clean as at beginning of shift.
- Respond to customer requests for spill cleanup within three minutes of request.
- Identify and report to maintenance any damage to furniture within one day of noticing it.
- Provide high chairs and other child-related items required by young diners.
- Carry order pad and pen and other necessary tools so no service is delayed for lack of tools.
- Set up tables with clean linen, napkins, and silverware so table can be returned to service within five minutes.

Order Taking/Processing

- Inform each customer of daily specials before taking the order.
- Make no more than one order-taking error per week that results in a delay in serving the correct order.
- Ensure that all cutlery and place settings are clean and proper before taking order.
- Tally bills and make no more than three errors per month that require correction at the cash register. ➡

- Process each payment within four minutes of receiving it at the table.
- Return to take dessert and coffee orders within four minutes after the patrons finish the main course.
- Take orders on behalf of other staff members if they are delayed.
- Inform patrons of the approximate time it will take to serve orders when delays are anticipated.
- Offer patrons water as part of the process of greeting them and taking their order.
- Greet each patron with spiel and a friendly smile.
- Make wine suggestions that are appropriate for the meals ordered.

Serving
- Serve food according to the procedures set by the supervisor.
- Return to each table within five minutes of initial serving to inquire about customer needs.
- Ensure that no customer waits more than five minutes after finishing eating to receive bill.
- Serve every food item within two minutes of being notified that it's "up."
- Identify any errors in food errors before serving items to customer.
- Serve food in an unobtrusive manner consistent with customer expectations.
- Offer coffee refills when cups become two-thirds empty.
- Remove plates within five minutes after the patrons finish their meal.
- Handle complaints about food quality service by immediately bringing them to the attention of the manager.

See also: Food Preparation

Transit/Transportation

Goals in this section can be used for employees directly involved in transporting people, including public bus and school bus drivers and taxi and limousine service personnel.

Customer Support

- Handle customer complaints so that the supervisor needs to deal with no more than one complaint a year.
- Provide accurate and courteous information to passengers when they ask.
- Assist elderly passengers into and out of vehicle.
- Receive at least one commendation per year from a passenger.
- Offer to help passengers with their baggage as they enter and exit the vehicle.
- Deliver passengers to airport at the appropriate terminal without loss of time.
- Ensure zero instances of a passenger missing a flight as a result of driver error.
- Arrive at each bus stop on route within two minutes of scheduled time except during weather emergencies.
- Discipline children on school bus in a consistent manner and inform the principal of all disciplinary problems.
- Take every passenger to his or her destination by the most direct or lowest-cost route.

General Operations

- Arrive for each shift ready and able to drive.
- Wear prescribed work clothing and begin shifts with clothing clean and neat.

➤

- Ensure that passengers arrive at their stops on schedule 95% of trips (excluding weather emergencies).
- Follow all tariff rates and procedures 100% of the time.
- Receive zero validated complaint judgments from the taxi board.
- Enforce no smoking laws as required, in polite and courteous fashion.
- Refrain from picking up fares in areas where it is illegal to make pickups.
- Arrive 10 minutes before route to check messages and perform pre-trip.
- Perform a pre-trip under-the-hood and drivetrain inspection daily.
- Ensure that each child boarding bus has a proper and visible identification tag.
- Maintain and submit trip logs to the supervisor at the end of each shift.
- Apply company rules on accepting large-denomination bills.

Safety and Maintenance
- Ensure that the vehicle does not go into service with any mechanical problems that might affect safety.
- Eliminate all passenger injuries caused by preventable mechanical problems.
- Receive no more than one validated complaint about vehicle operation in any calendar year.
- Receive zero tickets for speeding or other traffic violations.
- Receive no more than one validated complaint per year regarding cleanliness of vehicle.
- Maintain safety certification as required by local authority.

- Ensure that all passengers are in compliance with safety requirements before the vehicle moves.
- Inspect any safety exits at the beginning of each shift and report problems immediately.
- Refuse or delay trips when conditions constitute a safety hazard to passengers or equipment.
- Follow safety procedures for dealing with aggressive passengers.
- Complete a defensive driving course once every two years.
- Meet or exceed all physical fitness qualifications required by the company and the licensing authority.
- Remain in or with the bus at all times or otherwise secure access.
- Communicate emergency evacuation procedures to passengers as indicated in the procedures manual.
- Ensure that child passengers are legally and safely in child safety seats before putting vehicle into motion.

Vehicle Operation
- Ensure that no passenger injuries occur as a result of abrupt or extreme driving procedures.
- Drive vehicle to maximize fuel mileage, keeping mileage within 10% of average for vehicle type.
- Activate "No Passing" lights 100% of the time when children are boarding or leaving bus.
- Come to a complete stop at railroad crossings 100% of the time (or as legally required).
- Reduce vehicle repair costs by 10% next year.

See also: Customer Service and Support

Mechanical Repair and Trades

Goals in this section can be used for employees directly involved in the repair of machinery of various sorts and trades like plumbing, carpentry, auto mechanics, and welding.

Customer Communication

- Provide an estimate to the customer within the time span agreed upon.
- Inform the customer of any other mechanical problems found during repair.
- Explain clearly the consequences of not repairing a mechanical problem.
- Provide advice to the customer on whether a repair is worth doing.
- Notify the customer when the repair is completed.
- Contact each customer one week after repair to determine his or her satisfaction with the repair.
- Present a clear, itemized bill upon conclusion of repairs that comes within 10% of the estimate.
- Notify the client if arriving more than 10 minutes late.
- Inform the client of options regarding repair parts and the merits of each so he or she can make an informed choice.

Diagnosis and Quality of Work

- Diagnose problems accurately at least 95% of the time.
- Ensure that repairs do not have to be redone within one year.
- Ensure that repairs outlast warranty on repairs in at least 95% of cases.

- Attend appropriate training courses each year to refresh diagnostic skills and learn about changes in new models.
- Ensure that all repair work complies with all relevant safety guidelines.
- Ensure that no repairs fail inspection by third-party safety inspectors.
- Maintain area of repair so no injuries occur while repair is ongoing.
- Post appropriate signage to guide people away from repair area.
- Make repairs so that zero property damage occurs as a result of the poor quality of any repair.
- Meet customer needs so that 90% of customers are satisfied, as determined through follow-up calls.
- Test all repairs before leaving to ensure that they actually solve the problem.

Speed of Repair
- Complete every repair within the specified "book time" for that kind of repair 95% of the time.
- Ensure that no more than 5% of repairs are delayed due to lack of parts or tools.
- Arrive for every repair visit with all necessary tools and parts.
- Make every effort to minimize the amount of time the machinery is unavailable for customer use.

Work Planning and Estimating
- Plan projects so as to eliminate unproductive downtime attributable to poor planning.
- Provide accurate, fair, and honest estimates.
- Schedule field repairs to reduce mileage/transportation costs by 10%.

➡

- Plan so arrival at repair site is within 10 minutes of time promised.
- Schedule the shutdown of machinery for repair to have the least possible impact on the customer's business and/or life.
- Maximize billing hours through effective work planning.
- Maintain billable hours at an average of 30 hours per week level.

See also: Customer Service and Support

Human Resources and Personnel—Management

Goals in this section can be used with anyone working in Human Resource departments who has supervisory or managerial responsibilities.

Compensation/Benefits

- Ensure that salary and benefits packages are competitive to attract top-quality candidates, according to unit managers.
- Ensure that compensation levels are within 10% of industry norms.
- Keep project salary costs for next year within 5% of estimates.
- Research and suggest options for new profit-sharing program.
- Ensure that no more than 5% of job offers are rejected due to inadequate salary and benefits.
- Maintain overall overtime levels at less than 4% of total payroll per month.
- Contribute to corporate team investigating health insurance options and write the final report for executive management.
- Identify best practices in providing day care and recommend to the board of directors a course of action that takes into account practicality and financial issues.

Conformance

- Ensure that hiring practices conform to Equal Employment Opportunity Commission requirements.
- Reduce substantiated discrimination complaints to zero.
- Inform the CEO of potential illegal practices that put the company at risk.

- Procure expert legal advice on behalf of the company as needed.
- Complete Human Resources audit once every two years to determine conformance levels.
- Identify any illegal nonconformance to HR laws before external agencies do.

Hiring

- Ensure that job applications are representative of the diversity of the local workforce.
- Develop strategies to increase qualified applications from members of minority groups by 10% next year.
- Keep recruitment costs within 10% of industry average.
- Fill all jobs within six weeks of initial job posting.
- Reduce the time needed to fill vacancies by 10% from previous year.

Labor Relations

- Reduce union labor actions to zero, while staying within financial guidelines.
- Reduce total grievances to 15 or fewer a year.
- Reduce total grievance proceedings losses to three per year.
- Reduce by 20% the time needed to come to labor agreements.
- Report bargaining deadlocks to the CFO within three hours of occurrence.

Policy Development/Communication

- Prepare estimates of required staffing levels for next five years, to the satisfaction of the CFO.
- Research and report on potential outsourcing of HR functions, to the satisfaction of the CFO.

- Respond to requests from senior executives for advice or information within one working day.
- Develop a downsizing strategy that does not result in significant loss in productivity.

Staff Development
- With senior executives, prepare an annual staff development plan linked to the organization's strategic plan.
- Ensure that staff development planning is linked to work-unit performance management process.
- Develop a staff development plan that reflects the organization's skill needs for the upcoming year and incorporates input from executive, line managers, and employees.
- Keep current and knowledgeable about current HR trends and laws by attending annual government briefings on HR law and attending one national HR conference per year.
- Reduce staff development costs while increasing staff development hours delivered, by coordinating needs and solutions across the company and using economy of scale.

Staff Retention/Promotion
- Ensure that at least 95% of promoted employees succeed, as reflected in yearly performance reviews.
- Maintain staff turnover ratio between 5 and 8% per year.
- Reduce new hire turnover to less than 10%.
- Reduce dismissals related to substance abuse to less than 3% of total dismissals.
- Reduce staff loss resulting from "insufficient challenge in job" by 10%.

Staff Satisfaction

- Chair employee satisfaction committee that suggests at least five strategies for improving company morale that get implemented.
- Achieve company objective of being listed as one of the top 100 companies to work for.
- Advise senior executives on low-cost morale-building strategies.

See also: Managing Performance, Personnel/Hiring/Retention

Human Resources and Personnel

Goals in this section can be used with employees in Human Resource departments or elsewhere involved in hiring and retention, including work-unit managers.

Hiring

- Screen job applicants so hiring managers are satisfied with the pool of applicants.
- Develop and implement an online job application system by year-end.
- Ensure that job applications are representative of the diversity of the local workforce.
- Develop strategies to increase qualified applications from members of minority groups by 10% next year.
- Keep recruitment costs within 10% of industry average.
- Fill all jobs within six weeks of initial job posting.
- Reduce the time needed to fill vacancies by 10% from previous year.
- Ensure that managers understand steps to follow to request additional staffing so they can do so with no errors or requests for clarification.

Staff Development

- With senior executives, prepare an annual staff development plan linked to the organization's strategic plan.
- Incorporate staff development planning in work-unit performance management process.
- Help employees find the most effective means of maintaining professional certification.
- Advise employees on recommended development activities that will increase their potential for promotion.

- Ensure that employees are knowledgeable about all product lines.
- Provide basic orientation for new employees that they rate as "above average" in surveys.
- Help managers provide specific job orientations with new hires to reduce time required to get new employees up to speed.
- Use acting status appointments to develop at least four promising managerial candidates per year.
- Maintain a database of training options for specific positions that at least 30% of employees consult in any given year.
- Develop a staff development plan that reflects the organization's skill needs for the upcoming year and incorporates input from executive, line managers, and employees.
- Advise on organizational development issues and refer managers to competent resources, to the satisfaction of the managers.
- Keep current and knowledgeable about current HR trends and laws by attending annual government briefings on HR law and attending one national HR conference per year.
- Maintain database of local trainers, including quality review information, so managers can arrange seminars without the intervention of HR.
- Reduce staff development costs while increasing staff development hours delivered by coordinating needs and solutions across the company and using economy of scale.
- Ensure that staff development planning is linked to the work-unit performance management process.

Staff Retention/Promotion

- Ensure that at least 95% of promoted employees succeed, as reflected in yearly performance reviews.
- Maintain staff turnover ratio between 5 and 8% per year.
- Reduce new hire turnover to less than 10%.
- Reduce dismissals related to substance abuse to less than 3% of total dismissals.
- Reduce staff loss resulting from "insufficient challenge in job" by 10%.
- Conduct exit interviews for every employee and provide the HR manager a semiannual report on reasons for leaving.

Staff Satisfaction

- Conduct staff satisfaction surveys at least once every two years.
- Prepare recommendations to improve employee satisfaction, with at least two recommendations implemented each year.
- Use exit interview data to raise employee satisfaction levels.
- Chair employee satisfaction committee that suggests at least five strategies for improving company morale that get implemented.
- Achieve company objective of being listed as one of the top 100 companies to work for.

Conformance

- Ensure that hiring practices conform to Equal Employment Opportunity Commission requirements.
- Reduce substantiated discrimination complaints to zero.

- Advise the managers on legal interviewing techniques.
- Prepare and advise the managers for grievance hearings.
- Inform the CEO of potential illegal practices that put the company at risk.
- Procure expert legal advice on behalf of the company as needed.
- Complete Human Resources audit once every two years to determine conformance levels.
- Identify any illegal nonconformance to HR laws before external agencies do.

Policy Development/Communication
- Create a staff development policy that links staff development expenditures to the organization's needs.
- Communicate information about benefits package options in plain English, so most employees understand them.
- Consult with line managers on policy changes that affect them prior to rewriting policies.
- Write policies that managers can follow without asking additional questions.
- Prepare estimates of required staffing levels for next five years, to the satisfaction of the CFO.
- Research and report on potential outsourcing of HR functions, to the satisfaction of the CFO.
- Develop and communicate performance management policy to managers so that managers indicate they understand and can implement the policy.

Work-Unit Support
- Maintain job descriptions and update descriptions each year or as required by managers.

- Support managers in undertaking performance management so that managers complete 80% of appraisals on time.
- Provide employee assistance referrals to the satisfaction of managers and employees.
- Administer human resources database to maintain 98% uptime.
- Provide support to managers in handling layoff situations humanely.
- Develop a downsizing strategy that does not result in significant loss in productivity.
- Ensure that employees and managers complete forms provided by HR so that no more than 2% need revision.
- Respond to managers' requests for assistance within one working day.
- Help managers determine optimal staffing levels for work unit to maintain or increase effectiveness.
- Provide training to managers on conducting termination meetings safely and to satisfaction of the managers as indicated in feedback sheets.
- Provide at least three different forms from which managers can choose to track performance management.
- Provide legal interpretations to managers regarding personnel issues within two days of request and with at least 98% accuracy.
- Provide managers and employees with information about substance abuse rehabilitation resources available and increase the use of such resources to within 30% of the incidence of addiction in the population.

Compensation/Benefits

- Ensure that salary and benefits packages are competitive to attract top-quality candidates, according to unit managers.
- Ensure that compensation levels are within 10% of industry norms.
- Keep project salary costs for next year within 5% of estimates.
- Research and suggest options for new profit-sharing program.
- Ensure that no more than 5% of job offers are rejected due to inadequate salary and benefits.
- Maintain overall overtime levels at less than 4% of total payroll per month.
- Contribute to corporate team investigating health insurance options and write the final report for executive management.
- Identify best practices in providing day care and recommend to the board of directors a course of action that takes into account practicality and financial issues.

Labor Relations

- Reduce union labor actions to zero, while staying within financial guidelines.
- Reduce total grievances to 15 or fewer a year.
- Reduce total grievance proceedings losses to three per year.
- Reduce by 20% the time needed to come to labor agreements.
- Complete labor agreements for bargaining group by July 6 and stay within financial guidelines established by the CEO.

➡

- Report bargaining deadlocks to the CFO within three hours of occurrence.

Other

- Provide clear guidance to systems personnel about HR requirements for personnel tracking system.
- Review and recommend possible options for HR management software to satisfaction of the CFO.
- Lead systems development initiative to develop an integrated HR management system to be completed by year-end.
- Ensure employees receive all tax documentation at least three weeks prior to government set mandatory date.
- Attend local Human Resources Association meetings and present on at least one topic each year.
- Make employee assistance referrals quickly enough to maximize outcomes.

See also: Managing Performance, Personnel/Hiring/Retention

Physical Plant Maintenance—Management

Goals in this section can be used with management and supervisory staff involved in supervising maintenance, repair, and cleaning activities related to the physical space and equipment in the workplace.

Cleaning

- Ensure that department managers make no more than one complaint per month about cleaning service.
- Contract with outside cleaning agencies to provide required cleaning services within allocated cleaning budget.
- Schedule cleaning staff to minimize overtime and ensure that all required cleaning is done on time.
- Do spot checks of premises at least once a day to ensure cleanliness.
- Review cleaning logs to make sure washrooms are cleaned on schedule.
- Review customer feedback forms and alter cleaning schedules to increase "cleanliness" rating by 20%.
- Maintain cleaning supplies inventory to ensure zero need for employees to make special purchases due to shortages.
- Ensure that all volatile cleaning materials are kept secure, with access restricted to cleaning staff.
- Work with cleaning staff to research and recommend better cleaning products.

Plant Maintenance

- Ensure that plant downtime related to emergency repairs totals no more than three hours per month.

- Develop maintenance schedules for major equipment that result in a 10% reduction of total downtime due to equipment failures.
- Prioritize requests for maintenance, according to the potential impact on safety and productivity.
- Ensure that overall response time for requests for maintenance is within company requirements and specifications.
- Meet regularly with supervisors and line managers to identify ways the maintenance unit can provide better service to them.
- Ensure that unplanned emergency purchases constitute no more than 10% of the physical plant maintenance budget each year.
- Arrange for normal elevator maintenance to occur outside of peak work hours.
- Help the VP Operations identify major equipment replacements that will be necessary within next two years.
- Solicit from equipment users at least one maintenance improvement strategy to reduce unplanned failures.
- Review problem-reporting procedures and improve as necessary.

Safety
- Chair workplace safety and health committee during 2011.
- Ensure that all maintenance employees understand and follow emergency procedures.
- Arrange for immediate emergency repair of critical emergency systems within one hour of being notified.
- Assign and train staff in roles in emergency shutdown and evacuation situations.

- Coordinate third-party inspections of critical physical plant machinery (boilers, elevators) to comply with government certification requirements.
- Develop and implement a maintenance strategy to reduce customer injuries requiring medical attention to zero in the upcoming year.
- Review and stay current on government workplace safety and health regulations.
- Ensure that maintenance employees report and remedy violations of government guidelines before they are identified by outside inspectors.

See also: Workplace Health and Safety—Management

Goals in this section can be used with employees involved in any maintenance, repair, and cleaning activities related to the physical space and equipment in the workplace.

Cleaning

- Inspect washrooms at least once an hour and identify cleaning needs.
- Ensure that customers rate "cleanliness of establishment" as at least very good.
- Complete cleaning logs with no errors.
- Complete end-of-shift cleanup so employees on the following shift do not complain about tasks not completed.
- Use appropriate cleaning solutions and products for job, according to supervisor.
- Inform supervisor of upcoming shortages of cleaning supplies so no shortage interferes with maintenance.
- Respond to requests for aisle cleanup within 10 minutes and complete the cleanup within 20 minutes.
- Ensure that doorways into facility are clear of ice and snow or other impediments to customers.
- Place cleaning equipment so as to not block entryways for more than five minutes at a time during cleaning.
- Clean windows in public view to maintain clear, unobstructed vision and clean appearance.
- Maintain cleaning equipment inventory so all items are easily accessible and access to the items is not blocked.
- Process empty cleaning materials containers in prescribed and safe way.

Plant Maintenance

- Respond to emergency physical plant situations within 20 minutes of notification.
- Shut down the heating system in emergency situations according to manufacturer's shutdown instructions.
- Eliminate your own maintenance errors that affect plant productivity.
- Eliminate injuries to employees resulting from your own errors in maintaining assigned equipment.
- Inform supervisor of the progress of every repair so he or she can communicate effectively with plant supervisors as needed.
- Carry out preventative maintenance for assigned machines and as set out in manufacturers' guidelines.
- Identify probable causes of potential failure of major equipment and notify manager for preventive repair and replacement.
- Maintain maintenance and repair logs for all major physical plant machinery.
- Develop and maintain positive relationships with outside repair and maintenance personnel.

Safety

- Notify management and HAZMAT team of any potential hazardous substance spills within 10 minutes of identifying them.
- Spot and remove any items out of place that may constitute safety hazards.
- Place warning signs when cleaning floors so there are zero customer accidents related to improper signage.
- Eliminate all occurrences of spillage of hazardous material as a result of your own handling errors. ➡

- Participate and contribute to workplace safety and health committee.
- Participate in monthly checks and inspections of all safety equipment including fire alarms, smoke detectors, and carbon monoxide detectors.

See also: Workplace Health and Safety

Retail/Merchandising—Management

Goals in this section can be used with anyone working in the retail sector who supervises or manages employees.

Customer Service

- Handle customer complaints so no more than one per month go to head office.

- Talk with at least five customers per day to assess customer satisfaction.

- Ensure that average customer checkout time is less than four minutes.

- Provide customer service improvement suggestions to head office at least twice yearly.

- Ensure that floor workers have sufficient product knowledge to respond to customer inquiries effectively.

Scheduling/Staffing

- Reduce overtime 10% by hiring temporary and/or backup staff.

- Reduce staff absenteeism to less than 1% of total days worked in store.

- Ensure that all employees have adequate product knowledge, as indicated by customer feedback.

- Ensure that all employees are properly certified as required.

- Conform to staffing guidelines from the head office.

- Identify employees who are candidates for promotion within next year and forward the information to Human Resources.

- Develop and implement an employee-of-the-month system so that 80% of the employees surveyed find it constructive.

Store Management

- Reduce shrinkage by 2% per month from last year's figures.
- Completely eliminate health code violations in 2011.
- Ensure that the store follows the merchandising requirements of the company.
- Ensure that the store meets its revenue and budget targets for each month.
- Report anticipated monthly revenue shortfalls to head office by the 15th of each month.
- Maintain rating of at least 4 out of 5 from corporate mystery shoppers.
- Forecast customer demand for stock within 10% of actuals.
- Order stock to accommodate customer demand.
- Meet monthly projections of gross profit as compared with comparable stores.

See also: Customer Service and Support—Management, Financial, Security—Management, Food Preparation—Management, Retail/Merchandising

Retail/Merchandising

Goals in this section can be used with employees working in the retail sector at all levels of an organization, but particularly in retail locations.

Checkout/Cash Register

- Process 90% of customers within five minutes.
- Promote special offers to customers when appropriate to circumstances.
- Direct customers to proper aisle for desired products, without help.
- Balance the cash register and come within $1 98% of the time.
- Make sure that cash register discrepancies never exceed $10 per shift.
- Engage in friendly conversation with customers without sacrificing speed of scanning or otherwise entering items.
- Manage checkout lines and direct customers to other, faster lines.
- Process returns and refunds properly and without help from supervisor.
- Input items with no more than 1% error in amounts.
- Calculate change due to customers, both with and without machines.
- Wrap/package customer goods with no more than 2% reported damage.

Customer Service

- Fit customers with the proper size to the satisfaction of the customers.
- Offer the customers value-added services every time (e.g., parcel carryout).

- Teach customers about new features in store, as appropriate.
- Offer corporate credit cards to all customers, with a sign-up rate of at least 1%.
- Relay customer complaints to the manager at the end of each day.
- Smile and greet customers, to the satisfaction of the supervisor.
- Acknowledge customers waiting for service.

Retail Environment

- Place impulse buying items at checkout.
- Maintain the lights so no more than 2% are inoperative at any given time.
- Respond to emergency cleanup requests within four minutes of request.
- Ensure that all shelves under your control are neat and orderly by the end of each shift.
- Ensure that 98% of stock have UPCs and pricing codes in place at any given time.
- Keep aisles clear and free from debris.
- Maintain area so 95% of products are in proper locations.
- Keep food sampling tables clean and sanitary; empty garbage pails when they become three-quarters full.
- Rotate special feature displays around the store each week.
- Provide cooking instructions and recipes when customers ask for them.
- Ensure that seasonal displays are timely and removed immediately after the seasonal event.
- Check featured item displays at beginning of each shift to ensure that they are in place and in good condition.

Stock/Inventory

- Ensure that inventory on hand is sufficient to meet customer demand for sales items.
- Reduce issuing of rain checks by 20% in any given month.
- Ensure that 95% of expired products are removed from display.
- Reduce product wastage by 10%.
- Ensure that departmental shrinkage is below store average.
- Remove all damaged or unsellable merchandise from displays.
- Keep old product in front of new product.
- Operate stocking machines, forklifts, and ladders safely in accordance with operating procedures.
- Follow stock security procedures each time valuable items are accessed.
- Dispose of spoiled produce in accordance with procedures outlined in job aid.
- Ensure that 90% of high-demand items are safely accessible to all customers.
- Inform the manager of any inventory arriving damaged or spoiled within three hours of arrival.
- Ensure that all items are dated accurately.
- Report to the designated manager any discrepancies between inventory received and inventory expected as soon as you observe them.
- Ensure that the time lag between product being received at the loading dock and appearing on the shelves in saleable condition is no greater than three hours.

➡

- Put new items in the storage area as soon as they arrive so sales staff can access them easily.

See also: Retail/Merchandising—Management, Customer Service and Support, Financial, Security, Food Preparation

Sales and Business Development—Management

Goals in this section can be used with people supervising or managing sales functions in organizations.

Generating New Sales/Customers

- Improve sales to 18-24 age group demographic by 5%.
- Reduce cost per customer acquisition to $25.
- Coach sales staff in improving initial approaches to customers.
- Monitor cold calls to potential customers and provide feedback to staff.
- Coordinate conference presentations to generate a minimum of 10 new customers per appearance.
- Promote new products through media appearances at least six times this year.
- Conclude at least one new distributor agreement involving at least $1 million in sales.

Managing Current Sales/Customer Relations

- Increase average expenditure per visit by 10% across the department.
- Ensure delivery of sold products on schedule 97% of the time across the department.
- Contact all key accounts at least once every month to obtain feedback and offer help.
- Retain at least 95% of current distributors.

Sales Strategy Development

- Identify major reasons why sales aren't closed and suggest strategies to improve close ratio.
- Collect, summarize, and analyze customer input; generate suggestions for new products and submit them annually to the product director.

- Provide possible new product ideas to the director of product development, based on feedback from customers.
- Ensure that sales promotions result in 1-to-1.5 payback ratio.

Sales Training/Communication
- Conduct sales training seminars for subordinates at least once every two months.
- Develop strategy for sharing successful selling techniques.
- Diagnose and address skill gaps in supervised sales staff.
- Develop a modular training program for newly hired salespeople.
- Coordinate with marketing and production to prepare sales staff for new product rollout.
- Ensure that sales materials and brochures are available to sales staff when required.
- Provide sales projections to production to ensure that all orders can be filled on time.
- Provide monthly sales reports to VP Sales no later than 5th of next month.
- Notify VP Sales of anticipated sales shortfalls no later than 15th of sales month.
- Forecast monthly sales projections that are no more than +/- 12% off actuals.

See also: Retail/Merchandising—Management, Customer Service and Support—Management

Sales and Business Development

Goals in this section can be used with employees in sales positions or supervising sales staff.

Managing Current Sales/Customers

- Maintain personal customer retention ratio at 95% or higher.
- Cross-sell additional products to increase value secondary purchases to $10,000 per month.
- Increase average expenditure per client transaction to $200.
- Increase average expenditure per visit by 10%.
- Maintain monthly contact with customers spending more than $500/month for upselling purposes.
- Achieve or exceed sales quotes on monthly basis.
- Increase sales to current large accounts (> $50,000 annually) by 20%.
- Generate at least two customer referrals a month from current customers.

Generating New Sales/Customers

- Improve sales to 18-24 age group demographic by 5%.
- Close sales for 20% of new leads provided.
- Reduce cost per customer acquisition to $25.
- Reduce time per customer acquisition to one hour (face to face or phone).
- Promote new product/service X so it constitutes 15% of personal sales.
- Bring in one mega-account worth sales of $1 million.
- Reduce reliance on small account sales (< $10,000 per annum) by concentrating on developing large accounts.
- Introduce product/service X to three new markets.

Sales-Related Customer Relations

- Provide estimates to customers that are within 5% of customer cost.
- Provide estimates for project conclusion accurate within five days.
- Retain customers so that no more than five per year ask to be transferred to another sales rep.
- Maintain overall rating by customers of at least "good" on survey instrument.
- Be organized enough to meet customer contact commitments at least 95% of the time.
- Project a professional image to potential customers during sales presentations.
- Respond to sales inquiries within three hours.
- Ensure delivery of sold product on schedule 97% of the time.

Sales Strategy Development

- Identify major reasons why sales aren't closed and suggest strategies to improve close ratio.
- Identify customer issues/barriers to sales and participate in sales strategy development team.
- Collect, summarize, and analyze customer input; generate suggestions for new products and submit them annually to the product director.
- Work with marketing/advertising to develop new advertising strategies based on your understanding of your customers.
- As part of total sales team, contribute to sales increases of a minimum of 5% for each salesperson on team.
- Develop a modular training program for newly hired salespeople.
- Collect customer comments and pass them along to marketing.

➥

Sales Training

- Train peers in best practices in sales.
- Share sales techniques with peers at monthly sales meetings.
- Conduct sales training seminars for subordinates at least once every two months.
- Develop a strategy for sharing successful selling techniques.
- Diagnose and address skill gaps in supervised sales staff.
- As product expert, train other sales staff to sell new product/service X.
- Train other staff so their sales of new product constitute 15% of total sales.

See also: Retail/Merchandising, Customer Service and Support

Security—Management

Goals in this section can be used with anyone in supervisory or management positions in departments responsible for the security of people, data, products, and physical environment.

Communication

- Coordinate work with police and other agencies to the satisfaction of those agencies.
- Ensure that the emergency procedures manual is available and accessible to all employees.
- Provide employee assistance program information to victims within 10 hours of incident.
- Contact the employee assistance director within 24 hours of any violent incident, to arrange appropriate counseling available.
- Develop and communicate a disaster evacuation plan.
- Deliver refresher courses to security staff at least once a year.
- Provide information to employees about drug-testing procedures, to the satisfaction of employees.
- Write a yearly report summarizing security statistics and making recommendations to the CEO about required security upgrades.
- Research and report on the need for personal security devices to be furnished to employees.

Compliance

- Help line managers schedule so there are always at least two staff members in the store after dark.
- Ensure that all security-related policies conform to federal, state, and local laws and requirements.

- Ensure that all drug-screening programs are consistent with existing human rights legislation (zero court-upheld challenges).
- Respond to every customer complaint about security staff within one working day.

Improvement

- Reduce the cost of vandalism to less than $1,000 per year.
- Develop and implement at least two new theft-prevention techniques per year.
- Reduce incidents of physical violence against staff by 15% in 2011.
- Reduce drug test positives by 10% in the upcoming year.

Supervision and Training

- Schedule mobile patrols so each floor is checked at least once per hour.
- Ensure that all fixed-post security employees are alert (zero reports of inattentive security staff from building occupants).
- Ensure that main desk security employees use the visitor-tracking system as indicated in the security manual.
- Ensure that all security staff have, wear, and use appropriate uniforms and identification badges at all times.
- Help all security staff members procure and maintain "Certified Protection Professional" status.

Theft

- Implement an employee-monitoring strategy in high-risk areas.
- Maintain theft levels at less than 1% of total inventory.
- Work with managers in high-theft departments to reduce theft in those departments by 20% this year.

- Develop and implement key-tracking system to ensure that no unauthorized personnel have access to locked spaces.

See also: Workplace Health and Safety, Security

Security

Goals in this section can be used with employees responsible for security in the workplace, including those charged with the security of physical goods and facilities and the security and safety of people in the work environment.

Communication and Training

- Ensure that all employees understand emergency procedures for dealing with violent situations.
- Ensure that all employees are trained in techniques for preventing theft and violence.
- Ensure that all employees are trained and able to use observation and incident-reporting tools properly.
- Compile monthly incident reports and forward to head office before 15th of each month.
- Identify employee skill deficits that may negatively affect safety and security.
- Coordinate work with police and other agencies to the satisfaction of those agencies.

Compliance

- Follow cash-handling procedures as per company procedures.
- Schedule so there are always at least two staff members in the store after dark.
- Complete and pass training prescribed for security personnel each year.
- Maintain certification in CPR and other first aid techniques.
- With police, conduct annual safety audit inspections.
- Comply with policies governing professional appearance and conduct as specified by the employer.

Enforcement

- Use least possible force in dealing with shoplifters: no physical injuries that require hospitalization.
- Maintain your own fitness levels to company standards as measured each year.
- Reduce nonvalid shoplifting-related customer stops to less than 5% of total stops.
- Maintain validated customer complaints about enforcement practices to an average of less than one per month.
- Respond to staff requests for assistance within two minutes.
- Provide accurate follow-up and incident documentation promptly.
- Use verbal self-defense techniques to reduce the need for force, to the satisfaction of the supervisor.
- Involve or refer to law enforcement officers as needed and in accordance with company policy.
- Apply standard accident and criminal investigation techniques in each situation.
- Gather evidence and prepare cases successfully for filing complaints, as verified by courts and the police.
- Use proper legal techniques for searching suspects.
- Use proper procedures for search and seizure, as verified by police.
- Use vehicle safely for patrol and pursuit, with no accidents in which the police determine the security employee to be at fault.
- Interview witnesses using proper questioning techniques within the bounds of legality.
- Secure and monitor prisoners according to police guidelines.

- Receive zero validated serious complaints from employees or customers.
- Demonstrate proper weapons safety procedures at all times.

Improvement
- Reduce the cost of vandalism to less than $1,000 per year.
- Develop and implement at least two new theft-prevention techniques per year.
- Reduce physical violence incidents aimed at staff by 15% in 2011.

Theft
- Implement an employee-monitoring strategy in high-risk areas.
- Maintain theft levels at less than 1% of total inventory.
- Ensure that the electronic theft prevention system is working properly.
- Keep items identified as high-theft targets in secure cases until sold.

Personal Security
- Conduct an annual safety audit to identify potentially risky personal security habits.
- Conduct background checks on job applicants to ensure that nobody with a criminal record is hired.
- Report any employee "high-risk" warning signs to the Director of Security.
- Carry out high-risk activities (e.g., firing) ensuring that security help is available and notified in advance.
- Abide by personal safety procedures as set up by the Director of Security.
- Report suspicious persons on premises to security office.

➡

- Research and report on need for personal security devices to be furnished to employees.

Premises Security

- Secure premises when responsible for closing, 100% of the time.
- Maintain lighting system so 95% of lights work at any given time.
- Set alarm system properly at the end of the day, 100% of time.
- Patrol assigned areas on time and in the required manner.

Traffic Control

- Use clear and correct hand signals when directing traffic, to the supervisor's satisfaction.
- Reduce car-pedestrian parking lot accidents to one or none per year.
- Ensure that fire lanes are kept clear at all times.
- Arrange for removing any vehicles that impede fire lane access within 10 minutes of observing them.
- Keep traffic signage visible and in good repair as per supervisor evaluation.

See also: Workplace Health and Safety

Support—Management

Goals in this section can be used with anyone who manages or supervises support staff employees or who has members of support staff as direct reports.

Communication, Supervision, and Training

- Explain work task requirements to reports, in order to reduce error rates to 1%.
- Create and provide job aids for staff.
- Ensure that staff employees work within authority levels on all tasks.
- Conduct training on new technology systems.
- Monitor 3% of incoming calls to provide feedback to employees.
- Advise staff on methods to improve productivity.
- Interpret policy and advise staff on policy interpretations.
- Develop and maintain accurate job descriptions for supervised positions.
- Train new hires in operation of office machines within three days of hire.

Office Management

- Identify alternate sources for office supplies, to reduce costs by 10%.
- Increase throughput by 10% without additional staff.
- Respond to complaints from users about support functions within one working day.
- Reduce days lost due to injuries from ergonomic problems by 8%.
- Draft cost-benefit reports for technological improvements under consideration.

- Negotiate office equipment maintenance contracts to hold costs stable for 2011.

Scheduling and Work Assignments
- Ensure adequate job coverage of staff absences.
- Schedule staff to reduce overtime to 5% of total hours worked.
- Assign work to staff to make best use of time and skills.
- Accommodate the special needs of staff without sacrificing productivity.

See also: Support, Customer Service and Support—Management

Support

Goals in this section can be used with employees carrying out various support functions—filing, reception, switchboard, and handling phone calls.

Clerical/Filing

- Ensure that there are no more than 10 case files at one time in the "to file" basket.
- Log shared files taken by staff so that others needing the files can locate them.
- Review the filing system once each year to determine efficiency of system.
- Retrieve files within five minutes of file request.
- Ensure that other employees can retrieve files on their own without the help of a clerk.
- Check forms submitted for errors so that no more than 2% of the forms filed contain errors.
- Process forms within three days of receipt.
- Maintain file security and access control so that zero unauthorized accesses occur.
- Ensure that no more than 1% of files are lost or otherwise unavailable.
- Take outgoing mail to mailroom by 4 P.M. each day.

Reception

- Inform all visitors of the approximate wait time, accurate within 10 minutes.
- Greet all visitors within three minutes of arrival.
- Provide staff with enough information about the needs of visitors so they can reduce meeting time.
- Receive no more than one complaint per month about the service provided to visitors.

- Keep reception area clean and orderly.
- Track the availability of employees, in order to provide accurate information to visitors.
- Open the office promptly at 8:00 A.M. 95% of the time.

Secretarial

- Produce outgoing documents with no errors in the final draft.
- Schedule meetings with no conflicts.
- Make travel arrangements to take advantage of advance booking specials.
- Schedule so that all outgoing correspondence is dispatched within one day.
- Prioritize incoming mail and eliminate all unwanted mail to the satisfaction of the manager.
- Edit dictated copy to produce documents that the manager considers better than the text as dictated.
- Summarize and submit travel expense vouchers within three days of the trip.
- Prepare meeting briefing notes for the manager and have them available at least two hours before each meeting.
- Arrange and reserve meeting space and provide refreshments to the satisfaction of the participants.
- Order office supplies so that employees always have materials when they need them.
- Maintain accurate distribution lists for memos.
- Follow up on e-mails sent to ensure they were received and understood.
- Screen e-mails to reduce volume to staff by 50%.
- Fill requests for duplicating within four hours of request.

- Collate and staple documents for professional look, to the satisfaction of the document owner.

Switchboard/Phones

- Prioritize phone calls to the satisfaction of the manager.
- Take messages with sufficient detail to allow informed callbacks.
- Provide sufficient information to callers so return calls can be reduced by 10%.
- Route phone calls to the appropriate person 98% of the time.
- Process a minimum of 20 calls per hour, as needed.
- Answer all calls within three rings.
- Ensure that no caller is kept on hold longer than one minute.
- Screen calls and provide information to caller, to reduce the need for other employees to call back.
- Ensure that phones are covered during breaks, lunch, and short absences.
- Speak clearly so that no more than one complaint is received per month about being hard to understand.

See also: Customer Service and Support, Financial

Workplace Health and Safety—Management

Goals in this section can be used with managers, supervisors, and team leaders whose reports deal directly with workplace health and safety programs and issues.

Compliance

- Ensure the handling of hazardous material in compliance with federal regulations.
- Report hazardous material incidents to appropriate government agency within two days of identifying them.
- Ensure that warnings from inspectors are addressed and problems are resolved so that the governing organization takes no further action.
- Reduce government inspection warnings to zero for 2011.
- Eliminate any safety risks that could result in plant shutdowns.

Improvement and Investigation

- Work as a liaison with external investigators to the satisfaction of those investigators.
- Reduce workplace safety insurance fees by 10% in 2005.
- Reduce accidents requiring hospitalization by 10% per year.
- Reduce minor accidents requiring nurse's station involvement by 15% per year.
- Reduce days lost due to accidents to no more than 1% of total days worked.
- Reduce at-work fatalities to zero by 2005.
- Reduce the incidence of occupational disease by 15% by 2005.
- Develop enhanced systems for collecting accident data, to allow the development of concrete accident-reduction strategies.
- Keep and maintain complete, accurate, and timely records of safety violations and incidents.

Training and Communication

- Identify at least three sources for safety-related training and recommend the best option to the COO, based on cost and effectiveness.

- Ensure that 98% of employees are trained in the handling of hazardous materials.

- Ensure that courses receive an average rating of at least 3 out of 5 from participants for the potential of the training to reduce accidents.

- Maintain the no-show rate for training at less than 10% per month.

- Identify and prioritize corporate training requirements based on frequency and severity of accidents.

- Communicate health and safety objectives to all new hires within two weeks of hire.

- Create performance standards regarding safety for each employee supervised.

- Communicate workplace emergency evacuation procedures to all employees at least once every six months.

- Conduct emergency drills at least once every month, with complete compliance to standards (time needed to evaluate, shut down, etc.).

- Track changes in legislation and ensure that the company is in complete compliance within the time frame established by any new legislation.

- Develop and implement employee reward and recognition program for reducing accidents.

- Ensure that all employees can recite emergency phone numbers for various types of incidents.

- Ensure that job aids and safety posters are available and visible in all high-risk areas.

Work Environment

- Develop safe production shutdown procedures so the system can be shut down within five minutes after a safety problem is identified.

- Ensure that all subcontractors and service providers understand and abide by company safety procedures.
- Ensure that equipment maintenance schedules are followed.
- Ensure that the initial response time for treating injured workers is less than 15 minutes for each incident.
- Audit physical space arrangements and make recommendations to ensure staff safety in the event of violent incidents.
- Invite community law enforcement officials once a year to audit workplace procedures for preventing workplace violence.

See also: Security—Management

Workplace Health and Safety

Goals in this section can be used with employees responsible for managing and implementing workplace health and safety programs and issues, work teams with similar responsibilities, and individuals.

Compliance

- Ensure the handling of hazardous material in compliance with federal regulations.
- Report hazardous material incidents to appropriate government agency within two days of identifying them.
- Maintain your own HAZMAT certification in accordance with government requirements.
- Follow all safety-related guidelines for construction site procedures.
- Ensure that warnings from inspectors are addressed and problems are resolved so that the governing organization takes no further action.
- Reduce government inspection warnings to zero for 2011.
- Eliminate any safety risks that could result in plant shutdowns.

Improvement and Investigation

- Work as a liaison with external investigators to the satisfaction of those investigators.
- Reduce workplace safety insurance fees by 10% in 2011.
- Reduce accidents requiring hospitalization by 10% per year.
- Reduce minor accidents requiring nurse's station involvement by 15% per year.

- Reduce days lost due to accidents to no more than 1% of total days worked.
- Attend and contribute to Workplace Health and Safety Committee meetings, as perceived by other members.
- Reduce at-work fatalities to zero by 2011.
- Reduce the incidence of occupational disease by 15% by 2011.
- Develop enhanced systems for collecting accident data, to allow the development of concrete accident-reduction strategies.
- Keep and maintain complete, accurate, and timely records of safety violations and incidents.

Training and Communication
- Deliver safety-related training across company so that 90% of employees achieve a minimum of 80% on final course tests.
- Attend and pass defensive driving courses at least once every year.
- Identify at least three sources for safety-related training and recommend the best option to the COO, based on cost and effectiveness.
- Ensure that 98% of employees are trained in the handling of hazardous materials.
- Ensure that courses receive an average rating of at least 3 out of 5 from participants for the potential of the training to reduce accidents.
- Maintain the no-show rate for training at less than 10% per month.
- Identify and prioritize corporate training requirements based on frequency and severity of accidents.
- Communicate health and safety objectives to all new hires within two weeks of hire.

- Create performance standards regarding safety for each employee supervised.
- Communicate workplace emergency evacuation procedures to all employees at least once every six months.
- Conduct emergency drills at least once every month, with complete compliance with standards (time needed to evaluate, shut down, etc.).
- Track changes in legislation and ensure that the company is in complete compliance within the time frame established by any new legislation.
- Develop and implement employee reward and recognition program for reducing accidents.
- Ensure that all employees can recite emergency phone numbers for various types of incidents.
- Ensure that job aids and safety posters are available and visible in all high-risk areas.

Work Environment

- Develop safe production shutdown procedures so the system can be shut down within five minutes after a safety problem is identified.
- Ensure that all subcontractors and service providers understand and abide by company safety procedures.
- Keep all emergency exits repaired and functioning properly at all times.
- Conduct weekly inspections to ensure that all safety equipment is in place and operable.
- Ensure that equipment maintenance schedules are followed.
- Ensure that the initial response time for treating injured workers is less than 15 minutes for each incident.
- Audit physical space arrangements and make recommendations to ensure staff safety in the event of violent incidents.

- Invite community law enforcement officials once a year to audit workplace procedures for preventing workplace violence.
- Ensure that all workplace entrances and exits are secure and well lit at all times.

See also: Security

Section Three

Perfect Phrases for Motivating and Rewarding Employees

Hundreds of Ready-to-Use Phrases to Encourage and Recognize Excellence

Harriet Diamond
Linda Eve Diamond

Section Contents

Part II:
Perfect Phrases for Motivating Employees 407

Preface

Motivation is the force that drives us all in every aspect of our lives. Without motivation, we wouldn't work, diet, exercise, pursue hobbies, or even get out of bed in the morning. In business, motivation is the seed at the center of every success. In Thomas Edison's enduring words: "Genius is one percent inspiration and ninety-nine percent perspiration." Without motivation, we would all be reduced to that one percent mindset, daydreaming through a window wondering why nothing interesting ever seems to happen.

Luckily, motivation is all around us, and most of us have natural drives toward satisfaction and success. Unfortunately, de-motivating forces and de-motivating people also surround us. Negativity is like a contagious disease (and it *is* the cause of much *dis-ease*). The good news is that a motivational mindset is also contagious, but spreading it takes more than hanging *happy* posters. In order to become a motivating force, you have to believe those inspiring slogans and breathe a positively motivating attitude.

When we first told people we were writing a book on motivational phrases, the first suggestion we were given was, "How about: 'Your money or your life'?" We had to admit that's a pretty motivating phrase! Obviously, it was said as a joke, but threats seem to have a high results ratio. Fear-based motivation of employees is easy. A manager gives orders, maybe shouts them, then goes into the office and closes the door. If you disturb the manager, you had better have a darn good reason. If you mess up, you're in *big trouble*, and everyone knows what big trouble means. Negative motivation such as threats of being fired, demoted, or otherwise losing opportunities or privileges may *seem* to work, but any gains will be offset by employees feeling less dedicated and, most likely, resentful. Fear-based, *or else–style motivation* does not develop loyal self-starters with positive attitudes.

Motivation through inspiration, open communication, and results-oriented feedback (both positive and developmental) requires more thought and sensitivity. It requires a manager to have a motivational mindset and to use motivational language. Of course, the greatest challenge is implementing those skills in times of trouble. The motivational manager is one who maintains a positive mindset even in difficult times.

Today's work environment is not as secure as that of decades ago when workers received gold watches for spending a quarter of a century with their companies (often in the same roles). Today, employees might stay in the same job but work for three different companies in the space of a few years because of mergers and acquisitions. Others move on seeking greener pastures or looking to get out before the "other shoe drops."

Employers face the challenge of motivating employees to stay, to become and remain productive in the face of internal and external changes, and to ensure ongoing customer satisfaction in an increasingly competitive arena. Retail customers, for example, can shop in brick and mortar shops (specialty, chain, outlet, new, used, or antique) or online (at brick and mortar stores' Web sites, strictly online businesses, private sellers at their own dot coms, or online auctions). The competition within each of those options is staggering.

We all want to know that our efforts—successful or not—are noticed and appreciated. We want to know what employers expect and that we are or are not meeting those expectations and why. "Talk to me" is frequently a silent shout of the unmotivated and disillusioned. *Perfect Phrases for Motivating and Rewarding Employees* gives those who manage or supervise others a jumpstart in thinking about how to communicate in a variety of work situations. These phrases should help those who must motivate others to integrate positive and developmental feedback into their day-to-day interactions.

The most effective motivation is self-motivation. Choosing to reach a goal for your own reasons is far more motivating than striving to meet that goal for someone else's. In this book, you will find perfect phrases, not only to motivate externally, but to help people identify those triggers that will spur them to greater achievement for their own reasons as well as yours, creating a win-win success strategy.

Who Can Use This Book?

This book is designed for anyone in any industry who wants to develop the motivational mindset and to use motivational phrases to inspire employees. It can be used by those in office, hotel, restaurant, health-care, transportation, manufacturing, retail, and Web-based business settings, as well as by those employed in educational, government, and nonprofit work environments. Further, butchers, bakers, and, yes, even candlestick

makers, as long as they have employees to motivate, will fir
perfect phrases to suit them.

Please accept our broad use of the words *clients* and *cu*
tomers. We often refer to clients and customers interchangeab
For health-care or hospitality-specific examples, we use *patien*
or *guests*. Of course, we cannot refer to patients/guests/client
customers for all broad examples that may apply. As you can se
if we listed every substitution, this would no longer be a hand
little book.

Book Map

- **Part I** of this book lays the groundwork for successful
  motivational management. This section explores
  motivation and de-motivation, why motivation makes the
  difference, and gives you an opportunity to examine your
  own self-motivation and style. It encourages you to
  consider the importance of some fundamental
  characteristics of the motivational manager: Be a change
  agent, set clear expectations, and lead by example.

- **Part II** offers phrases for motivating employees in various
  situations. Many of the phrases will transfer directly to you
  own situation; others will give you a framework for
  substituting a relevant phrase or trigger an idea for
  addressing a particular case. For each, you will find
  Motivational Mindsets (motivation for the motivator) and
  Motivational Phrases (phrases you would say to motivate
  employees). The mindsets are as important as the phrases
  A motivational mindset lends foundation and context to
  the phrases and helps you create an environment in whic

employees thrive. Successful managers know that the best motivation is open, honest communication.

■ **Part III** focuses on benefits, perks, and rewards. Benefits, a critical component of any job package, may include insurance, wellness programs, retirement plans, and flextime. This section covers benefits that allow for different styles, energies, and employee needs. For instance, flexing the work schedule, if possible, is a motivator for many. The more you can tailor the job to the individual, the more appreciative and fulfilled that person feels coming to work. Perks and rewards include public recognition, gifts, and more. The "something extra" not only motivates and inspires but sends a clear message of appreciation.

Enter Here

Perfect Phrases for Motivating and Rewarding Employees is designed to help you strengthen your motivational force. Used as a reference, a guide, a companion, or jumping-off point, this book offers a solid foundation for motivational managers, but the structure you build will always reflect your own vision and style. If your current style needs some tweaking, it is never too late. If some of the phrases in this book feel foreign to you, try them on. If you find yourself quick to say, "That won't work," stop to think about why you feel such resistance. Maybe it won't, but maybe it will; maybe it will with some minor changes. Put the concept in your own words; adapt it to your style.

You were motivated to pick up this book and you are moti-vated to motivate, inspired to inspire. So allow yourself to take some calculated risks to allow for the greatest payoffs. Even difficult situations are opportunities to motivate or to model grace under fire. Whether you are looking for phrases for specific situations or looking for more context surrounding the mind of the motivational manager, like most self-help books, *Perfect Phrases* offers an opportunity for you to learn more about yourself. Enter here…

Acknowledgments

Our sincere gratitude to the senior executives, managers, supervisors, and employees in the companies that opened their doors to our training and consulting services during the past two decades and continue to welcome Diamond Associates. These span industries including pharmaceutical, health-care, transportation, retail, banking, manufacturing, and utility, as well as government agencies. We especially appreciate the thousands of employees who attended Diamond Associates' seminars. We all learn by teaching, and whether we or one of our trainers conducted the course, no one returned without having learned about those behaviors, phrases, and actions large and small that shape a company's workforce.

Included on several chapter opening pages in Parts II and III are comments from people in current leadership positions. Our thanks to these motivators for sharing their insights with us: Maria Bordas, manager of strategic planning and policy, Aviation Department, The Port Authority of NY and NJ (NY); Dr. Susan Brenner, senior vice president, Bright Horizons Family Solutions (MA); Marcie Gorman, president and CEO, Weight Watchers of Palm Beach County, Inc. and president of the W.W. Franchisee Association, Inc. (FL); Roger Hillman, manager, Litigation Practice, law firm of Garvey Schubert Barer (WA); Armand Pasquini , area director of Human Resources, Starwood Hotels (DC); Denise Rounds, owner of Bellezza Salons at the Hilton, Caesars, and Bally's Park Place (NJ); and Monica Smiley, publisher of *Enterprising Women* (NC). We also are grateful to Ellen Diamond for her insights from the perspective of the motivated employee.

We are thankful to Peter Tomolonis for reading an early draft of this book and for making suggestions that strengthened it. Peter worked in management positions in the Human Resources and Aviation Departments of the Port Authority of NY and NJ for almost three decades before retiring. He has directly motivated or developed programs and/or systems to assist others in motivating and rewarding thousands of employees.

Clemente Toglia, a principal of Dominion Financial Group in Red Bank, NJ, advised us on financial options and incentives for employees. Motivation is one of Clem's strengths. Before launching his company, he was one of Diamond Associates' most dynamic trainers.

Finally, we acknowledge our editor, Donya Dickerson, who is a model of motivation, for her assistance and enthusiasm throughout this project, and Grace Freedson, our agent, for introducing us to McGraw-Hill and for her continuing energetic efforts on our behalf.

Part I

The manager plays a crucial role when it comes to motivation. In this part, you will explore your style and ways to establish a motivating environment. Such an environment is fostered by a motivator who sets a good example, clarifies expectations, and is flexible in the face of change. Also critical to establishing a motivational environment is the understanding that employees are individuals with varied drives, dreams, and personal goals.

Motivation is much more than a tool for energizing the demotivated; it puts an added spring in anyone's step. Managers may overlook high-potential performers who are doing more with less and doing it well. As essential as it is to help less productive employees become better, it is equally essential to help your most productive employees be their best.

Chapter 1

Why Motivate?

"If you want to build a ship, don't herd people together to collect wood and don't assign them tasks and work, but rather teach them to long for the endless immensity of the sea."

—Antoine de Saint-Exupéry

Motivation vs. De-motivation

Most people understand the benefits of motivating employees. We have all been de-motivated and felt undervalued. Those words work in tandem. As you read about motivational phrases and behaviors, you will notice a pattern of open communication and respect. Remember those who motivated you and those who had the opposite effect. Which ones made you feel like a valuable contributor?

The reasons for motivating are far more compelling than the excuses used for not motivating.

Excuses for Not Motivating

- "I, as the employer or manager, have the option of cycling people out as they fail to meet my expectations." Constant turnover not only stresses the "survivors" but also seriously impacts your bottom line.
- "No one motivated me. I motivated myself." Did you? How? Did any outside influences play a role? A worthwhile exploration, perhaps.
- "The paycheck is motivation enough." In today's economy, the paycheck alone is rarely enough to retain quality employees.
- "Each employee was hired to do the best possible job and should just do it." This is the workplace variation of, "I don't have to tell her I love her, I married her didn't I?"

This theory of *motivate yourself management* does little to promote self-motivation, which, if nurtured, is a powerful force. The first excuse costs time and money, not to mention lost customer confidence, while the last three obviously fail to take into account human nature.

Motivation includes both incentives and positive reinforcement, and it provides a reason beyond the paycheck for employees to care about the company. Employees who care about the company and its customers positively affect the company's success. Those who don't care have the opposite effect.

Reasons *for* Motivating

Motivated employees:
- Contribute to a positive work environment.
- Affect the morale of those around them.

Perfect Phrases for Motivating and Rewarding Employees

- Are team players.
- Are willing (if able) to go the extra mile in a crisis.
- Motivate clients and customers to return.
- Put a friendly face to your good name.
- Care about their company's image and success, and it shows.
- Are more likely to be self-starters and innovators.
- Have strong personal goals.
- Want to keep their jobs or move within the company.
- Have a healthy work ethic.
- Are committed to problem solving.
- Are good for business.

Unmotivated employees:
- Do not attract or retain clients or customers.
- Negatively affect the morale of those around them.
- Often quit or get themselves fired at the company's expense.
- Do not care about the company's image and success, and it shows.
- Call in sick more often than satisfied employees in order to go do *anything* else (and may even *become* ill from the anxiety of going to a job where they feel unappreciated, even mistreated).
- Will "punch out" in the middle of a crisis.
- May do what is asked of them, but will rarely do more.

Great coaches know how to motivate. They know what pushes people need to start their internal engines. So, we send you forward with the words of Vince Lombardi: "The difference between a successful person and others is not a lack of strength, not a lack of knowledge, but rather a lack of will."

Chapter 2

The Wise Motivator

"Example is not the main thing in influencing others; it is the only thing."

—Albert Schweitzer

Self-Motivation

How motivated are you to do your job? Think big picture *and* specific projects or tasks. A highly motivated leader will keep others motivated. You want high-energy, productive, focused, and motivated employees. Who doesn't? Self-motivation trickles down to both internal and external customers, creates a positive work environment, contributes to financial profit and personal fulfillment, and leads to team success. The manager or business owner who exudes high energy and a positive outlook is motivational before ever trying. "Enthusiasm," said Ralph Waldo Emerson, "is contagious."

Your Style

Think about leaders you admire (public figures or people with or for whom you have worked) and the characteristics that describe them. What about the first manager who motivated you? The teacher who made you feel you could succeed when you doubted yourself? An inspiring family member? Pick one or two of these people and jot down some *characteristics* that define them (such as enthusiastic, energetic, calm under fire, honest, decisive, focused, flexible, careful listener). You might also include some *actions* they took that you admire (gave back to the community, found creative financing options to avoid layoffs, never shouted in the office). Underline the characteristics and actions you hold as ideals. How many describe *your* style? If you match up in all or most areas, great! If not, keep the list as a reminder of worthwhile goals.

Now look at those behaviors that detract from your effectiveness as a leader. What do you need to change? Are you typically late for meetings? Are you known as a shouter? Although everyone mutters, "That's just her style," no one appreciates it or looks forward to being on the receiving end. You are also setting a standard. Model the behavior you would like to see. Focus and build on those behaviors that define a strong leader. If it takes time, stick with it. We all have the capacity for change.

Be a Change Agent

Most people fear or feel intimidated by change; even positive change can put people off kilter. A supervisor whose feathers are easily ruffled by the winds of change will only add to the tension. On the other hand, a supervisor who expects the unexpected and doesn't get flustered is not only a calming force but also a role model for handling change.

Perfect Phrases for Motivating and Rewarding Employees

As a manager, supervisor, foreman, or team leader, you feel the winds of change as they blow in from many directions. Corporate or company changes require your introduction to your staff or team. Often, you are in the role of salesperson convincing others of the merits of a change and the benefits to them, the company, the customers or clients, and your work product. You may have to sell a change in which you don't believe. Be honest, but supportive of the necessity for that change. The impetus for change may also come from those who report to you. You may be the one who can implement change or the only link between direct reports and decision makers. Change might also be inspired by client feedback, industry news, or, of course, your own personal insight. Your next big business idea might come from hearing someone on the street say, "Hey, I wish someone would _____ (make, write, teach, create)!" The idea is not to wait until the business is faltering or stale, but to be *always* listening, *always* looking, and *always* open to the next idea.

As a business owner, you receive motivation for change from many directions as well: change in markets, demand, customer requests, the economy, those who report to you, or your own innovation, to name a few. Positive change may come from a seemingly negative event. You lose a contract; you lose a star employee; your staple product becomes obsolete, and it feels like your darkest hours. Then, you reevaluate how you lost the contract and find ways to strengthen your presentation that put you in a better position with future prospects; your new employee has contacts and skills that make your business surge; you bring on a new product that is in greater demand than the old one had been in 20 years. When you feel blindsided by unexpected change, don't despair; think—and get your best people thinking with you.

Change is both inevitable and necessary in the process of moving forward. Not only do those in leadership roles need the ability to handle changes as they arise, but great leadership will never resist change simply because it's "not the way we do things." If you want to inspire innovators, innovate. Innovation doesn't come from rigid notions of "We *should* do this; we *should* do that, and by all means, we *shouldn't* do the other thing!" Relax. Stretch out your *shoulds*. It's good for you *and* for business to be flexible and open to new ideas.

Set Clear Expectations

The number one rule for getting what you want is to ask for it clearly. Many employees miss the mark because of misunderstandings or, as they say, managers expect them to "be mind readers." Those who report to you want to know what you expect, how you want it done, and when.

Clear expectations create a strong framework for a common purpose. Whether assigning a single task or a major project, or setting the tone for your work environment, save everyone time by stating your expectations clearly. Be clear about what behaviors are or are not acceptable. Clarify deadlines. Clear deadlines are relationship savers, face-savers, and client savers.

Clarify language. The simplest words can be misinterpreted. Don't assume that everyone's understanding of "first draft," "customer care," or "early" is the same. Clear communication goes beyond giving information. It incorporates asking questions and listening—*really* listening.

Lead by Example

Think of all the behaviors that you want your employees to demonstrate. Do you demonstrate them? For example: You want employees to be available to work overtime occasionally when deadlines are pressing, unforeseen circumstances have interfered, or things just take longer than anticipated. Are you running out the door at 5:00 or even 5:15, thanking others for carrying on the work? That won't be graciously accepted too often. Of course, if you have an obligation that prevents your staying, explain it humbly; however, don't assume that your participation—or presence—is not important. Too many late night crunches for others as you head out on time will sabotage any other efforts to motivate.

You want employees to pitch in and help others as needed. Roll up your own sleeves, too. An excellent restaurant recently closed. Shortly before this thriving start-up took a dive, the following happened: A waiter did not show up. The place was mobbed. As staff scrambled and customers waited, the owner/maitre d' maintained his role of welcoming guests and walking around and smiling and chatting. As one disgruntled diner explained, "He didn't carry out a meal or clear a table. They were clearly shorthanded. The customers waited too long for their dinners; the waiters were frazzled; and he just strolled around." By contrast, during an unusual rush at another restaurant, the manager was taking orders before the next wave of customers hit. Diners were impressed to see that they rated such care. Imagine how grateful the staff was!

Think about crises in your work environment and ways you can pitch in and help. In a crunch, no one should be above typing, collating, working a register, clearing a table, or finding a file.

Respect is another lead-by-example opportunity. You expect every employee to treat every client or customer with respect. After all, they are your organization's lifeblood. Don't badmouth the tough customers as they leave or quip about them in the presence of other clients or customers. Treating customers the way you want your employees to treat them should top your list, along with treating employees the way you want them to treat customers. Like the restaurant described above, a local shop quietly closed its doors to no one's surprise. It was typical for customers browsing in the store to hear the owner and salespeople complain about browsers who waste their time and don't buy or to be snickering about one customer in front of another. The store closed within two months.

Always remember that your behavior is setting a standard for the behavior of others. If your department has to work closely with another, prevent turf wars and interdepartmental friction by setting the tone for diplomacy. Look in your internal mirror now and then. Do you see a leader who communicates well, shows respect for others, accepts responsibility for his/her actions, shares the limelight, and demonstrates a strong work ethic? If so, these characteristics are more likely to be reflected in those who report to you. The behavior you model—whatever your intent—is the behavior others will see as the standard. "Leadership," said George Van Valkenburg, "is doing what is right when no one is watching."

Motivating Employees

You may know what motivates you, but what motivates others? Of course, not everyone fits into the same mold and not all motivational approaches work for all employees. It's easy to say someone *should* be motivated by a manager who gives out specialty chocolates, but do you know whether you're giving a box of chocolates to a diabetic, someone who is allergic to chocolate, or someone who—believe it or not—just doesn't like chocolate? Forget what you think people *should want* and find out what they *really want*. Great motivators are not self-centered. They are other-centered. They understand the difference between the employee motivated by "space to work" and the one who works best with periodic oversight. Just as everyone doesn't like chocolate, everyone doesn't like space or lack of it. Some people are most creative working alone; others are energized by a group dynamic.

Your role as motivator begins with your mindset. In Part II of this book, you will find *Motivational Mindsets* and sample *Motivational Phrases* that support them.

Part II

Perfect Phrases for Motivating Employees

Words carry immense power. They can motivate, encourage, promise hope, and make people feel like part of something special; conversely, they can de-motivate, discourage, and make people feel alienated or taken for granted. In the wrong hands (or mouths, we should say), words can be weapons, even when that's not the intent. Some people simply believe others would be embarrassed by praise, or that a little shouting or name-calling is part of the process and that no one really takes jabs at their competence to heart. Your best bet is to assume people take words at face value and that they may be more sensitive than you think. Remember, too, that no one has ever been hurt by well-deserved, genuine praise.

So, choose your words carefully—those you use out loud, as well as those you use in your own inner dialogue. Your life, it is said, is a reflection of your thoughts. As a supervisor or business owner your work environment, too, is very much a reflection of your thoughts. Your words contribute to the experience of those around you. Everyone has off days, but if you've created a truly motivational environment, you or the employee with the off day will be supported, maybe even uplifted, instead of pulling everyone down. Positive environments give off a positive charge; the first step in motivation is creating that environment.

Chapter 3

A Positively Motivating Environment

"Life is what we make it. Always has been, always will be."

—Grandma Moses

Motivation thrives under managers and supervisors who create a positive atmosphere, one in which people feel supported, valued, and respected. A motivational work environment is charged with energy. Working in an environment without motivation is similar to slogging through mud. You can have all of the "rah rah" meetings you want and use positive slogans, but if you allow an employee to be harassed or to be treated disrespectfully, your positive efforts will appear hypocritical. Pushing through negativity to get the job done takes a great deal more effort than being encouraged by positive language and feedback, feeling appreciated, and working with an overall sense of team spirit.

A number of leaders describe a positive environment as one that encourages risk and allows room for error when taking risks. Armand Pasquini, area director of Human Resources, Starwood

Hotels, put it this way: "So many managers are concerned about zero errors or doing things by the letter that they stifle creativity and initiative. Early in my career, one manager said something to me that had a profound impact and released my creativity. Recognizing that my focus on not making mistakes was holding me back, he said, 'I dare you to make a mistake that I can't fix.' I find myself saying the same thing to those whom I manage today." Marcie Gorman, president and CEO, Weight Watchers of Palm Beach County, Inc. and president of the W.W. Franchisee Association, Inc., transferred a two-word mantra she used successfully with the nation's #1 weight loss program to any work situation. "Just stop! If you discover that you made an error, don't feel guilty, don't dwell on it, don't cover it up, don't make it any worse: just stop. Then, regroup, learn, and forge ahead."

A Positive Workplace

The Motivational Mindset

- The positively motivating environment is one in which employees feel welcome, comfortable, and appreciated.

- Start the day with a friendly greeting. Show a sincere interest in employees.

- Positive phrases can often replace negative ones. Instead of saying, "I can't stand this project," try, "This project is really challenging!" Positive words change your tone.

- *Yes* is more inspiring than *no*, even if it's a *Yes, but*… If you cannot say *yes* because of timing, say, *Yes, but not right away*. Instead of dismissing a new idea completely, is there some part of that idea to which you can say *yes*? Would you accept the idea with certain revisions? If *yes* is a possibility but not a certainty, then *maybe* is appropriate.

- Of course, *no* is a necessity, too. Without *no*, you would be doing everything for everyone, joining countless committees and crusades, and taking on responsibility for every organization that reaches out to you. *No's* can be polite and even supportive and encouraging. Most importantly, they can be critical to self- and employee-preservation.

- Champion family-friendly policies (without creating an environment in which single people are penalized with extra work and late hours to accommodate).

- Acknowledge employees' rights to life outside of work. Understand that people having made previous plans that are hard to change does not mean they don't want to contribute and would not stay late under other circumstances.

- More and more family-friendly companies offer on-site daycare. The employee who knows that his/her child is in a safe, caring environment just steps away, focuses on work rather than worrying.
- Create a positive physical environment. Consider fresh paint, temperature, ergonomics, cleanliness, and lighting.
- Keep a library of motivational books that employees can borrow. Encourage people to share helpful resources that they find on their own.

Motivational Phrases

- "Good morning."
- "How are you?"
- "Yes."
- "Yes, as soon as I complete this _____ (project, phone call, letter…)." *or* "Yes, if you can help me by _____ (researching one aspect, making a few phone calls, staying a half-hour late…)."
- "Maybe. Let me see how long this _____ (report, reconciliation, inventory, phone call will take…)."
- "What a beautiful picture of your _____ (son, daughter, husband, wife…)."
- "I know you are concerned about your _____ (mother, husband, child…). Please feel comfortable calling _____ (home, the hospital, the daycare center…) a few times today to check. Let me know if you need to leave early."
- "It's going to be a challenging day. Grab your coffee and let's get started."
- "I'm glad we have such a strong crew here. We're short staffed and it's going to be a busy day."

➡

- "I appreciate your _____ (helping Sally, covering for Joe, coming in early, staying late…)."
- "You're right to be upset about what that _____ (customer, client, coworker, supervisor…) did, but what can we do to get back on track or maintain a positive focus? Is there anything we can learn from that interaction?"
- "I'm excited about this new project, and I look forward to hearing your ideas."
- "I would like to see you leave early for your son's soccer game, but we have a lot to get done. Can you come in an hour early tomorrow?"
- "We are now offering pre- and after-school programs as well as all-day child care. All employees who are parents are invited to attend one of the scheduled orientations."
- "What a great day! Thanks for all of your hard work."

Respect

The Motivational Mindset

- *Respected* is not synonymous with *feared*. You will gain more genuine respect by being other-centered, open, communicative, and friendly than you will by being autocratic. The supportive leader is no less capable of getting the job done than the feared one. In fact, your employees will be more motivated and more loyal. Fear is a shortsighted, short-term motivator with limited returns.

- Just as support staff is there to support you, you are there to support them. When a manager loses sight of the give-and-take required, support staff is more likely to give only the very minimum. Give, on the manager's part, can be anything from coaching or providing training to praise for good work.

- Be consistent with everyone. Be flexible and make exceptions, when appropriate, but not always for one person or based on favoritism. You will breed resentment for you *and* the person receiving your favors.

- Not everyone feels positive about every employee all the time. Showing respect is especially important when an employee disappoints you or pushes your buttons. Sometimes, what's in your head just shouldn't come out of your mouth. Any goodwill or show of respect you have developed will be immediately demolished by phrases such as "How stupid can you be?," "You did *what* again?," "I don't have time for this nonsense," or "For crying out loud!" Deal with problems head on, but even the most difficult situations can be handled with respect and self-control.

- You won't earn respect if you don't follow through on promises. If you cannot follow through, say so, explain why, and suggest alternatives.
- Take responsibility. In some corporate cultures, it's nearly a lost art and will be highly respected.
- Admit to being wrong. You will gain more respect than you might lose by insisting you were right in the face of all reasonable evidence.
- Admit to not knowing something. You couldn't possibly know everything. No one does. Say you will find out, refer the employee to the right person to ask, or ask the employee to track down the answer.
- All employees deserve respect and common courtesy, no matter what their role in the organization. Employees must also feel respected by other employees, feel safe in the workplace, and know that all complaints are taken seriously.
- A clear message that harassment or discrimination of any kind is unacceptable creates a positive environment.

Motivational Phrases

- "Please" and "Thank you."
- "Even great ball players don't hit home runs all the time, but their fans continue to believe in them. You did your best, and I believe in you."
- "I know I promised to make time for that _____ (meeting, presentation, discussion…) on Friday, but I have to deal with a problem that just came to my attention. Can we reschedule for Monday morning? How is 10 A.M.?"
- "It's clear that we don't see eye to eye on this issue, but I respect your point of view."

➡

- "I have faith in your abilities."
- "I don't know the answer to that question. Let me find out for you."
- "Our policies are designed to protect your rights."
- "You must have been upset by that comment. I'll talk with X immediately."
- "Harassment is unacceptable." *Or any reprimand of someone who is not showing respect and any action that makes an employee (a victim of persecution or harassment) know that he or she is in a safe, respectful environment.*
- "Sexual, racial, or ethnic jokes or any comments that may compromise someone's sense of dignity have no place in this office."
- "I don't expect you to accept disrespectful behavior from anyone. I encourage you to clearly tell Lisa that she may not speak to you that way. If the problem persists, please let me know and I will speak to her."
- "I understand that you felt insulted and the customer was wrong, but you cannot talk to customers that way."
- "Have you met William? He's the _____ (writer, researcher, point person…) who makes me look so good at management meetings."
- "You were right."
- "I was wrong. I'm sorry."

The "Everyone Counts" Attitude

The Motivational Mindset

- No one is "just a…" The most demoralizing phrase in business is "just a _____ (secretary, assistant, maintenance worker, sales clerk, receptionist, order taker, store manager, foreman…)."

- If someone says, "I'm just a…" say, "You're not *just* anything! Here's why what you do is important…"

- The motivated autoworker is building a car. The unmotivated one is tightening bolts.

- People need to believe that the work they do is valuable, and it *is* or you wouldn't have hired them. Let them know how important they are to the company, the process, and the outcome.

- Employees who naturally take pride in their work will stop taking pride if they're knocked down a peg or two.

- Self-esteem is motivational and feeling valued by supervisors and coworkers strengthens self-esteem.

- Even employees with good self-esteem want to feel valued in the workplace.

- Employees making others feel small cannot be tolerated in a motivational environment.

- Some employees put themselves down. Be sure to give them specific examples of why they shouldn't.

- A manager who makes an employee feel small gets less of an employee.

Motivational Phrases

- "You're the one out front. To a customer at your register, you're the face of this company."

- "The way you deal with customer complaints adds to customer retention, and those customers are telling others about us and how well our company treated them."
- "You're not just a _____ (paralegal, research assistant, fact checker…). Your work is critical to the _____ (accuracy, success, substance…) of my work."
- "If we didn't have you proofreading, think of all of the mistakes that would have left this office on our company letterhead. You do your share to uphold our company image."
- "When you answer that phone, you're the voice of this company and the way you make people feel comfortable tells them that this company cares."
- "As the receptionist, you're the one receiving all clients and customers. In many cases, you're their first impression of our company."
- "You're not just ringing sales. The customer's interaction with you shapes that person's experience with our store and your sense of humor certainly keeps this place bright and cheerful."
- "Client relations are the very heart of this business."
- "You're not 'just a driver.' You are responsible for ensuring the safety and comfort of our _____ (customers, executives, passengers…)."
- "Packaging is a critical last link in the sales process. When customers receive damaged goods it can risk the sale and the relationship."
- "Your job is essential to everything we do. If supplies aren't stocked, everyone is scrambling. We count on you to keep things running smoothly."

- "If the shelves aren't stocked, customers will go elsewhere looking for items we have right in the back. Your efficiency affects the whole sales process."

- "Keeping this _____ (hotel, restaurant, spa…) clean is as important as every other service we offer. If people come in and see dirty (floors, carpets, dishes…) they're likely to turn around and leave."

- "I realize this position is a stepping stone for you. Any experience you gain here will help you in the future. In the meantime, the work you do is valuable, and we all appreciate your competence and enthusiasm."

- "Your position is important to this company's _____ (bottom line, sales process, production, customer retention, finished product…) because _____."

Stress Less

The Motivational Mindset

- Excessive stress causes illness, lower morale, and a feeling of dread, in many, of coming to work. No one wants to live in a constant state of high stress.

- Your decisions, behaviors, and ability to handle stress have a direct impact over the stress of employees who report to you. Know your own stress levels and take command of your reactions. In hectic times, your state will either add to the problem or be part of the solution.

- Are you overextending your department? Are you overextending yourself, and by extension, your department? Assess what you can do to change the state of your office.

- A well placed *no* could keep you from crossing the line from a "bustling workplace" to an out-of-control environment in which frenzied mistakes and burn out are the norm. Before you say *yes*, consider the importance of the request and available resources. It's okay to say, "I'll think about it," "Let me check our workload," or "Can it wait until next week?"

- Do you praise employees for coming in horrendously sick? Would the company really have folded if they stayed home? How productive were they? What mistakes could have resulted from a groggy work state? How many work hours were lost when others caught the bug and had to stay home? If someone's that sick, recommend bed rest (and maybe some soup).

- Burning out your staff won't help you build momentum. If you own your own business and it's growing too fast, you may want to extend yourself to meet demands. (Hire one or two more people if, to satisfy you, one would have to work around the clock.) Usually, the additional financial output comes back in multiples. If that won't work for you, slow down until you're ready to consider expansion.

- Not every fire is a fire; not every tragedy is a tragedy. Being selective in emergency responses helps *real* emergencies get the immediate attention they deserve. What would happen to emergency response systems if people called 911 every time a cat was stuck in a tree or they wanted to ask a general question?
- A short break—one for fresh air, a phone call, meditation, stretching, or simply not doing anything at all, maybe even just thinking (or not thinking)—can change the tenor of a day.
- Any investment in teaching stress management techniques is worthwhile for handling both long- and short-term stresses. Fight or flight is a defense mechanism that physically geared us to react in the wild. In the office, the urge to fight or flee often leads to explosion (conflict) or implosion (self-doubt, depression, anxiety).
- Do you have a sense of humor? Do you encourage openness to humor (that doesn't target any person or group)? Laughter is a wonderful de-stressor.

Motivational Phrases

- "The scope of this proposal grows with every client conversation. Let's stop and assess what we can realistically do within our deadline."
- "I know everyone already has a packed agenda, but the XO contract is a big opportunity for us, and David

needs some assistance in preparing for tomorrow's meeting. Let's figure out how we can pool our resources to pitch in."

- "Machinery does break down—usually at the worst time. Take a deep breath and explore your options for completing this project."
- "That customer was totally out of line in dumping on you like that. I appreciate your diplomacy in handling her. Why don't you take a five-minute break?"
- "You cannot control everything that happens. You *can* control how things affect you. Take three slow, deep breaths. It really does help."
- "Losing that _____ (sale, client, computer file…) must be upsetting. We've all been there. What steps are you thinking about for recovery or for moving forward?"
- "Mistakes are part of the learning process. Let's look at the lessons this situation presents."
- "I'm not blaming you for what happened. I understand what led you to make that decision. Let's address that cause and see how we can keep that same mistake from happening again to you or someone else."
- "You sound terrible! Stay home and get well."
- "You cannot control how customers speak to you but you *can* keep your stress level down by controlling your reaction."
- "Don't take a client's anger personally. Odds are the anger has nothing to do with you and is simply frustration with the situation. Stay calm and try to help. Your concern will usually turn that client's mood around."
- "We pushed hard for that deadline, but we did it! I appreciate your efforts."

- "Are you sure you want to take on that added responsibility? You already seem to be on overload. I don't want to see you burn out."
- "I know how hard you worked on this project, and it's frustrating that its success is in someone else's hands now. But you can relax knowing you did your part and, whatever the outcome, you did a great job."
- "Let's take a 10-minute break to stretch and get some fresh air."

Team Spirit

The Motivational Mindset

- Everyone has ideas, and diverse perspectives are always useful.
- Every member of the team must be treated as equal. No one should be talked down to by a manager or team member.
- If you are creating multiple teams and have conflicting personalities among your staff, put them on separate teams. Interpersonal trials arise within any team, but you do not need to set the stage unnecessarily. Your goal is not to test their abilities to deal with one another; your goal is to create a team that will get the job done.
- The most talented member is not necessarily the best choice for team leader. Look for someone who is fair minded, has good organizational skills, and is respectful of other team members.
- No task within a team project is small or menial. All contributions are part of the end result.
- Develop a staff with a customer-centric team spirit.
- A hierarchy in which the _____ (manager, supervisor, team leader…) shoulders all responsibility and takes all credit is less likely to create buy-in and dedication among members.
- Everyone deserves credit when the team does well.
- Individuals who put in extra time and energy or act beyond the call of duty deserve individual recognition as well as being recognized as part of a successful team.

Motivational Phrases

- "I don't want anyone to feel isolated. We are all part of a team."
- "Each member of this department is valuable."
- "We are here to support each other, not judge. If someone is stuck with a problem, we need the team to pull together and offer solutions."
- "Your team has done an exceptional job."
- "Your team has done very well and your work within the team has been outstanding."
- "Your team had some issues with this project, but I appreciate your hard work and leadership."
- "Personalities always come into play in team situations, but we all have to be careful not to take things personally or to make personal criticisms. Feedback should be relevant to the team's success."
- "You are a strong group of individuals, and I predict you will gain even more strength as a team."
- "Even the most creative thinkers cannot access the level of perspective that a group of people with differing points of view can generate. I expect the outcome of your working together to be especially interesting since you are all creative thinkers on your own."
- "You are dependent on each other, so trust is important. If you have had interpersonal issues that will start you off on the wrong foot, I suggest that you address them early on."
- "The team needs to take responsibility without blaming individuals; at the same time, individuals must take responsibility if we are to learn from mistakes and strengthen the team."

- "I suggest brainstorming _____ (ideas, solutions, ways to raise money, low-cost marketing solutions…) on your own, then brainstorm as a team. You may be surprised to see how many possibilities present themselves after you think you've exhausted every avenue."
- "Strong personalities working together are bound to have disagreements, but the process of resolving those differences will open up new avenues that may not have been explored otherwise."
- "Please share your knowledge and expertise. You will not diminish your value by helping to strengthen others; in fact, management will appreciate you even more."
- "I have a great feeling about what this team can accomplish."

Productive Meetings

The Motivational Mindset

- Begin on time.
- Share and follow an agenda, and keep the discussion focused and moving forward.
- Encourage sharing ideas and strategies. Allow the group to brainstorm solutions to problems.
- Control the flow, slowing down when critical issues arise.
- Avoid putting people on the spot unless it's unavoidable. If you want someone to publicly present an idea or explain an issue, ask that person ahead of time.
- Talk about achievements and give kudos and thanks to those who have earned them.
- Talk about challenges from the perspective of seeking solutions.
- Share positive customer service reviews of the company and of individuals by name. Share negative comments, but do not name names. Speak to those employees privately.
- Discourage *groupthink*, which may be exhibited by consistent blanket agreement. A manager who encourages individuality and is comfortable with dissent can prevent perpetual groupthink.
- End on time and conclude with clear direction.

Motivational Phrases

- "Thank you all for coming. I know this meeting was called last minute, but I hit a snag and I need everyone's creative thinking on this one."

➡

- "Our _____ (guest relations, sales initiatives, production…) has been doing well. How can we go from good to great?"
- "Daniel and Christie, tell us how your project is going. Have you encountered any areas where you have questions or need support from the team?"
- "Sonya came to me with an interesting idea. Sonya, would you please share your idea with everyone?"
- "We recently received a lot of customer complaints about _____ (our new product, turnaround time, service wait, service quality…). I called this meeting to generate ideas about ways we can be _____ (more helpful, faster, more responsive…)."
- "We're on schedule with most of our projects, but this one seems to be lagging. Please share your ideas about what might be holding up its progress and what we can do to get it up to speed."
- "Our new Web site has attracted a lot of interest. The design team is to be commended. Now we need someone to take on the responsibility of tracking traffic and sales. Who can volunteer? That report will be a significant contribution to our monthly meeting."
- "We laid out a lot of new initiatives recently. Let's review how we're doing so far."
- "Our regular contributors always offer excellent suggestions. I suspect we have other good ideas at the table. I'd like everyone to have a chance to speak."
- "I would like to go back to Gordon's statement…"
- "Vi received an award from _____ for _____. Let's all give him a round of applause."

- "Gloria, as always, I appreciate your many suggestions. However, we only have a half-hour for this meeting and a tight agenda. Can we go into greater detail later?"
- "Let's summarize our decisions and review who has agreed to complete what tasks by when."
- "We'll circulate a summary. Please review and react within three days of receiving it."
- "Does this time work for everyone? Good. See you next week. Thank you."

Chapter 4

Ongoing Performance Management

"Continuous effort—not strength or intelligence—is the key to unlocking our potential."

—Winston Churchill

Performance management is more than just an annual or semi-annual isolated review meeting. Performance management is a process that builds on continual feedback—both positive and developmental. The process includes setting clear expectations and goals, observing behavior, providing feedback, support, corrective action, and, at regular intervals, the performance review meeting. Ongoing performance management should communicate and reinforce the organization's mission, vision, and values. Employees need to and are entitled to know expectations, priorities, success measures, and their status in meeting these expectations.

Clearly, ongoing communication is key to a successful process. Roger Hillman, Esq., manager of the Litigation Practice of the law firm, Garvey Schubert Barer, advocates initiating ongoing dialogue: "It's not enough to say, 'My door is always open.' You have to stand up and walk through it."

Skill development is also an important part of the performance management process. Encourage employees to tap into internal or external training programs, online courses, mentoring, or on-the-job training. Don't forget to help your high-potential performers continue to grow.

Following is an actual quote: "Of course, you can't receive an 'Excellent' rating on your review. You're only a secretary and don't contribute to the company's bottom line." This quote is anonymous, for obvious reasons.

Ongoing Positive Feedback

The Motivational Mindset

- Positive feedback builds self-esteem, confidence, and goodwill.

- Think of the phrase: "Catch them doing something right," coined by Ken Blanchard in *The One Minute Manager,* to remind yourself to give the always-appreciated pat on the back.

- Kudos need no special occasion. Minor accomplishments are *still* accomplishments and *all* skills and positive behaviors add value.

- The employee who rarely excels needs the boost of an occasional "Way to go!" more than anyone. Find something to praise.

- Even your top performers need to know that you are aware of their efforts and successes. Without positive feedback, they may eventually wonder, "Why bother?" or decide to move to a more constructive environment.

- Major accomplishments deserve major praise.

- The best positive feedback is specific and goes beyond vague accolades to praise specific behaviors. *So-So Positive Feedback*: "You were great in that meeting." (That's fine to say, but add why or how.) *Useful Positive Feedback*: "Your tactfully bringing that meeting back on track saved our client relationship. I appreciate your initiative."

- Start to notice how often you give positive feedback and to whom you give it.

- Praise is positive feedback for a job well done, but positive feedback encourages the good efforts of even those who are struggling. Even if it's only a small part within the whole of an effort that has not gone well, praise the good efforts as something to build upon.

- Praise can be given privately, publicly, in writing, online, and in letters or e-mails copied to appropriate people.

Motivational Phrases

- "Great job!"
- "You really have a knack for _____."
- "I wish I could ____ as well as you."
- "I'm so glad we have you here to _____!"
- "I noticed the way you _____ (handled that difficult situation, encouraged someone, worked through a problem…). Good work!"
- "I appreciate your _____ (working late, coming in early, going out of your way to make this project a success…)."
- "I was impressed by your _____ (skills, ingenuity, commitment, desire to learn, creativity, depth of knowledge, way of dealing with that customer complaint…)."
- "I know you hit some snags, but that's all part of the learning process. Overall, I am impressed with the way you handled that task. Good work!"
- "You significantly improved on my _____ (writing, suggestion, design, marketing plan…)."
- "Would you mind sharing that idea at our next staff meeting? I think everyone could benefit from it."
- "I know how much you've struggled with writing that report. The results are excellent—clear and concise."
- "Your going out of your way to assist guests with directions and to answer questions contributes to the environment we want."

434

- "Your changes to that _____ (recipe, method, program, display…) have gotten us rave reviews."
- "Thank you for taking on that job and doing it so well. I know that our clients appreciated your thoroughness and availability throughout."
- "Nicely done! Your command of crowd control during that sudden rush of customers was incredible. You remained calm and directed."

Ongoing Developmental Feedback

The Motivational Mindset

■ Developmental feedback may not seem motivational on the surface. However, specific, supportive developmental feedback *is* motivational. It tells each employee *specifically* what you want and why, and how to become a stronger, more valued member of the team.

■ Without developmental feedback, people think they're doing exactly what you expect of them when they're not, and they'll continue doing it, thinking they're doing a good job. They will be far less effective than they would be with a little guidance.

■ Putting the responsibility on the employee to determine the solution to his/her behavior problem motivates that employee to follow through. By dictating a solution, you can add to the problem.

■ Never say *always* and never say *never*. Employees who are told that they *never* answer the phone are likely to feel that any time they *did* answer the phone was totally unappreciated. They begin to wonder, "What's the point?" rather than continuing (or trying) to improve.

■ Don't build up a war chest of "You dids." Address problems when you see them; after resolution, let them go. Of course, if the problem is part of a pattern, it may be important to bring it up again and, in instances of serious breaches, take corrective action. Keep a record of your feedback discussions.

■ When giving developmental feedback, focus on behaviors, not judgments. *Negative or Inflammatory Feedback:* "You're not a team player." *Specific Developmental Feedback:* ➡

"When Richard was under the gun and asked you for help in preparing his presentation, you said it wasn't your job. That behavior goes against the strong team environment that benefits all of us."

- Phrases to strike from your vocabulary: "You're so dumb/stupid/incompetent." "What's wrong with you?" "You're not the sharpest tool in the shed, brightest bulb, etc." "Well that's *your* problem, isn't it?" "Shut up!" *Cursing* (in any form or context). *Shouting*.

- Explain what the consequences will be (and why) if a detrimental behavior continues.

- If a serious problem exists, describe the problem and its history. If prior warnings have been given regarding this problem, remind the employee. Inform the employee that failure to improve could result in another warning, downgrading, or termination. Document this discussion. Follow your company's progressive discipline policy.

- If a negative behavior seems out of character, say you recognize that it is and offer an opportunity to talk. You may need to recommend or require attending programs such as anger management, sexual harassment, diversity, or counseling.

Motivational Phrases

- "I have noticed that you're quick to say to coworkers, 'I'm too busy' or 'I can't help you.' We all need to support each other and to keep a positive tone. If you're too busy, you might say, 'I can look at that in an hour. I hope that's okay' or 'I'm pushing a deadline. Will tomorrow work?' Or you could suggest someone else who might be more available."

➡

- "Snapping at coworkers is out of character for you. Do you want to talk about what's wrong?"
- "Losing your temper on the phone with that client was inappropriate. What can you do to turn this situation around and not lose your temper next time?"
- "I realize that your mother's illness hasn't allowed you the time you need for this assignment. What can I do to help you access the resources and provide the assistance that you need to complete it?"
- "Here comes the customer who nearly inspired the phrase, 'no substitutions' on our menu. Last time, she really ruffled your feathers. I know you can juggle her requests and our chef's boundaries although that is quite a challenge."
- "You do not make eye contact with or greet customers at your register. We're here to make their shopping experience pleasant. These small things do that. You'll also find that people will be friendlier to you, and you'll enjoy your work more."
- "Have you ever walked into a store and felt that you were interrupting a meeting by requesting assistance? We all have. We don't want our customers to feel that way."
- "Mary Simms is frustrated because she's left a corrected phone number with our office twice before. Would you mind cross-checking all records, and e-mail everyone who may have reason to call her? Let's prevent any of us from calling the wrong number again. Thank you."
- "I've noticed a lot of errors in your typing since you've had to cover the phones. It's hard to keep picking up the thread if you are in and out of a document. I know the extra responsibility is interfering, but please use spell-

check and proof carefully before releasing anything. Do you have any ideas for keeping your place in the face of ongoing interruptions?"

- "Your morning meetings are productive, but they routinely run into overtime. Let's review the protocol for morning meetings so you can see how a streamlined procedure might move things along more efficiently."

- "We have no place in this office for shouting or cursing. We can resolve our issues by communicating reasonably."

- "Coworkers need your support, just as you need theirs. We are not here to knock each other down; we're here to build a strong company. I know I can count on you."

- "I don't often see you smile when you greet people. You're focused on doing a good job, but a friendly greeting is important for maintaining good customer and coworker relations. Those good relations will make your job easier and more pleasant."

- "We all enjoy your friendly attitude. However, continual chatting during work adds to everyone's end-of-day pressures. We'll all be more relaxed if we save personal conversations for personal time."

- "In the office, the Internet is used for business. Please save your personal instant messages and cyber shopping for home or your breaks. Popping on for a quick look always takes more time than we realize."

Planning for the Performance Review Meeting

The Motivational Mindset

- Communicate the process mechanics to employees.
- Schedule annual or semi-annual performance reviews and make sure to keep the appointments you've set. Nothing is more unsettling than waiting for the ever-postponed review.
- Schedule, in advance, to allow you and the employee time to prepare.
- Approach the process with a "total picture." Do not focus on the most recent events—positive *or* negative.
- Review your own notes regarding the employee's performance during this time period as well as any coaching and feedback discussions and their results.
- Determine specific changes that you want as a result of this discussion and plan open questions to focus on these changes.
- A well-planned and conducted performance review will inspire, not deflate. The goal is to help employees reach their full potential and provide guidance and support so they can.
- Ask yourself: "How will this session maintain or enhance the employee's self-esteem and self-image?" "How will this session help the employee become more effective?"
- Avoid these common pitfalls: comparing one employee to another, focusing on one aspect and generalizing, assuming the person who has your work style must be doing everything right, or attributing motives without facts.
- If your company does not have a standard form, you have a few options:

➡

- A number of good books on the market include performance review forms.
- Shop the Web for automated or Web-based performance appraisals or downloadable appraisal forms.
- You can try your hand at writing a form that makes sense for your company, but don't recreate the wheel. Use resources. Reuse what works, then add or alter to make statements more relevant.

Motivational Phrases

- "Performance reviews help me keep in touch with how you are doing and what your needs are."
- "Your performance review is scheduled for Tuesday, March 3rd, at 9:00 A.M. Please bring questions or comments."
- "The review is the time to discuss your performance goals and how you are meeting them. Please come prepared to share your specific ideas about how you are doing."
- "The performance review is nothing to be nervous about. It's a benchmark that will be useful to both of us."
- "Think about contributions you've made of which I might not be aware. I'll want to learn about them at the meeting."
- "Don't be afraid to toot your own horn."
- "Salary increases are/are not directly tied to performance review ratings."
- "Think about steps you'll want to take for your personal improvement plan. Are there courses you might want to attend or projects to work on that will help you stretch your skills?"

- "Look back at your previous review so you are aware of improvements you've made and ways you have met your goals."
- "Think about ways you exceeded the expectations we set last time."
- "I know this is a busy time for everyone, but these performance review meetings are essential. Your direct reports deserve your input."
- "John, when writing reviews, remember that the form is a guide. By following it, you maintain objectivity and review everyone according to the same guidelines."
- "I know reviewing others' performance is new to you. I suggest that you avoid using labels, such as 'uncooperative.' Focus on specific behaviors, for example: 'Your refusal to _____ (greet a customer arriving to meet someone else, check e-mails regularly, turn your cell phone on…) is bad for business and impedes team success.'"
- "Think about action words when giving feedback. Whether describing what the employee does well or pointing out areas for improvement, action words give specific, meaningful feedback. For example: 'You prevented a major panic with your decisive action during the blackout.' or 'When you interrupt others during meetings, we lose time, and often, the point being made.'"
- "Be prepared to tell me how organizational policies, senior management, or I may have helped you attain your goals or prevented you from achieving them."

The Performance Review Meeting

The Motivational Mindset

- By the time the employee and employer sit down for "the talk," there should be no surprises. This meeting should be part of an ongoing dialogue in a workplace with clear communication and feedback; the employee should have a fairly good sense of what issues might arise.

- Do not allow interruptions. Your employee is counting on your feedback and undivided attention.

- Focus on specific behaviors rather than generalizations. Descriptive words and phrases such as *exceptional*, *nice job*, and *needs improvement* are fine for summing up, but do not tell the story. Identify specific actions and give details.

- Do not paraphrase general statements on the form. Use specific examples.

- Your comments should reflect employees' work in relation to their job descriptions. Filter out feelings and focus on actions. Discuss strengths and developmental needs in key performance areas. Reference objectives and previous action plans. Focus on job-related behavior and performance expectations.

- Developmental feedback is more effective when it involves the problem's causes and corrections, its effect on others within the workplace, and, if applicable, its impact on company goals, image, or client/customer relations.

- Seek to identify areas for new skill development and/or increased responsibility. Help your high-potential performers reach greater goals.

- Jointly develop an action plan with the employee and

schedule interim follow-up meetings. *Follow-up is critical.* Revise goals if necessary.

- Employees should leave the performance review meeting with your comments in writing.

- Conclude on a positive note and express your interest in the employee's success. Schedule a follow-up meeting to review progress toward developmental and growth decisions.

Motivational Phrases
General

- "Are you pleased with your overall performance? Why? Why not?"

- "What would you like to change? Why? How?"

- "What changes would you like to see—in the organization, department, division, yourself—that would help you do your job? How would you suggest implementing these changes?"

- "Can you think of anything specific that I've done that helped or hindered your performance?"

- "I know you have been working to make changes we discussed in the last meeting. Are you having any problems with that?"

- "I noticed that you are implementing those changes we talked about. Keep up the good work."

- "Do you have any concerns?"

- "Do you have any suggestions?"

- "How would you feel about taking on more responsibility?"

- "I would like you to develop an action plan based on the goals we identified in the meeting. Let's review it next week."

- "I understand I've given you a lot to think about in terms of choosing a direction. Let's schedule a follow-up meeting so you can take some time to consider your options."

- "I have confidence in your ability to initiate the changes we discussed. Please let me know if you have any problems and let's review your progress next month."

- "I'm very pleased with your improvement since our last discussion. I hope you are, too."

- "Once you start _____ (reworking that system, using some of the customer service skills we discussed, working on the new project team, revising your schedule…), let's meet to review progress. Put it down for two weeks from today."

- "Is there anything else you would like to discuss with me?"

Addressing Concerns

For more phrases that address concerns, refer to the earlier section in this chapter titled: "Ongoing Developmental Feedback."

- "You often seem frustrated. You start to say something and back off. I value you and your work. Let's talk about what's been bothering you."

- "Help me understand why you want a transfer. You're our top performer. Clients love you; colleagues respect you. I don't want to lose you. What led to this decision?"

- "We have all been on overload, but when you don't keep up it adds to everyone else's burden. Last week, as you know, we almost lost one of your clients who was frustrated with continual delays. What can we do to remedy this situation?"

- "Sometimes, you seem to blaze ahead without following directions. I appreciate your initiative, but it's important that our team members work together and follow some proven courses."
- "I know that this process is confusing. Mastering it is essential to your job. What aids or tools will help you?"
- "When you come in late, others have to interrupt their work to cover for you. What can you do to get here on time?"
- "According to the action plan we created in the last meeting, you were going to _____. I noticed that you haven't begun. What is getting in the way?"
- "We have talked about what the problems are. What solutions do you see? How would you go about moving forward from here?"
- "I have noticed that you sound abrupt on the telephone. Are you aware of that?"
- "We have received a number of complaints from people who describe you as 'rude.' I'm sorry to say I don't have specifics. Are you aware of the actions or tone of voice that would lead people to say that? What are they? How do you think you could modify your _____ (tone, actions, behaviors...) to rectify this problem?"
- "You haven't been transitioning into your new role. I know you don't feel fully confident in this role yet, but I need the job done. I'm here to support you and I believe you can do it. Are you with me? Do you have reservations that I should know about?"
- "Do you realize there will be serious consequences if you continue telling racial jokes in the office? Let's review the company's definition of offensive language and the consequences for using it."

- "When you lose a sale, I can hear you shouting all the way in here! You know it's a numbers game. You just have to move on. Shouting affects everyone's morale. Please find another outlet for this frustration."
- "I appreciate your acceptance of some strong developmental feedback. Please know that my role is to help you succeed."
- "We covered a number of rough spots, but I want to stress that, overall, your work has improved significantly."

Praise

For more phrases of praise, refer to the earlier section in this chapter titled: "Ongoing Positive Feedback."

- "You've initiated three new projects during the past two quarters. That's impressive. What do you have in mind going forward?"
- "I appreciate your frankness when directions aren't clear. You save us all a lot of time."
- "You have gone above and beyond on every assignment. Your commitment to following through despite the time drain has helped not only our department, but also the entire company."
- "Your ability to jump in with creative solutions has saved a lot of time and money. I've shared that with upper management."
- "Your work is exceptional. You are detail oriented yet don't get bogged down in minutia. You continually exceed expectations."
- "You are not stopped in your tracks by problems; you create solutions."
- "I am impressed by your initiation of new projects."

- "I appreciate your eagerness to assist coworkers and to pitch in without being asked."
- "Since our discussion several months ago, I notice that you are more patient with the service department. That helps us keep things running smoothly. Thanks."
- "You are a clear communicator and I appreciate that you are quick to request explanations when I'm not as clear as I could be."
- "You have shown tremendous improvement in your ability to juggle multiple tasks. Keep up the good work!"
- "Your positive attitude is inspiring to those around you. Keep smiling!"
- "I believe that you're ready for more responsibility. How would you feel about being the team leader on our upcoming project?"
- "I just received another customer letter praising your problem-solving initiative. This customer was very appreciative that when she had to speak to someone else you handed her off personally and then went out of your way to follow up. I'm proud to have you on our team. Here is a copy of the letter."
- "I frequently pass by when you are speaking with a customer and overhear how service-oriented you are. Your keeping a friendly demeanor even under the most difficult circumstances is impressive."

Employee Goals and Growth

The Motivational Mindset

- Understand that skill development is a worthwhile investment of time and money, and plan for it. Skill development has a variety of approaches: classroom training, computer-based training, on-the-job training, cross training, mentoring, shadowing, and jumping in with both feet. Varied methods are best suited to different employees and different skill sets.

- When setting goals with employees, look beyond today or this year. Where does this employee want to go within the organization? How can he/she get there?

- Goals set *with* employees are more effective than goals set *for* employees. Use the performance appraisal process as an opportunity to help employees create development plans. Establish a clear method for tracking progress.

- Employee performance goals should be specific and should support departmental and company goals.

- Some people want to climb as high as possible; some people are happy closer to the ground and just want to feel secure in their jobs, do good work, and go home worry free. All personality types and levels of aspiration offer value and need to feel supported in their individual goals.

- Someone who is resistant to moving up should not be pushed because someone else believes his/her 'talents are wasted.' Express your appreciation and admiration of the employee's performance and abilities. You may (or may not) inspire that person to new heights. Praise is motivating, but an employee also needs to believe that his/her work is important and treating a job as "menial" is demoralizing.

- Both fears of success and fears of failure can often be overcome in a supportive atmosphere.
- Help employees look at the next step on the career path. Though a part of us may want to selfishly hold people in place when they are doing their jobs especially well, we all know that focusing on what's best for the employee is ultimately best for everyone.
- Find out the employee's dreams. If you have or can create a position that aligns in some way with someone's dreams, there is no greater motivator and no limit to the potential for success.
- Make availability and benchmarks for promotions clear. If true potential is ahead, use the news to inspire, but if the chances are marginal don't try to inspire by building false hopes. An employee who feels he or she was led around by a fake carrot will be thoroughly de-motivated.

Motivational Phrases

- "What do you (as an individual) or we (as a department, team, or company) want to achieve? When do we want to achieve this goal? How can we achieve this goal?"
- "What goals can you set for yourself that support our department and company goals?"
- "Where do you want to go within the organization? What specific objectives and actions will help you achieve those goals? What support will you need from me? From others?"
- "Please develop a realistic timeline that we can review."
- "What skills do you have to reach the goals you've set? What training and/or support do you need?"
- "How can you help others reach mutual goals while staying on track and on purpose?"

- "You have moved up rather quickly with glowing recommendations along the way. What career path do you envision?"
- "Your strong accounting background led you to finance, but your people skills are outstanding. Have you considered transferring to Human Resources?"
- "Where do you see yourself in five years? Ten years?"
- "You have a natural talent for _____. Have you considered honing that skill?"
- "If you learn to _____, you are in a stronger position to get a promotion."
- "Not many people in this department know how to _____. It would be a valuable skill for you to develop."
- "Times are changing and it's important for someone in your position to know how to _____. If you add this to your already strong skill set, you will further your opportunities for advancement."
- "You clearly have command of the technical aspects of the job. With improved writing skills, you could be eligible for a promotion."
- "I couldn't be more pleased with your job performance. As you can see, you've exceeded expectations in every area. What can I do to ensure that we continue to challenge you?"

Chapter 5

Modeling and Encouraging Communication Skills

"He who has a why can endure any how."

—Friedrich Nietzsche

Communication skills, both face-to-face and via technology, are critical to the success of any business. Ironically, in many cases, the advance of technology has increased the importance of people skills. With so many modes of communication, each of us needs to be the central pilot, the human at the hub, following up. Did the message get through? Was it comprehensible? Is this a situation that requires a human voice or presence? People who work together have differing styles, expectations, and temperaments and must understand each other explicitly to get the job done.

In 1967, Marshall McLuhan coined the phrase "the medium is the message," emphasizing that the *how* impacts the *what*. Today, more than ever, with so many media at our disposal and real and perceived time crunches and emergencies pulling at us, choosing the medium that suits both the message and the audience, making the *clear communication choice*, is more important than ever.

Clear Communication

The Motivational Mindset

- Think about the consequences of poor communication: mistakes; misinformation; lack of commitment; untapped potential; failure to implement change; and lost time, money, and resources.

- Be question friendly. Some people surround themselves with invisible walls that say, 'Do not disturb.' These discourage questions that, if answered, provide timesaving clarification.

- Understand that everyone doesn't process information the same way. Some people respond better to verbal instructions or information, others to written, and still others may need a hands-on demonstration. Communication styles may include paraphrasing, using examples, empathizing, or reflecting.

- Be clear about what you want and be appreciative when you get it.

- Explain new tasks clearly, step by step, demonstrating (if appropriate) and stopping along the way to ensure comprehension. Complex instructions may be best written out as well as explained. You may want to write out key points or ask the employee to take notes. If the instruction will be repeated, the document will become a handy tool for training or reference.

- Clarify deadlines and be specific. How complete do you want the task by that deadline? Do you want a status report before the final deadline? When asking someone to work overtime, be specific about times and dates.

- Everyone processes information in the framework of their own priorities unless given clear expectations and clear time frames.

- Involve people in the big picture. The more information you share, the easier it is for each person to succeed at his or her part of the whole.

- Do not use jargon with anyone who is new in the industry or not in your industry. Encourage employees to do the same.

- Actively seek feedback on your own performance. Liberally use the phrase, "Tell me more." Ask for clarification on points that seem unclear or unfounded. Carefully evaluate the accuracy and potential value of what you hear.

Motivational Phrases

- "Our internal deadline is February 24 to allow us time to incorporate input from other departments and have a final review. Our goal is to send out the completed package by March 8."

- "We get so used to using these words every day that we forget which are jargon. I heard you telling a customer about (some jargon phrase) and want to remind you that customers may feel intimidated by terms they don't know. What would be a customer-friendly way to say it?"

- "What problems are you having with the new _____ (computer, checkout, registration, inventory…) system? How do you think we can address them?"

- "How can we revise signage to clarify directions and limit travelers' frustration?"

- "I'm so glad you spotted that woman's briefcase under the table. You saved her a great deal of trouble and reinforced our reputation of caring for customers."

- "I'll be on vacation next week, so if you want my input, please get to me by Thursday."
- "Let me show you how that works."
- "I don't want to waste your time. Why not give me a brief outline or summary before you dive into writing that report."
- "Your dedication is admirable; however, your safety comes first. Please stay where you are until the weather advisory lifts the travel warning."
- "I had no idea how that additional responsibility impacted on your current workload. Let's review some options. First, what would you suggest?"
- "I apologize for transposing that phone number. You must have been going crazy."
- "Thank you for bringing that problem to my attention. It does need to be addressed immediately. I'll let senior management know—and tell them that you picked it up. Nice work."
- "Let's not take anything for granted. I know you should have no problem making the arrangements we discussed, but please call or e-mail me to confirm that all scheduling details are completed."
- "Check online for step-by-step procedures. It's a lot to remember until you are completely familiar with each process."
- "I know you're pushing a deadline, but I do have to explain this to you before I leave. Please take a moment out to focus on this."

Listening for Clear Communication

The Motivational Mindset

- Show that you are listening: Make eye contact, respond, and focus on the person speaking to you.
- Ask open questions. Open questions encourage more than one-word responses. They typically start with: *what, where, how, why*, or phrases such as *tell me*, or *please explain*.
- Summarize to be certain you understand and/or are understood.
- Make clarification a way of life. Ask employees to repeat important information to you and do the same for them.
- Identify people who have good ideas but may be shy about expressing them. Encourage them to share.
- Do not interrupt, complete others' sentences, or jump to conclusions.
- Use open, attentive body language. Leaning forward, making eye contact, and keeping your arms uncrossed are all expressions of open body language.
- When people start talking to you at times when you cannot focus or listen, it is important to express that you're busy but interested and to suggest a time (or time frame) when you can listen.
- Don't assume someone heard you just because you muttered something as you walked by while that person was otherwise engaged. Make eye contact and, if necessary, schedule a better time to talk.
- Tone of voice, word choice, and body language are all-important cues that may easily be misinterpreted. Beware of jumping to conclusions regarding these listening cues. When in doubt, ask.

➡

Motivational Phrases

- "Let's talk in here, where we won't be interrupted. I know you've been trying to catch up with me."
- "If I understand you correctly, what you're saying is _____."
- "You've made a lot of interesting points. I'd like to summarize to be certain I understand."
- "I'm sorry if I misunderstood you. Let's see where we can go from here."
- "Let's all allow each other to share ideas without comment or criticism. Later, we'll evaluate more carefully, but I'd like everyone to feel free to let ideas flow."
- "How would that work?"
- "Why do you prefer that method?"
- "Please explain your thinking on that."
- "I'm sorry I don't have time to give you my full attention right now. Can we talk later this afternoon?" (If possible, schedule a time.)
- "You sounded upset when I called this morning. Did I misread you or is something wrong?"
- "I just blurted out this meeting information, but I see that you're focused on something else. Since I'm running out and won't be available, please jot it down so I know you have it."
- "That's a great idea, but I'm not sure it's right for us at this time because _____. Can the plan be tweaked to meet our needs more precisely?"
- "I like that idea. Tell me more."
- "That's an interesting idea. Let's explore it at our next meeting."
- "I put my phone on voice mail so we can talk without interruption."

Clear Communication Choices

The Motivational Mindset

- All communication choices are not equal. Use the right medium for your message. For example, a message e-mailed at 3:00 P.M. regarding a 5:00 P.M. meeting or e-mailed late in the day regarding an 8 A.M. meeting, can easily be missed. Don't rely exclusively on e-mail for time-sensitive issues.

- Some people get hundreds of e-mails each day and just can't wade through—or may be out of the office or in meetings all day. If a message is critical, try e-mail and voice mail—or, better yet, track someone down in person if possible.

- Not everyone has the same comfort level with technology. Know your audience.

- Never assume your whole message got through while a cell phone was cutting out.

- Create short, clear voice mail messages for those calling you and leave short, clear voice mail messages when calling others.

- Leaving key information such as what you need to know and by when, your availability, and your contact information, eliminates or greatly reduces phone tag.

- Use specific subject lines in e-mails.

- Don't write mystery e-mails where the most important point is buried in the middle or saved for the end. Write the most important information up front.

- Sometimes, instead of instant messaging, e-mailing, calling, or enabling your video conferencing equipment, you might just walk down the hall and talk face to face.

➡

- Your face and body language are communication media, too. Do they fight with your message? Be aware of the visual cues you give.

Motivational Phrases

- "If you cannot reach someone through text messaging, try another method. You might be text messaging a person who doesn't use that feature. You might even be sending to a phone that does not record text messages at all."
- "I know you're discouraged by not getting a callback, and I know you said you called all day yesterday, but you also said you didn't leave a message. It's often hard to catch people, but they do check in. You'll save yourself time and frustration by leaving specific messages."
- "If your e-mails are not getting a response, try another method. Servers go down, e-mail programs can have glitches, and your name could accidentally be set to fall into the junk file. Make a call and when you connect with a live person, confirm that you have the right address and explain your problems getting through."
- "Communicating with that department is beyond frustrating. I admire your patience."
- "If you cannot be there to join us for the meeting, can you be there via phone or video conferencing?"
- "E-mail is not always my top priority, and I may not get to it the day it is sent. Please mark all urgent requests 'time sensitive' in the subject line."
- "Instant messaging does not mean the recipient is available to respond instantly."
- "Don't include anything in an e-mail that you wouldn't want to see on a billboard."

- "Don't assume everyone knows e-mail and instant messaging abbreviations."
- "Even if you don't have all of the information yet, please leave me a message filling me in as much as you can before 2:00 P.M. That will be my last chance to check in today."
- "If a message is urgent or has to be returned ASAP, I need to be told about it the minute I come in. If you are stepping out, please leave a message on my _____ (door, desk, chair, voice mail, e-mail…)."
- "Thank you so much for thinking to send the contracts by overnight mail. I hadn't thought of that and would have had a real problem if you didn't."
- "Specific e-mail subject lines are helpful: *Thursday's Meeting Agenda; Friday's 10:00 A.M. phone conference rescheduled; Thanks to those who helped with the March event; New Healthcare Policy; This Month's Contest; Company All Stars; Kudos.*"
- "Spell-check is not a mindless activity. Read the choices. *Always* spell-check and *never* rely on spelling or grammar checks without engaging your own bank of knowledge."
- "I really do like your suggestion. I've been told I have 'that face.' Don't let my expression throw you. Your idea is superb."

Chapter 6

Motivating Critical Skills

"Whatever you are, be a good one." —Abraham Lincoln

Whatever your field, certain life skills translate to good business practices. Some of these come naturally to people and others are cultivated with a little guidance and a good role model or two. Creativity, initiative, critical thinking skills, and a flexible mindset keep people thinking, contributing, and moving the company forward. Time management and organizational skills keep business, business relationships, and workflow running smoothly. Presentation skills to large and small audiences enhance information sharing. The motivational manager gently encourages building or honing these critical skills.

Developing skills requires time and effort—yours and your employees'. When that investment seems unreasonable, think of Thomas Jefferson's words: "I am a great believer in luck, and I find the harder I work, the more I have of it."

Creativity

The Motivational Mindset

- Creativity may require quiet time to think. Don't always expect a creative answer on the spot.
- People are often more creative than they realize. Giving people a chance to access their creativity will often boost self-esteem.
- Encourage the search for new solutions to persistent problems.
- If employees have creative interests outside of work, tapping into the same skills in the office might spark their creative spirits. Before you hire a company to design your brochure cover, consider the talents in your office.
- Consider a monthly (or quarterly) creativity caucus to encourage and hear employee ideas.
- Encourage brainstorming, allowing as many ideas as possible to come to the surface for consideration. The #1 rule of brainstorming: All ideas are welcome and nothing is ridiculed or put down. No ideas are wrong.
- Compliment creativity when you see it.
- When is the last time you looked through your staff's résumés? Are you overlooking skills and talents that didn't apply two or three years ago but would help you and give your employee an opportunity?
- Stark walls, fluorescent lights, and unadorned cubicles don't inspire creativity.
- Have a library available for employees that includes brief meditations or relaxation techniques. Used on breaks, these can lead to a refreshed, creative mindset.

Motivational Phrases

- "Do you have a suggestion for a new _____ (product, initiative, promotion…)?"
- "In what kind of environment do you do your most creative thinking?"
- "Take your mind off the issue for a while (perhaps over lunch). Sometimes creativity flows as soon as you stop consciously searching."
- "Why did you seem hesitant about this plan? I value your opinion and would like to know your thoughts on it. Would you mind sharing?"
- "Choose a partner to brainstorm solutions. Even wild ideas are allowed here. Whichever team gets the longest list (with no repetitions) wins a free lunch (or some small token reward)."
- "I imagine you'll find a creative solution."
- "I need some creative juices on this project. Can I have your input?"
- "How many new approaches can you come up with for dealing with this issue?"
- "What thoughts do you have on how we can turn this problem into an opportunity?"
- "We need your creative sparks in tomorrow's meeting."
- "What is your instinct on this? You have great intuition."
- "Can you find a new angle for tackling this issue?"
- "How would you approach a new client about our product line?"
- "We've used the same format for our company awards program for five years. The planning committee is requesting suggestions for changes."

- "We're having a contest to rename the newsletter. The employee who submits the selected title wins a $100 gift certificate."

Initiative

The Motivational Mindset

- Initiative is not always moving *up*. Initiative can also mean stepping in to help a team member, *any* team member in need. In a crisis, everyone pitches in—including the manager. If cashiers, customer service reps, or waiters are on overload, it hurts your customers and doesn't look good for anyone. If your administrative assistant can't meet your deadline, it's your problem, too.

- Intrapreneurship has become a watchword in successful companies. The concept brings the fire and passion of the entrepreneur to employees in larger work environments. Create a sense of ownership among employees for your department's or company's success and the intrapreneurial spirit will motivate.

- Two major initiative roadblocks are indifference and negative reinforcement.

- Showing appreciation and respect for the employee who attempts to chart new ground—whether or not successful—encourages that employee and others to think outside the box.

- Employees who are encouraged to take initiative and who can see the results of their initiative in action are more likely to be motivated and take interest in the company's success.

- Forget the old adage: "If you want something done right, you have to do it yourself." Remember, instead, this new adage: "If you want something done right, delegate to the right person."

➡

- Delegation is not dumping. Delegate to the right person; then be available to answer questions and provide support and guidance.
- Delegate the responsibilities that will keep business running smoothly. Do not foster an environment where no one takes initiative and, for example, supplies run out causing rush, panic, or complaints. Little things, even supplies, mean a lot.
- Time invested in explaining, demonstrating, and answering questions will pay off later, when an employee has the confidence and competence to take over the role.
- By offering small windows for big thinking, employers encourage staff to reach beyond their grasp.

Motivational Phrases

- "I need someone skilled to take over this assignment. I will be here to support and train you. Would you be comfortable with the added responsibility?"
- "How are you doing on that project? I knew you would be able to run with it on your own."
- "Please check in with me as you take on your new responsibilities. I have to approve decisions during this learning phase, but I know you will be quick to pick this up and will do an excellent job."
- "Tell me how you would improve nurse-to-patient response time. You seem to be able to be in three places at once."
- "I am confident in your abilities, but feel free to ask questions anytime."
- "I'm always open to new ideas. Can you think of another approach for _____ (guest check-out, patient intake, client follow-up, work order processing…)?"

➡

- "What a fantastic idea! I'm 100 percent behind you. How can I support you?"
- "What are your ideas for solving this problem (or resolving this issue)?"
- "I have been working closely with management on reviewing our strategic plan for the next five years. I'd like to share some ideas with you and get your opinion. You're really in touch with day-to-day operations."
- "You know that we all believed that the new approach you initiated would be successful and we all share your disappointment. Try those few changes that we talked about in the meeting. Your creativity moved us forward a few steps. Your next try will help us leap ahead."
- "Our new guest relations handbook is almost ready for press. You have made excellent editing suggestions on other projects. Would you mind reviewing this?"
- "You have such great ideas, but you seem hesitant to share them. I think it would be to everyone's benefit if you could become confident about how much you have to offer."
- "You know this project inside out. My travel schedule is interfering with my role as project manager. I'd like you to take over."
- "Thanks for taking the initiative in putting passengers for the 10:15 A.M. flight in front of that incredibly long line."
- "I'll be out of the country next month. I'm confident having you present our recent initiatives at the interdepartmental meeting. Let's get together so I can explain how I typically do that."
- "You don't even have to run _____ (the changes, your ideas, your edits, the proposal…) by me. Everything you do is so on target."

Critical Thinking

The Motivational Mindset

- Critical thinking is a search for reason through a problem-solving process.
- Critical thinkers don't blindly believe everything or nothing. They see full spectrums of colors and shades, not just black and white.
- Skepticism is not necessarily negative. Healthy skepticism raises necessary questions.
- Brainstorming can continue even after you think you've hit upon the best idea. It may only be the best idea *yet*. You also may need backup plans.
- Monday morning quarterbacking should not be played as a form of regret, but as a catalyst for growth. It can be helpful to replay an incident that did not go well in order to prepare for successful future outcomes.
- Avoid jumping to simple cause and effect conclusions. For example, Bob spilled his coffee during the presentation. The client chose to contract with a competitor. Of all possible reasons for a client to choose a competitor, don't decide it was because Bob spilled his coffee.
- Encourage employees to consider other points of view, even those that sound the most outrageous.
- Look at prior experiences and consider their relevance to the current situation.
- Use and teach a simple problem-solving strategy:

    1. Identify the problem.

    2. Analyze the problem and consider possible causes.

    3. Generate possible solutions and select one.

➡

4. Implement the solution.

5. Follow up by evaluating the solution.

- Conduct problem-solving sessions that allow everyone to participate. Allow for additional questions and creativity to broaden the experience.

Motivational Phrases

- "How can we define this problem? What are possible causes of this problem?"
- "What do we know from prior experience? How relevant is that prior experience to this situation?"
- "How many possible solutions can we find? Which solution or solutions will help us achieve our desired result?"
- "How should we prioritize solutions?"
- "Which solutions address the cause?"
- "Is it necessary for our solution to address the cause or is this clearly a one-time issue?"
- "How will we implement this solution?"
- "What process will measure the solution's success or rate its effectiveness?"
- "What new ideas can we generate?"
- "What possible outcomes can we imagine?"
- "It's not important right now who forgot to confirm the hotel. What is important is how we relocate a conference of 500 people in three weeks."
- "We're facing a difficult challenge—satisfying customers, stockholders, and regulatory agencies. Let's review common stakeholder requirements and start with those."
- "That incident was an embarrassment to all of us. Let's explore what happened so we won't duplicate it."

- "Statistics, intuition, numbers, past experience, and logic are all useful tools, but relying solely on any one of them can be a mistake."
- "Never underestimate your gut instinct. Factor it in."

Flexibility

The Motivational Mindset

- Change is life; it is the natural state of all things. A work environment that does not change stagnates.
- Complaining about change sets a counterproductive tone. Rather, determine ways to work with the change.
- Embrace change enthusiastically, and encourage others to recognize inherent opportunities.
- Fear of change is a learned response. Even learned responses can be changed. Model the positive response.
- Every time a new employee joins a company or a department, the dynamic changes slightly. The flexible leader is in tune with the shift and able to help it maintain a positive direction.
- Being flexible means remaining open to suggestions and willing to change your plan or direction if change is best—whether or not it's comfortable.
- Change, even positive change, can be a major cause of stress for many people. Our reactions to change, not the change, cause us stress. Be open to new ideas and approaches. Encourage that openness in others.
- Stressing out or stewing over a problem does not bring about change. Explore options and be proactive.
- Don't rush to judgment, good or bad; evaluate the situation and consider possible courses of action. We have all experienced so-called *blessings in disguise*.
- Once a policy change is in place and you know the time for questioning it is over, help those who report to you accept it and move on.

Motivational Phrases

- "I understand that change can be stressful, but this reorganization will ultimately be positive."
- "New technology can be daunting, but we have to stay current. Group training is available every morning at 7:30 A.M. and individual training is available upon request."
- "These are exciting times for the company, and we know that you are all behind our success. Opening a new store pulls resources from existing ones. Please bear with us during this phase."
- "The new office will be different, but we can look forward to _____ (more windows, being downtown, having a conference room…)."
- "The new branch will be a place for expanded opportunities."
- "The new management does things differently. You may like some of their methods and not others, but we ask that you reserve judgment during the transition."
- "I know this is not how we've done it in the past, but let's consider whether it's the best method for the future."
- "What benefits can you see from this change?"
- "I like your new idea. We have never tried this before, so we have many possible outcomes. Let's run a few scenarios to see how it might play out."
- "This is not working out as we had planned, but the results are interesting; let's stay the course. You never know what you may discover. The inventors of post-its were trying to make glue."
- "The only constant is change. If we can be comfortable with change and expect the unexpected, we won't feel thrown 'off course' when it comes."

- "What computer upgrades would make this project run more smoothly?"
- "Let's pause to assess our progress. Are we on track? Is 'on track' still where we want to be or should we consider a new direction?"
- "I'm very comfortable with the current progress, but your suggestion is interesting. Let's try it for one quarter."
- "I realize that the promotion you're considering is a major step, but I believe you have the qualities to succeed at that level. Let's talk about what your new responsibilities would be."

Time Management

The Motivational Mindset

- Time is money—to you, your company, your clients, and your employees.
- Compressed time, poorly managed time, and not enough time lead to errors, lost opportunities, and stress.
- Increased media at increased speed, such as e-mail and cell phones, have created a general sense of urgency in the workplace (and beyond). Most people believe they do not have enough time to do their jobs and meet others' expectations. Control the frenzy.
- Planning saves time—yours and others'. Plan and help others plan to achieve long- and short-term goals and, sometimes, to just get through the day.
- Time management tools aren't in everyone's toolbox. Don't assume that all employees know how to plan. Offer guidance, seminars, and resources.
- Help employees anticipate the unexpected. Establish a mindset where the unexpected won't have the power to wreak havoc.
- Controlling interruptions is key to time management. Respect others' uninterrupted time and request your own.
- Setting and synchronizing priorities is essential to good time management.
- Understand whose crisis is your crisis.
- Help supervisors who report to you learn to delegate appropriately. Delegating is selecting the right person for the right job, not pushing unwanted tasks on others.

➡

Motivational Phrases

- "I know that recent layoffs have increased everyone's work load. Think about these questions as you review those tasks that you now face: Is this necessary? Can it be consolidated? Can it be eliminated? Can it be delegated?"

- "I know that time tracking seems like yet another job, but it *does* help you evaluate how you spend your time. We're only doing this for one week."

- "When you are focused on typing a document, I hate to interrupt. Sometimes, like now, I just have no choice."

- "I appreciate your covering Sam's phone while he's at the conference. I know it's a constant interruption. Why not let his calls go to his voice mail and check it every hour so you can stay focused on your work?"

- "Myrna from Marketing seems to think our department is her social obligation each time she passes through. It is not rude to smile at her and go right back to work."

- "Just because the request came in by e-mail doesn't mean that the response is required within minutes. Your priorities are important. Unless the message is urgent, plan the best time for *you* to respond."

- "I noticed that toward the end of the day, you are playing major catch up. I used to struggle with managing priorities, but then took this great course. Would you like some time management suggestions from the pros?"

- "Bouncing between priorities can slow you down. Have you considered giving yourself a telephone-free time slot?"

- "Joseph can keep you on the phone until next week. I've learned to never ask him an open-ended question. Also, I begin my call by saying, 'I only have a few minutes, but I wanted to return your call quickly.'"

- "Telephone tag is very time-consuming. The more specific your message, the better chance you have of getting a call back when you are available or of getting a message that ends the game."
- "I know you have project A as a priority, but Ali has encountered some setbacks with project B and needs extra help. Where are you with project A? Can you afford to take a few hours out to help Ali? We need to meet that deadline, too."
- "I know you handle customer complaints with great diplomacy. Eva has a similar style. You could free up some valuable time by training her to share that role."
- "This proposal just came in and is due in a few days. What can we clear from your schedule so you can run with this?"
- "I need this data by 5:00 P.M. Can you get this to me and still meet your other deadlines? If not, we need to find additional help or make some calls. We cannot afford to let any of these items fall through the cracks."
- "Establishing a timeline early with other personnel involved will save time later."

Organization

The Motivational Mindset

- Despite the occasional employee who can reach into a seemingly disorganized landslide of papers and pull out the appropriate item, most people function better when organized.
- A well-organized business, filing system (hard copy and computer), and workspace save time, money, and anguish.
- The office must be organized in a way that everyone can understand. No one person should be the only one who can find anything.
- Even the people who can keep everything in their heads without ever writing anything down get sick, win the lottery, move on. Good organization is something that can be picked up on by someone else when necessary.
- Improving organizational skills can improve time management and reduce stress. Obviously, scrambling to find things wastes time and, depending on the urgency of the item, can raise the stress level of everyone in the vicinity.
- Good organizational skills can also reduce the risk of missed deadlines or last-minute rushes.
- People with true organizational skills get things done. Others are so busy organizing that they spend more time arranging planners than doing actual work. Learn to recognize the difference so that you can support people and get them on the right track.
- Some people are very good at their jobs but are hindered by a lack of organization. Don't stifle creative people by saddling them with rigorous organizational systems,

➡

but encourage everyone to use a system that works for them.

■ Be open to new technology that can organize, synch calendars, and back up computer files. If your employees are more comfortable with new methods that would be improvements on the old, let them train you.

■ For critical data, back up your backup.

Motivational Phrases

■ "I like the way you organized the _____ (office, filing system, data, team assignments). Thank you."

■ "I am always impressed by how you keep things running so smoothly around here."

■ "I'm sure your new organizational system is more streamlined than our old one, but we all need to understand how it works. Let's hold a meeting so you can explain the new system."

■ "Many people on our team find it difficult to find files on the computer. Everyone seems to be using their own systems, leaving files scattered and hard to find. Let's work together to come up with a system that we can all use."

■ "The business has been growing so fast, I think that's why certain things have slipped through the cracks. What ideas do you have for recreating organizational systems?"

■ "Would you like to attend a class on organization to learn ways you can bring our office up to speed in light of our recent expansion? Check the training catalogue to see what's available."

■ "What organizational system works best for you? You will be more inclined to stay with one that suits your style."

- "Keeping up with all the paperwork can be overwhelming. Several people found this _____ (course, system, process) useful. What do you think?"
- "You seem to have your finger on the pulse of any given moment's priority. What system do you use for keeping priorities in order?"
- "I realize this project is not on the A list because it's not time sensitive, but it *is* important. Do you have ideas about how to schedule this into the workday/week over the next few months?"
- "Please put your important dates on the master calendar. We all depend on each other at one time or another, so it is always helpful to know who will be here when and when others might or might not be available to offer support."
- "You must have been frustrated to have missed that meeting because of a computer glitch. Let's find software that keeps our calendars updated and synchronized."
- "Please be sure to keep everyone in your department posted when your contact information changes. We want clients and customers to know you have the strong support system you deserve."
- "Whom can I entrust with the responsibility of backing up the main database? None of us can afford the time it would take to track down lost data."
- "Everyone has a different process for organizing leads for follow-up. Let's share so we can learn from one another."

The Motivational Mindset

- Many employees must present new ideas to their peers or to management; plans, proposals, or findings to other parts of the company; or company initiatives to existing or prospective clients.
- Presentation skills do not come naturally to everyone.
- Comfort and knowledge play key roles in effective presentations.
- Ensure that employees know that they've been selected to present or serve on a panel because of their knowledge. Praise their backgrounds and understanding of specific topics and issues, emphasizing that's why you've asked them to be out front.
- Build confidence through offering courses and/or opportunities for small group presentations with supportive feedback.
- Provide necessary equipment and tips on the most effective ways to use it.
- Encourage employees to watch strong, effective speakers on TV, videos, or in person.
- Have an instructional video available and offer basic tips online or in hard copy.
- Assure others that they can learn to relax, speak up, speak slowly and clearly, make eye contact, and connect with their audiences.
- Provide positive feedback and supportive suggestions for improvement. Encourage practice.

Motivational Phrases

- "I'd like you to present our marketing plan to the management team. Are you comfortable?"
- "You know this product's features and benefits better than anyone. We need an additional rep at our booth at the national conference. Would you like some presentation skills coaching before that comes up?"
- "Your presentation last week was strong. I have a few suggestions to make you an even more effective speaker."
- "By using focused, dynamic gestures, you can strengthen your delivery."
- "I usually choose several friendly faces throughout the audience and make eye contact with them."
- "Remember, everyone is attending this meeting to learn about your _____ (approach, development, initiative, findings, recent meeting with XYZ…), not to criticize your presentation."
- "You would be surprised at how a smile warms up an audience."
- "I was very impressed with your handling of the Q and A. Your answers were succinct and to the point. Clearly, you were the expert in the room."
- "When you review your talk, eliminate unnecessary words, phrases, jargon, and irrelevant details."
- "Your soft-spoken manner tends to make people feel comfortable in one-to-one discussions, but you'll have to practice projecting when you make presentations, even at our committee meetings."
- "I noticed that your voice tightens when you speak up at meetings. Try drinking hot tea or coffee instead of cold water."

- "Your presentations have become quite polished. My one suggestion is that you work on inflection."
- "I saw a very motivational speech on television last night. I taped it for anyone who would like to use it for pointers on presentation style." (Do not use religious or political figures. No matter how motivational they may be, when emotions get involved the points you hope to make will be lost.)
- "That was a tough Q and A that you fielded. One way to control the 'question bully' is to use eye contact and body language. As soon as you complete your answer, turn and acknowledge someone in another part of the room."
- "Wow! You were dynamic, well versed, and succinct. We could not have asked for a better representative."

Chapter 7

Motivational Challenges

"Others will underestimate us, for although we judge ourselves by what we feel capable of doing, others judge us only by what we have already done."

—Henry Wadsworth Longfellow

M otivational challenges can seem overwhelming at times. It's easy to say "I would be a great motivator, but how can anyone motivate under these circumstances? I'm supervising people who seem not to care, who are negative, are constantly complaining about the rules, or just don't get along." This is not the time to give up; you need to double your efforts to both motivate yourself and overcome these challenges to motivate others. Sometimes an employer must recognize a poor fit or realize that the employee cannot develop the requisite skills. The motivational employer can turn most employees around by tapping into the smallest window of opportunity to help them make positive changes. Norman Vincent Peale, author of *The Power of Positive Thinking*, wrote: "People become really quite remarkable when they start thinking that they can do things. When they believe in themselves, they have the first secret of success."

The diversity challenge is also ever-increasing. People who came up the ranks with a traditional hierarchy are working later in life and mixing at all levels with a new breed of young people who come in with strong skills and high expectations. The virtual commuter has been quickly finding where to fit into it all; and the current level of cultural diversity would have seemed extraordinary not long ago. Each category brings its own set of challenges.

A Culturally Diverse Workforce

The Motivational Mindset

- Ensure that everyone is treated equally. Do not tolerate discrimination based on *any* difference. Be aware of your own biases and limiting perceptions so that you can keep yourself in check, as well as others.

- The culturally diverse workforce has become the norm rather than the exception in many areas of the country. Just as a culturally homogeneous group benefits from diversities such as age or educational backgrounds, the culturally diverse workforce brings new benefits.

- Often, the diverse workforce reflects the customer base within that geographical area. Diversity within the workforce increases the organization's understanding of the customer.

- Whether a culturally diverse workforce is seen or experienced as an advantage is a matter of perspective. It does often present unique challenges and those who see any change as a downside will be quick to see diversity as a negative. Your job as motivator is to focus on the positive aspects and navigate the challenges.

- Take advantage of everyone's unique strengths. Respect differences and build on common values.

- Model and demand language and accent sensitivity. As possible, offer English classes for those who don't speak English and foreign language classes for those who supervise or manage employees with limited English abilities.

- English speakers can be discouraged and feel left out when bilingual employees are speaking other languages around them. Make clear that same-language communication among employees, when possible, is the ideal. Communication is challenging enough when we're all speaking the same language.

- Don't tell (or allow) jokes about race, religion, or nationality —including the joke-teller's own. Even when we can laugh at ourselves, telling those jokes gives mixed signals to others.
- The evolution of our workforce requires sensitivity to multiple holidays.
- Understand and explain, when necessary, that levels of eye contact and personal space are different in various cultures and that body language we would take as clear cues from Americans may not mean the same at all when expressed by someone from another culture.

Motivational Phrases

- "We're lucky to have such diversity among us. The more perspectives we have, the greater our advantage."
- "We will not tolerate racial or religious slurs. I've spoken with X. If anyone ever makes you uncomfortable again, please tell me so I can resolve the situation."
- "Many of our clients are not used to your accent. If you try speaking just a little bit more slowly you might notice a big difference in how well people understand. I know it's frustrating when you have to repeat yourself."
- "I understand that you feel like an outsider when you walk onto the dock and everyone is speaking Spanish, but you're only passing through and they all speak Spanish more comfortably than English. I'll talk to them about making you feel comfortable, but we need to think of their comfort, too."

- "We're offering English classes for employees and Spanish for supervisors."

- "Our workforce has changed dramatically. We will provide cultural diversity seminars to help each of us understand the nuances of one another's cultures."

- "When you order sandwiches for meetings, please select some vegetarian options, including nondairy, to ensure that there's something for everyone."

- "Tapas, I could use your help. I have a new client from India and I just came from a meeting that felt strained. I'm having trouble reading him. If I fill you in, can you tell me whether his reactions reflect cultural norms or whether I should be concerned?"

- "Nguyen is not showing disrespect by avoiding eye contact. Actually, in his culture, lack of eye contact is a sign of respect."

- "Personal space and comfort zones vary among different cultures. Let's work to raise our awareness out of respect for each other and our clients."

- "Our Hispanic customer base has increased significantly. In addition to our bilingual support staff, I strongly recommend our in-house Spanish for Business course for all managers and supervisors."

- "I realize that we can't all become proficient in the many languages of our housekeeping staff, but we can learn a few phrases in their languages to show that while they're struggling to learn English, we're trying, too."

- "We are adding glossaries to our upward mobility manuals to assist those attendees whose first language is not English."

- "You did the right thing by telling me about the offensive statements you overheard. I will talk with everyone who was there immediately and if it happens again, please do not hesitate to tell me. We have a zero tolerance policy for that kind of language and I'm sorry you were subjected to it."
- "Different cultures use different greetings. Mirror the greeting you receive."

Generations at Work

Four generations now share the workplace. They are often referred to as: The Silent Generation, Baby Boomers, Generation X, and Generation Next. In brief, the Silent Generation remembers when the executives were men (in dark suits and white shirts) and secretaries (in dresses and high heels) used old-fashioned typewriters, carbon paper, and microfiche. Baby Boomers raised the status of women in the workplace and changed traditional notions of family roles at home. Gen Xers grew up alongside the technology boom. They brought a wave of dress-down, flextime, work-at-home, and play-at-work attitudes to the office. Gen Nexters come to the table with technology as a second skin. The first rung on the corporate ladder is not always their first step. Their workplace is so different from the one where the Silent Generation got its start, that a Nexter might guess that *microfiche* is a small French fish. However, specific age groups and profiles of each group are less important than understanding some common issues that arise when generations come together at work.

The Motivational Mindset

- For a long time workplace advancement was guided by a simple, reliable formula: age = experience = opportunities for advancement. Being supervised by much younger people may be a difficult adjustment for many.

- If you look or are considered "too young" for your position, don't make threats or unreasonable power plays to show your strength. Most new managers need to earn respect. Being solid, rational, and doing what needs to be done will earn you that respect.

- Young workers are starting out at salaries many senior employees would never have dreamed of at their ages. Sometimes a simple matter of economics can feel personal or feed resentment.
- Be open to the "voice of experience." Sometimes, you can save time and effort by building on a past approach or document and by learning about past pitfalls.
- If an older report is directly refusing to "answer to you" or making jokes about your age, initiate a frank discussion. If reasoning fails, deal with the action as you would any other disruptive, counterproductive behavior that does not belong in a business environment.
- If you're having trouble getting buy-in for your ideas from the "old guard," consider your presentation style and whether you put down the old methods that served their purpose well. Consider also whether you've given a reasonable time frame for transitions.
- Younger generations may feel frustrated when others are not as technologically savvy. Praise technological prowess, but encourage patience.
- Before you say, "We tried that 10 years ago; it didn't work," or "I know what works; I've tried it all," consider how much has changed. Could an approach that didn't work then have simply been before its time?
- Don't make people "pay their dues" on principle. Times, entry-level skills, competitive offerings, and expectations have changed.
- If you believe that younger workers don't respect experience, pause to consider whether *you* respect new ideas. If you believe older workers don't respect new ideas, pause to consider whether *you* respect experience.

➡

Motivational Phrases

- "I've been doing this so long I sometimes get stuck in my ways. I know you have a lot of great ideas. Let's schedule a time to sit down and talk about them."

- "Before you completely dismiss old methods, consider whether it might be best to build on them. Looking at all angles will ultimately make your idea stronger."

- "When suggesting something new, don't put down the old. Be careful in your phrasing. People may take it personally and feel put down. When you present new ideas, you don't want to start by putting people on the defensive."

- "Barbara has been here a long time. You will never gain her respect without showing yours."

- "I'm impressed with your training. It took me a few years in the business to get to the level you're at now."

- "Many management trainees in this company have the same level of technical skill that you have. Your way of making people feel valued is your unique edge."

- "The board is open to new ideas as long as they are presented in a traditional format. Observe another meeting as you prepare your presentation."

- "Seniority weighs very heavily with upper management. Get some experienced staffers on your side before you go in."

- "I understand that you're upset about senior employees who refer to you as 'kid.' Have you asked them not to? I'm sure they mean well and will make the effort to stop if you tell them it makes you uncomfortable. If you tell them and they continue, let me know."

- "I know you're eager to get ahead. We do carefully consider those with seniority when filling management positions. We are a very loyal company and that's one way we can show appreciation for those who have stuck with us over the years, but you do have upward mobility opportunities. Let's meet to talk about your future."

- "Please share your knowledge from prior experiences and work with us to determine what is relevant to our present circumstances."

- "When you resent a request or behavior by a young new employee, consider whether your expectation or judgment is based on your own past experience. Ask yourself whether the belief you formed is still valid. Is your expectation reasonable at this time?"

- "Before you resent not being approached for advice or expertise, consider whether you've made yourself available. Let others know that you're eager to help and that their questions are not an imposition."

- "I know you're upset about Keri getting an expense account after only three months when you were here for six years before you got one. It's no longer a matter of status—it's practicality. She entertains clients, we have room in the budget, and these accounts cut down on bookkeeping."

- "I know you cringe when Jake calls you 'old timer.' Have you told him? I know that he respects you, and he may just think of it as a friendly nickname. I'm sure he'll stop if you tell him it makes you uncomfortable. If not, let me know."

The Underachiever

Underachiever can have two distinct meanings. One sends your overnight package, but doesn't follow up to see that it arrived. The other sends your package overnight, follows up to see that it arrived, and has at hand the name of the person he or she spoke to. That second person (who follows up), if resistant when offered a promotion, would be referred to by many as an underachiever. However, in that job, daily, that person is achieving high-quality performance. Let's call that person the *career underachiever* and let's call the underachiever who doesn't follow up on the overnight package and doesn't seem to care the *blasé underachiever*.

The Motivational Mindset
(for the blasé underachiever)

- Some people feel overwhelmed or have trouble looking at the big picture and seeing where to begin. Help by breaking down large projects into smaller, manageable tasks.

- Some underachievers may never have been appreciated or told that their work made any significant contribution. Or, they may have learned how to just "get by" years ago and may come alive if inspired by some spark of interest.

- You might be supervising someone who has felt "used by the system" in the past and is on the defensive regarding his or her personal time and space. Show that you are not going to take advantage, and you may see the individual's defenses come down and work performance improve.

- Explain how the employee fits in with the organization and the importance of the job he or she is doing.

- Give developmental feedback. Don't worry so much about crushing the spirit of the blasé underachiever that you

➡

refrain from giving solid, developmental feedback. Such feedback has the potential to turn around an apparent lack of motivation and follow-through.

- Clarify your expectations and give clear direction. Often, people don't realize the little steps that complete a job.
- Be diligent about praising even small, positive changes and jobs well done.
- Assess whether additional training in a particular skill set will improve confidence, abilities, and drive.
- Encourage attendance at professional conferences.
- Examine whether a person is over- or underqualified. Sometimes someone is just the wrong fit for the job.

Motivational Phrases
(for the blasé underachiever)

- "You tend to procrastinate routine tasks. Why do you think that is?"
- "What do you enjoy most about your workday?"
- "You have so much talent, but something seems to be holding you back. I'd like to discuss this with you. Is there anything I can do?"
- "You say you're getting bored with your job. What changes would motivate you?"
- "What would make this job (or specific task) more interesting/challenging for you?"
- "You seem overwhelmed by this project. Why not break it down? Where would you start?"
- "I know that _____ is repetitive work, but without it, our department would be in big trouble."
- "Small steps lead to great achievements."

➡

- "Your role in our organization is more valuable than you may realize. When you walk past any customer during your day, please smile and say, 'Hello.' Your interactions are important."
- "Never lose your long-range vision."
- "A clean environment is important to everyone. That makes your role particularly important."
- "It may seem like a small thing, but greeting _____ (guests, tenants, shoppers, clients…) makes a big difference."
- "I appreciate your staying on top of routine maintenance problems. You save us time and the company money."
- "I was impressed with the way you handled _____ (the crowd, the complaint, the confusion…) today. Good work!"

The Motivational Mindset (for the career underachiever)

- Be certain that employees are *aware* of possible upward moves and their access to steps that lead there.
- Always ask when you see potential, and encourage if you see a glimmer of interest. However, don't make a mission out of making your dreams come true for someone else. Respect employees' choices and let them feel good about where they are.
- Some people have enough and don't want more. They don't need the bigger paycheck or want more hours *or* responsibility. They are where they are for a reason—it's where they want to be.
- The *career underachiever* is like the big fish in a little pond—highly successful in the present position and seemingly overqualified with wasted talents. If someone is

happy in a position and doesn't want to change, what does *wasted* mean? A promotion could mean longer hours, less time at home, or less contact with people all day. You have to know what someone enjoys in order to motivate.

- Never hold someone back, but show your appreciation for those who choose to stay where they are. If someone is doing a highly competent job and wants to stay put, be happy for that employee and grateful to have such a competent person in that position.
- There are no small parts on any business stage. Whether someone is working behind the scenes or out in front of clients or customers, everyone has some impact on how the product functions, how it's packaged, how the customer sees the company, or the morale of other employees around them. Everyone has some impact. Make sure everyone knows the importance of his or her role.
- For the *career underachiever* who does not realize his or her potential, your role in noticing, acknowledging, and encouraging that potential is critical.
- Confidence and self-esteem may be issues for both the *blasé underachiever* and the *career underachiever*.
- Positive feedback is important for everyone, but may make all the difference for an underachiever.
- Be sensitive to the *career underachiever's* underlying motivation. Avoid variations of "What's a smart girl like you doing in a joint like this?"

Motivational Phrases (for the career underachiever)

- "In what ways do you think your job could be more challenging?"

- "What do you enjoy most about your current position?"
- "You have so much talent, but something seems to be holding you back. Would you like to discuss it?"
- "You have tremendous ability. I'd love to have you continue assisting me, but I'd like to help you go further in the organization."
- "You seem happy in your present job; however, I see potential for promotion to the next level. Does this interest you?"
- "Your work is outstanding! Would you be interested in taking steps toward moving up?"
- "A position for _____ is opening up and I think you would be ideal."
- "What training, resources, information, or skills would make you comfortable in moving to the next level?"
- "You know I value your contribution to our department, but your _____ skills could help you take off. Do you want to know about other opportunities in the organization?"
- "You have such a good grasp of the floater's role. Would you consider training others?"
- "Your understanding of this process is beyond that of most in your position. Would you be interested in working on a handbook?"
- "You've managed every department in the store successfully. There's an opening in our San Francisco branch for a store manager. Would you like to discuss what's involved?"
- "What are your career goals?"
- "Most of our managers started _____ (in sales, as cashiers, behind the counter…). Let's look at an upward mobility path that suits your skills and abilities."

The Powerhouse Overachiever

As with underachievers, you will find a few types of over-achievers. Of course, many super-achievers work like whirling dervishes, efficiently making things happen all in a day's work without paying a toll. However, some overachievers are motivational challenges. Some will do just about anything to achieve and can wreak havoc on workplace harmony. (We'll call these *reckless overachievers*.) Others will work beyond their own limits at the risk of sacrificing health and well-being, which, in the end, isn't good for anyone. (We'll call these *workaholic overachievers*.)

The Motivational Mindset (for the reckless overachiever)

- While overachievers can be wonderfully productive, they may also be so focused on the prize they miss slowing down for critical details. Their good efforts should be recognized, even when they need to be reminded to check for accuracy.

- When accuracy is essential, a system of checks and balances should be in place that applies to everyone. Help the overachiever understand that this is the standard process because mistakes can and do happen to everyone, and we're all too close to our own work to see certain things.

- Overachievers may be more focused on the next job than the one they're in now.

- Overachievers may be critical of others who are working at a different pace.

- The overachiever may have maxed out at his/her skill level. If Sasha is an outstanding salesperson with no

➡

patience for those learning the ropes, don't promote her to sales supervisor. Give strong reinforcement that she is valued as the right person for her current position.

- The overachiever who is told that it's okay to slow down may be relieved. Some people push beyond reasonable limits to meet wrongly assumed expectations.

- Overachievers may want the next position so badly that they will plow ahead without pausing for training or asking questions. When delegating, be clear about the importance of checkpoints and questions during the learning process.

- Do not allow employees to self-impose a supervisory role over others.

Motivational Phrases
(for the reckless overachiever)

- "Great work! Did everyone on the team get a chance to review it?"

- "Thank you for working so late last night. This is outstanding work! I know that your team members were geared up to work on this during business hours. Please show this to them to review and finalize the details together. Again, great work, but I encourage you not going it alone next time."

- "I appreciate the work you did on project Q. At the same time, I still need project A completed by 3 P.M., Thursday. How is that coming? A is the priority now and if you can put in the same energy you put into Q we'll be in great shape. Thanks."

- "I can't believe how quickly you finished the inventory! As you know, accuracy is critical. Did you check it over? Has anyone else helped you with a final check?"

➡

- "I expected that repair to continue into next week. Well done! Take a long lunch. You deserve it."
- "I know how well you can multitask. Often, it's necessary. When serving a customer, though, the best course is to focus on the customer. Almost anything else can wait."
- "I notice that you posted for department manager. I hope you get the job. I'd be happy to chat with you about what you might expect in that role."
- "I'm sure you know that there's a sales manager position opening. Your sales skills are outstanding and produce great income for you and the company. I hope you decide to stay in your active role on the sales team. I don't see you behind a desk pushing papers."
- "One of Martin's clients told him you said he was unavailable yesterday, but he never knew the call came in. Yes, we're in a competitive industry, but trust among colleagues is important. Your last company may have done things differently, but I think you will enjoy the benefits of the cooperative environment we've created."
- "You were right about the return policy and your jumping in was important. However, I encourage you to be more tactful when correcting a coworker, especially in front of a customer."
- "We have a system in this restaurant. If someone cannot get to a table immediately, we pitch in, but we don't take over tables in someone else's section. That creates a competitive environment that doesn't benefit staff or customers."
- "I know that the balance has been weighted more heavily on your shoulders lately. Thank you for stepping up."
- "You completed the inventory ahead of schedule; however, you overlooked some categories. Speed without

accuracy is not fast. With your abilities, you can slow down and still stay ahead of schedule."

- "Tom, you've been spending a lot of time talking with people in the Finance Department. When there's an opening, that's a good move for you and I'll support it. Right now, Marketing needs all your energy."

- "Suzanne, I understand your drive to complete each project and move to the next. That's a great work ethic; however, we have an editing protocol that everyone—even top-notch writers like you—must follow. Please help me out."

The Motivational Mindset (for the workaholic overachiever)

- These overachievers may be so dedicated to being "all they can be" for the organization that they are neglecting personal relationships and/or themselves.

- The *workaholic overachiever* will eventually burn out.

- Work-life balance is as important to forward-looking companies as it is to employees.

- Don't punish competence by placing a much heavier workload on the one who is getting things done.

- While some overachievers can be careless, missing details in their rush to get more done, some present the opposite challenge of pushing themselves to be perfect. Your role includes reminding them of the time factor and that "cooked is better than overcooked."

- If someone is suddenly burying him/herself in work and insists this is the best course of action "for now," don't take advantage by setting the bar to that new level of output.

- Beware of taking the overachiever for granted. When someone is *consistently* doing good work quickly, don't underestimate the value of *consistent* praise and recognition.

- Some workaholics run on stress; others are running *from* personal stress. Don't play shrink, but be aware of motivation.
- *Workaholic overachievers* may glow when burning the midnight oil, but if they are not careful, they could burn out their staff.
- The *workaholic overachiever*, if unaware of his/her style and its drawbacks, can be a detriment in a management position.

**Motivational Phrases
(for the workaholic overachiever)**

- "I notice you've worked every night this week. That must be difficult with the new baby at home."
- "You do fantastic work all day long. I hope you don't take the problems of the day home with you."
- "I don't want to pry, but when do you get time for you and your family? I'm ecstatic about your dedication, but I hope you realize that the organization also respects your need for work-life balance."
- "I know how dedicated you are to the monthly accounting, but your long hours here during your post-op period are more than anyone should handle. Let's get a temp to help you."
- "I know you've been late in the mornings because you have been working late. I wish we could offer comp time, but we can't right now and we need your high energy in the mornings."

➡

- "I notice that you've been taking shorter and shorter lunches. I hope you know how much I appreciate the quality of your work. Your eating a leisurely lunch will not put the company in jeopardy. I care about your health as well as your work."
- "You look exhausted. How late were you here last night? Don't make me set a curfew!"
- "We're growing too fast, but the solution is not for you to become superhuman. I do appreciate your trying!"
- "The promotion means longer hours and travel. I know you can handle it, but I also know that you have a new family. This position fits your work goals, but I want you to feel certain that it also fits your life and family goals. I will support any decision you make."
- "Your redesign of the Orientation Program and related manual and visual aids is phenomenal. I know that you and your staff put in many late nights. Our budget allows for a celebration lunch. I also urge you to let them work at only 110 percent for the next few weeks."
- "Your energy is inspiring! Keep a little in reserve and take care of yourself. We need you strong for the long haul."
- "Thank you so much for that extra effort. It really paid off."
- "What made you stay late last night to double-check the number of giveaways for the trade show? Boy, did you save us!"
- "You put in a great day's work. Go home and relax!"

The Part-Time Employee

The Motivational Mindset

- The part-time employee needs to feel as much a part of the team as the full-time staff. A part-time commitment is still a commitment.
- Ensure that part timers know that their roles are critical to customer satisfaction and company success.
- Include part-time employees as much as possible in office meetings and celebrations.
- Mentors help part timers learn their jobs and help them see their work in the context of the larger picture.
- Some organizations are entirely staffed by part timers because of customer needs or business demands.
- Part timers may be overqualified but need the scheduling convenience of part-time work. Know who's working in your midst and access talent.
- Consider small incentives. Offer a gift card or cash reward for perfect on-time attendance, outstanding customer service, or any other one-time or ongoing behavior you would like to reinforce.
- Ensure that part-time employees have all the information they need to represent your company or department effectively. Don't just give them "need to know" information.
- Often part timers report to more than one supervisor. Ensure a consistent message regarding work, policies, and customer care. Also ensure that all supervisors understand the need to coordinate priorities when sharing the support of a part timer.
- Share with your part timers the mechanics behind juggling schedules. Part-time work is not a casual commitment.

Motivational Phrases

- "Please give as much notice as possible if you have to change your schedule. You're part of a team, so your schedule affects others."
- "Thanks for always leaving such clear notes for those who work the next shift."
- "Although you are only here three days each week, your effect on the _____ (patients, residents, customers, guests…) is noticeable."
- "Thank you for your contributions to the project."
- "Please feel free to ask questions. I want you to understand the process."
- "I called you in to give you this gift card as a bonus. You're always here on schedule, on time, always ready to do what's needed. Keep up the good work!"
- "Each month you will be eligible for a 'perfect on-time attendance' bonus. Changing your schedule with 24-hour notice will not affect eligibility."
- "You're doing an excellent job. If you become interested in a full-time position here, I would be happy to help you find one."
- "I'm very impressed by what you are able to accomplish within a part-time schedule."
- "Most of the staff is part time. Part timers are our backbone."
- "Because we have a number of part-time sales associates, we have established a system for sharing customer inquiries and complaints. Following it carefully simplifies everyone's job."
- "All of our blackjack dealers pool their tips. I know not every casino does this, but that's our policy. It has resulted in improved customer service and larger tips for everyone."

➡

- "Thank you for agreeing to work Saturdays."
- "I know that Tuesday/Thursday has been your schedule for years. Would you consider helping out Sobie by trying Wednesday/Thursday for a few months?"
- "Even though you are not here full time, your work product has full-time value."

The Virtual Commuter

The Motivational Mindset

- These days, entire offices may be virtual.
- Though working offsite has become an acceptable standard for many, transitioning from the traditional office may be difficult.
- Virtual commuting can be combined with physical office time.
- Many managers are satisfied as long as the work gets done. Hours logged may be less important than results.
- Unique communication issues arise between virtual commuters and those working in-house. You will need to be sensitive to these.
- Virtual commuters should be treated with the same respect and support as people who are physically there.
- If the number of hours logged by an offsite employee is important, create a uniform, consistent system for recording.
- Some people in the office may treat the offsite employee as a second-class citizen; it is important that everyone understand the virtual commuter is an important part of the team.
- Just as those in the office periodically chat, an occasional friendly e-mail, instant message, or telephone chat with the virtual commuter is good for mental health and team spirit.
- If you, as a supervisor, are the virtual commuter, make yourself as accessible as possible.

➡

Motivational Phrases

- "You are as much a part of this team as anyone who is physically in the office, and you are entitled to support."
- "Please sync your schedule with the office's online calendar."
- "Please give support staff as much lead time as possible to integrate your priorities into their schedules. In order for them to keep you in the scheduling loop, you need to keep them in yours."
- "Sometimes, some of you seem to forget that Raul is part of the team. Please remember that it's not 'Raul's project'; it is *our* project and is just as important as others on the table."
- "Our Thursday morning staff meetings are a great energy exchange. We'll make arrangements to conference you in."
- "Our monthly staff meetings are the best way for you to stay connected and for everyone to get to know you. Please make them a top priority."
- "Please check with Sally before you choose a format or font. When integrating your work is time-consuming, everyone gets frustrated."
- "You can't see our smiles, but that design is awesome."
- "That number crunching was dynamite. Thank you for getting it to us so quickly."
- "You've been having some problems with your server. Please call our service company today. A major project is coming your way in a few days."
- "You seem to have instinctively fit right into the virtual commuter role. Would you consider training others?"
- "Getting in tune with the time difference is a challenge. Our project planning chart accounts for that to ensure

that no one is waiting for material while someone is sleeping."

- "Don't feel guilty about working in the sunshine. We have other advantages, like cafeteria food."

- "We will miss you when you move. Please consider the virtual commuting option."

- "You are our first virtual commuter, so please don't be discouraged by any little snags in the system. I'm sure we can work them out as we all adjust."

The Naysayer

The Motivational Mindset

- The naysayer can affect the energy and motivation of a team.
- Don't fall into the trap of treating the naysayer as the boy who cried wolf. Sometimes there really is a wolf.
- Positive attitudes spread; so do negative ones.
- Sometimes, the naysayer just needs to be validated and will be willing to come onboard after feeling heard and appreciated.
- Often, naysayers are unaware of the frequency and/or impact of their negative comments.
- Model for others ways to deflect the naysayer's comments.
- Offer suggestions and model ways for the naysayer to turn negative approaches or phrases into positive ones.
- Talk with the naysayer about his/her negativity (using specifics) and its effect on others.
- Understand that you may not be able to encourage someone to change an ingrained habit or personality trait. However, the positive environment you create will help bring balance and may begin to turn the naysayer around.

Motivational Phrases

- "I appreciate your voicing reasonable concerns, but once we decide to move forward, we need positive support."
- "I understand the problems you've pointed out and your concerns are valid. What solutions can you offer and what data do you have to support them?"
- "We get back what we put out. Let's put out some positive energy."

- "Often, your questions ensure that we explore all options. This time, however, we have time constraints and strong reasons to go forward. Can you suspend your doubts in order for us all to put high energy into making this work?"

- "I understand your reservations. Let's review the pros and cons."

- "Your team's work product is outstanding. I agree with you about the need for some modification, but when you present this idea at the management meeting, please focus on all the positive elements and mention the minor changes after generating enthusiasm."

- "You know how shy Maria is. She rarely offers suggestions at meetings. Your criticizing her idea as she spoke not only clammed her up but prevented our learning more about her proposal. I'm sure you didn't intend to stop her cold. How might you have handled that differently?"

- "I know Harry will find a chink in the armor, but please stand your ground. This is a great proposal."

- "I know you have some doubts, but what do you think is valuable about our new security system?"

- "The management team's plan seems to cover all bases. Do you agree?"

- "Where do you think we fell short? What could we have done differently?"

- "Others would be more responsive to your valuable suggestions if you precede them with a positive statement about what is right."

- "Rather than jump in with a 'better idea,' why not ask your reports how they might make this work more effectively?"

- "Implementing a new, company-wide accounting system is a daunting task. Despite the learning curve it will save us time and money. I'm counting on you to focus on the positive when you present the change-over to your staff."

Complaints About the Rules

The Motivational Mindset

- Rules, policies, procedures, and informal guidelines should be governed by logic and support your organization's values, mission, and goals.

- If "Because I said so" was frustrating as a kid, it's even more frustrating as an adult. Give cogent reasons, not flip responses.

- If someone requests that rules be bent for a good reason, be flexible. Reconsider the rule or consider carefully why this could be an exception.

- You may have a policy allowing a certain number of days off after the death of a family member, but if a dedicated worker needs more time, the bottom line is that we're all human behind those policies and sometimes we need a little understanding.

- If a request is made for a particularly good reason, but the exception cannot be made for everyone, explain your decision.

- Don't apply rules to some and not others. Favoritism de-motivates.

- Of course, if breaking a rule for one would cause a problem, stand your ground. But don't underestimate employees who might be more understanding than you think of a clearly explained exception.

- The more involved employees are in creating policies and procedures, the more interested they are in supporting them. Include those directly affected in determining and enforcing informal guidelines (e.g., keeping the coffee room neat, starting meetings on time, covering others' phones).

➡

- Some rules are dated or, without context, may seem random. People will be more likely to respect rules that make sense to them.
- Work to get ineffective and/or outdated rules changed. Explain what you're trying to accomplish.
- Safety policies are inviolate. These are "no exceptions" rules.

Motivational Phrases

- "The reason behind this rule is _____."
- "I'm sorry I cannot make an exception here. I have considered it carefully. I wish I could."
- "Please give me all the reasons you think we can or should make an exception in your case so that I can give your request thorough consideration."
- "A lot of people seem to have a problem with this rule. It was designed for a specific purpose. (Be clear about the purpose.) If anyone has ideas about how to modify this rule while maintaining its ability to achieve that purpose, I would be happy to consider them."
- "This rule ensures everyone's safety during an emergency evacuation. We cannot bend it—ever."
- "I know safety goggles sometimes seem unnecessary; however, we count on your vision in many ways and don't want to jeopardize it."
- "Privacy rules may be inconvenient at times, but we all appreciate them when our own privacy is at stake."
- "Since 9/11 we lock the courtyard door. The need for a convenient place to smoke does not supercede everyone's safety."
- "Yes, we can bend that rule in this case."

➡

- "You have gone above and beyond so many times. I would be happy to make this request for you."
- "With technology changing daily, we must keep pace with privacy rules."
- "The occasional call to check on a lunch date or a child at home is fine. Lengthy personal phone calls are not. I'm sure you understand why."
- "I know it seems like a lot of red tape, but we have legal issues to consider."
- "I agree that the single earring per ear rule is dated. The dress code was established in 1991. No one has updated it. Human Resources is revising the guidelines."
- "That's a great outfit for a private party or dinner out. However, bare midriffs are not appropriate in this office."

Employee Conflicts

The Motivational Mindset

- Conflict thrives in an atmosphere of self-interest, unrealistic expectations, unfounded assumptions, poor communication, and limited access to information.
- Unchecked conflict leads to stress, polarization, and mistrust, creating an unproductive work environment.
- When conflict arises among employees, always get all sides of the story so that you can mediate logically and fairly. Describe or recap the situation succinctly, and ask all parties involved what result they would like to see.
- Leave your personal biases of what you think must have happened outside the door.
- Specify what you will do or what you would like to have happen.
- Don't be one to spread rumors—or listen to them. Make clear that the rumor mill is not a viable communication vehicle.
- Model and encourage respectful behavior, rational dialogue, and discussion of different points of view.
- Don't pit one employee against another or encourage rivalries. You have more positive vehicles to promote a drive for excellence.
- Address problems without blame.
- *Never* yell or curse.

Motivational Phrases

- "Excuse me; may I see you in my office, please?" (instead of public reprimands)

- "I have received complaints that you _____ (shouted at Dan in front of customers, wouldn't share quarterly figures with Andrea…). I'd like to hear your side."

- "Jake, what I hear you saying is that you think Maya intentionally stole your client. Is that correct? Maya, you said you didn't know that this was Jake's client. Is that correct? Let's get to the bottom of this. What happened when the call came in? What can you do now to move forward with this client and to prevent this misunderstanding from occurring again?"

- "I understand you're upset, but I cannot focus on what you're saying when you are shouting."

- "You were both rushing. Isn't it possible that you misunderstood each other?"

- "Let's start with the assumption that no one lied. Misinformation and misperceptions do not mean someone intended to deceive. If we're going to get to the bottom of this, let's start by giving everyone the benefit of the doubt and see where that leads."

- "Clearly, you each have a different perception of what happened. Please tell me yours."

- "The situation, as I understand it, is this: _____. What resolution does each of you propose?"

- "I can see the anxiety this has caused. Let's slow down and look at the facts. We all want this to succeed."

- "Colin, what did you hear Jack say? Jack, what do you remember saying?"

- "It doesn't matter whose fault the mistake was. Let's pull together to fix the problem and determine how to prevent a similar one."

- "It was my mistake. I'm sorry for the extra work it caused."

➡

- "We are all under a great deal of pressure; however, shouting at one another and slamming papers down on desks doesn't help. No one here is the problem. Let's focus on the work and be respectful of each other in the process."
- "I realize that Sven did not include you in the initial planning meeting. That would upset me also. Sven, you can understand that, right? However, now we must move on. What remaining issues must you address? You two can certainly work that out."
- "I can see both sides. How would each of you like to resolve this?"

Chapter 8

Raising Morale in Tough Times

"If you would lift me up you must be on higher ground."
—Ralph Waldo Emerson

The difference between working for one bank, department store, or manufacturer and another used to be minimal. Most people stayed with a company throughout their entire work life, many earning gold watches for 25 years of service. Stability was a virtue: the *company man* stayed put and the company remained *the company*. Today, as companies merge, acquire, and disappear, any sense of a stable work environment is challenged. When the company cannot guarantee that it—or you—will be there, you tend to look for that next place to land. The wise employer maintains a pulse check for signs of career dissatisfaction and keeps lines of communication open. Lack of information during challenging times leaves people frustrated and, often, assuming the worst of all possible scenarios.

Catching people before they fall, fail, or leave maintains a positive environment during the most trying times. Monica Smiley, publisher of *Enterprising Women*, sees a "common thread among the country's top women business owners: the ability to persevere in the face of daily adversity." Successful leaders in all business cultures bring that entrepreneurial spirit and the mindset to *tough it out* to any challenge. Dr. Susan Brenner, senior vice president of Bright Horizons Family Solutions, advises: "It's easy to get mired in the day-to-day problems of the job and lose sight of the work's purpose. Look beyond the details, and remember the reason you do what you do, the goodness of your work. Then take on the daily issues, knowing that they are necessary steps to reaching your goals."

The Motivational Mindset

- Mergers and acquisitions are major transitions. In the event of a merger or acquisition, you *can* set the tone as to how the news is received. Set a positive one.

- If your company is acquired by one that it has publicly criticized, don't pretend there was never any bad blood. You're not fooling anyone. Talk about where you are *now*, what has changed, and what makes you believe this union will bring specific improvements.

- Avoid surprises. Share information. Missing and misinformation fuel the rumor mill.

- Don't just toss out facts for general consumption. Think about those receiving the information. What is important for employees to know? What information is threatening to employees? Hold meetings; answer what questions you can.

- Stay positive, but don't sugarcoat reality.

- Plan your message; don't improvise.

- Deliver the news and move on—but be prepared to revisit the topic as delayed reactions occur and additional questions arise.

- When someone leaves the company for positive reasons, celebrate in a way that lets people say goodbye. Most employees form strong bonds at work. A coworker or colleague's leaving constitutes a major change.

- Fresh initiatives, a new name, and a new logo may breathe fresh air into the atmosphere, but if management does not follow through, the air quickly gets stale and people feel let down. Future initiatives will seem meaningless

➡

and are unlikely to find buy-in among people who have come to see them as the *flavor of the month*.

- If you start something new, be fully committed to it. If it's not working, fix it. Drop it if you have to, but don't let it fade away. Acknowledge what came out of it and explain why you're dropping it. Then move on.

Motivational Phrases

As always, say only what is true. This can be a tricky situation if corporate policy restricts what you can say. Use the following phrases if they apply.

- "We need your help through this tough time. If you can hang in with us, when we get back on track and our numbers are better, we will all benefit."
- "I know change is difficult. If you have any questions during the transition, please feel free to ask." (or refer questions to the appropriate person)
- "I know how much you value everyone in your department. You've built a great team. Whomever you decide to let go will be a loss for us all."
- "We are doing everything we can to reduce your stress during the acquisition process. Additional suggestions are welcome."
- "We will all miss Karthik. He was our top performer and a great guy. As we restructure, the field is wide open for new top performers. I hope you will all join me in looking to the future."
- "Please disregard the conflicting rumors about why Ari left the company. Of course, the rumor mill is not the most reliable place to get information. I'm sure Ari shared the reasons at his own discretion."

- "We have gone through a lot of changes. Change can cause stress, but it also can bring opportunities."
- "I would like your input on our new direction."
- "The layoffs will not affect your job."
- "I've always been honest with you and will continue to be. Clearly, we will have some staff reassignments. That's not always a bad thing. I'll share what I learn as soon as I can."
- "I have talked with senior management about the crowded working conditions during the renovation. Unfortunately, so much is top priority right now that, although we have their ear and understanding, nothing will happen as quickly as we'd like."
- "Our informal management style is quite different from that of our new parent company. Please try to understand that they are bringing a style that has worked for them. In time, we might see the changes as beneficial overall."
- "You can all expect to be interviewed by the new management team. Be honest in your answers. If you believe that a process or policy has been a problem, say so. Also, champion what you think we're doing right or they won't know and it could change."
- "The acquisition process is lengthy. You can expect focus groups and individual interviews as the new management team learns about our processes and you, the people who made this company so successful."
- "Our company is in a position to make most personnel decisions. We will, however, be building a hybrid team that represents both companies. I appreciate all of you and your contributions and will do everything I can to retain you."

Tough Economic Conditions

The Motivational Mindset

- Expect mature, rational responses. What you expect is often what you get.
- Avoid the urge to be a cliché dispenser. "Buck up" and "It's always darkest before the dawn" won't help anyone.
- Be as honest as you can be about why firing or layoff decisions were made.
- If you are cutting the dental plan, present possible resources for reasonably priced alternatives.
- In supporting employees, never bash upper management. Usually they are doing the best they can with the cards they were dealt. Undermining confidence in their leadership stresses the process.
- In supporting management, never put down employees or make them feel devalued. Explain how their participation in the process is essential to success.
- If you are cutting benefits or perks, always be clear that the decision is driven by economics, not performance.
- Explain the rationale behind across-the-board cuts or salary freezes. Be sensitive to the effects a hiring freeze will have on those already carrying a heavy load.
- Enlist staff support when deciding upon equipment/ material costs. They are usually the experts.
- If you are taking raises while employees are getting fired for economic reasons and facing cuts in pay or benefits, there are no words you can say. People will feel slighted, undervalued, and resentful. Many will be looking to move on.

Motivational Phrases

As always, say only what is true. This can be a tricky situation if you are restricted by corporate policy in what you can say. Use the following phrases if they apply.

- "We can no longer afford _____, but we can offer you _____. I know that you deserve more, but this is the best we can do right now."

- "We have to temporarily cut back on overtime opportunities because of our current economic situation. I have every confidence we will be able to restore it within the year."

- "I wish we could pay you what you're worth."

- "The company values your contributions."

- "We can't provide raises this year, but we can look at flextime options to ease the situation."

- "I know we're understaffed right now, but there is nothing we can do about that at this time. We just have to pull together and do our best. I appreciate your efforts during this trying time."

- "I wish I could tell you the layoffs would not affect our department. I am as much in the dark as you are. As soon as I hear anything, you will."

- "All we can do is stay positive and put out our best work. To the best of my knowledge, our department is not in danger of layoffs."

- "We have to cut dental benefits, but I have a list of resources for low-cost alternatives. Benefits will be effective through June."

- "In order to continue providing health insurance, we've had to raise the co-pay. I'm sorry, but rates have skyrocketed and we want to be able to continue coverage for everyone."

- "Okay, so the memo titled, 'Blue skies are gonna clear up' was corny, but at least management is trying."
- "I was trying to grow my business too fast during tough economic times, but I would hate to lose you. Would you consider buying in with sweat equity as a partner?"
- "We cannot offer holiday bonuses this year. I hope the days off with pay during the holiday season soften the blow for everyone."
- "Summers are becoming very slow. Would anyone like an additional week off at half pay?"
- "You know I can't offer you an increase, but I will work with you to ensure some additional time off."

Bad Company Publicity

The Motivational Mindset

- Hold meetings to address concerns.
- Disclose only what is allowable, but answer questions honestly.
- If the company's actions were immoral or illegal, don't defend them. Talk about changes and what it will take to make corrections and move forward.
- If someone in the company or an executive of the company was wrongly accused, inspire support from the ranks.
- Even if the company or executive were in the wrong, inspire support for the work to be done to turn the situation around and retain (or regain) respect in the community.
- You may lose some people along the way. It's to be expected.
- Do not allow whistleblowers to be abused. Even if you disagree with their actions, even if they could have used other channels, and even if their suspicions were wrong, these are usually not people who want to hurt anyone. In fact, their motivation is likely to protect as many people as possible, and they risk their own comfort to do so.
- Be a model of ethical behavior, no matter what's happening around you.
- Clearly follow your company's legal and public relations guidelines when addressing employees.
- Inform employees of legal and public relations guidelines to ensure their compliance.

Motivational Phrases

- "Do you have any questions?"

- "We need your support during this difficult time."
- "We have made mistakes." (*If* you're allowed to say that, say it.)
- "We've been hearing a lot about what's *wrong* with the company and we have people working on that. Let's work on faith that they're doing their jobs and continue to do ours. Let's be what's *right* with this company."
- "Let's generate some *positive* press."
- "Let's explore ideas for positive things we can do to rebuild trust _____ (in our company, within the community, among clients and stockholders…)."
- "We are at a crossroads, about to enter unknown territory. We need your intuition and creativity more than ever before."
- "Let's not give power to the rumor mill. Please hold off on making judgments until we have all the facts."
- "Setbacks are an opportunity for reevaluating strategy and trying new ideas."
- "The news may be skewed for sensationalism. Let's focus on what we know is real."
- "Let's ignore the headlines and keep a clear perspective."
- "We would like to take responsibility for where we've gone wrong and go forward in a positive direction. We need your help in creating a positive, forward-thinking environment."
- "Setbacks are opportunities to develop new strategies and create fresh starts."
- "You will be besieged by family and friends for 'the dirt.' Please use discretion in discussing information and focus on the company-wide effort to turn this problem around."
- "We don't have time for 'management bashing.' We, in the trenches, are fighting to redeem the company's image."

The Whole Team Is Down

The Motivational Mindset

- If people aren't meeting your expectations or they seem frustrated or overworked, ask yourself whether your expectations are reasonable. If you were in their positions, would you be making the sacrifices you're asking them to make?
- Are the lead times you give before deadlines realistic?
- Look at the company, your offerings, the skill levels you have hired, and current workplace trends.
- If your expectations are unreasonable, no amount of motivation will sustain a workforce's exhilaration in the task of climbing uphill.
- People need goals they can meet and small successes they can achieve daily or weekly.
- If your employees are continually failing, look at ways to motivate, but also look at their realistic chances for success within the parameters given to them.
- Are people putting a negative buzz in the air every day? Why?
- Do the surroundings feel conducive to success? Or would someone describe them as bleak or run down? It doesn't take much to get a coat of paint on the walls, hang something cheerful, or get a few plants.
- Did you just renovate and now everyone seems to be hitting a slump, with some suddenly out sick more than usual? Sick building syndrome is real and certain chemicals can cause *brain fog* or a myriad of other physical symptoms. If you've just painted or put in new carpeting or walls, air out the area well and consider an air filter, especially if you don't have windows.

➡

- Maintain your enthusiasm and support others in rediscovering theirs.

Motivational Phrases

- "What problems interfere with your meeting deadlines?"
- "What do you believe held you back from completing this project on time?"
- "What skills do you believe you need to develop through additional training in order to meet our goals?"
- "Let's brainstorm ideas to get some energy back into this operation."
- "Everyone seems to be sleepwalking this week. What do you think is going on?"
- "This month is crammed with 'must meet' deadlines. Can I bribe this group to include a few working lunches with some pizzas and Chinese food?"
- "These temporary digs are rather drab. Does anyone have a few posters or pictures that have been relegated to storage? They might work wonders here."
- "Some of us are sensitive to the new paint (or carpeting). Let's put up with a little cold air to clear out the fumes."
- "The fumes from the _____ (new paint job, new carpeting, renovations…) are pretty strong. We've rented an air purifier for the week."
- "Let's take a group coffee break. I ordered doughnuts and fruit. We can afford 20 minutes away from this."
- "Maybe completing all these projects as promised was an unrealistic goal. I think Client X has some leeway and might give us a few more days. Would that help?"

➡

- "This has been a rough quarter, but we've got a lot of talent here. Let's focus on our past accomplishments and go forward to repeat them."
- "We are starting a new incentive program with great rewards for your hard work. Let's schedule a meeting early next week to kick off the new program."
- "We have so much to accomplish before the new store opening. I suggest everyone focus on key tasks. Worrying about how we'll get it all done depletes needed time and energy."
- "Losing Customer X was a major setback. Let's examine why we did and discuss ways to make up the lost revenue."

Part III

Motivational Rewards: Perfect Benefits, Perks, and Rewards

Beyond the energy, the kudos, the recognition, the support, *and* the paycheck are tangible (and sometimes intangible) rewards, perks, and benefits. Yes, most people work because they must earn a living. The fortunate work at jobs they love—or at least like—in environments that make going to work a positive experience. So, what else do they want? And what about those who are not tuned in or turned on by their jobs, those who view going to work as one notch above or below going to the dentist? What can make them want to give their all?

The number and types of benefits, perks, and rewards you can provide are all, of course, based on your organization's financial ability, corporate policy, and union agreements. No one can afford to provide all, but considering the full spectrum will help you choose which would be most valuable to your employees. When you factor in what you can afford, remember the costs of nonmotivated employees, especially when they leave and must be replaced. The effects of a motivated, dedicated workforce must be crunched into the hard number calculations.

Chapter 9

Perfect Benefits

"No one does anything from a single motive."

—Samuel Taylor Coleridge

The demand for new and changing skills, the perceived demise of loyalty on the part of employee and employer, the skyrocketing costs of health care, and the fear of cracks and leaks in once-secure nest eggs, have affected what attracts and keeps employees. Potential employees look at flexibility, family-friendly policies, and strong benefit packages when considering where to work. Employees look at practical financials as well as flexibility and appreciation when deciding where to stay.

Benefits are what an employer offers above and beyond the basics. Maria Bordas, general manager of strategic planning and policy for the Port Authority of New York and New Jersey's Aviation Department, is known among colleagues and employees for her favorite quote: "What I think and what I believe are of no consequence… What is of consequence is what I do." Think about what you do to show that you care.

The phrases that follow are the positives, the ones you can say when you are able to offer the proposed benefit; for phrases to use when you cannot offer the benefit, refer to Chapter 8: "Raising Morale in Tough Times," in the section titled "Tough Economic Conditions."

Health Insurance

The Motivational Mindset

- With the high cost of health insurance, employees value good coverage and factor it in with earnings. Health insurance is a valuable benefit that shows employees you care about their well-being.

- Consider a variety of approaches before selecting a program for your company.

- Shop for the best deal on health insurance so that you can pass the savings on to your employees.

- Ensure that employees have all necessary information about options and providers. Give employees the direct contact information for your broker or insurance carrier.

- Many people don't bother to learn the requirements and regulations on their own and can be hurt financially in a health crisis by not following certain protocols. Ask your broker to provide free seminars to help employees become knowledgeable health-care consumers and to fully understand their benefits.

- Alternative health care is becoming a mainstream demand. Be aware of options.

- Employees have diverse health-care needs. One employee might choose a lower premium and higher deductible than another. A split plan allows employees to choose from different plans, even different companies.

- A cafeteria plan (also called a "flexible benefit plan" or a "Section 125 plan") allows each employee to select from a menu of coverage options. Someone may, for instance, choose health, life, and disability insurance but not dental, while another employee might choose only health and dental. Cafeteria plans offer a tax advantage as well.

- Smaller companies may consider providing "Volunteer Plans" for insurance such as dental, life, or long-term disability to allow employees the *option* of buying in without the employer having to meet participation requirements.

Motivational Phrases

- "You will find information about our health plan in this packet and on the Web site."

- "Feel free to _____ (ask me; call Karen at extension 286; call the agent, whose number is on the front of your packet) if you have any questions."

- "We're researching health insurance plans. What's most important to you? Low co-pay? Having a particular doctor in network? Preventative health-care rider?"

- "Our plan offers a low co-pay and a preventative health-care rider. We've found that those are most important to the majority of our workforce."

- "Let me (or my assistant) know what insurance companies your doctor works with so we can try to choose a plan that works for most. I'm sorry, I can't make any guarantees that we will succeed in pleasing everyone, but of course, we'll do our best."

- "I'm sorry about your daughter's illness. Our plan manager is a stickler for following the rules. I want you to get all the help you need, so please follow the protocol."

- "I realize that the referral process is frustrating, but that kind of plan allows us to pay a larger portion for all employees."

- "So many employees have requested alternative care coverage, dental coverage, PPO rather than HMO, that we are instituting a menu format for health-care benefits. Please review all options and related co-pays carefully before selecting."

- "Rest assured that your medical information remains confidential."

- "Many employees are investigating assisted living for their parents. Our lunchtime lecture will address that topic."

- "Of course you're angry about having your emergency care payment denied. Call Marie in HR to help you through the process of resubmitting."

- "I encourage everyone to take advantage of the reduced-rate annual physical. That's a key reason we chose this provider."

- "Call the provider's customer service line to ask your questions about precertification. Yes, you will reach a person."

- "Please attend the seminar. If you understand how your health insurance works you will be able to take full advantage of its benefits."

Wellness Programs

The Motivational Mindset

- A healthy organization is made up of healthy people. Wellness programs will provide a healthier, more motivated workforce. Investigate and share the wealth of available information regarding money saved by companies whose programs have resulted in reduced illness and injury, lowering the bottom line of health-care costs.

- Wellness program targets may include nutrition, weight loss, smoking cessation programs, exercise, and stress reduction.

- Onsite fitness centers, reimbursements for gym memberships, work/life balance programs, health and nutrition programs, ergonomic assessments, injury prevention programs, and educational materials are among the contributions companies can make to a wellness environment.

- Exercise programs can be tailored to work-specific areas that are at risk of strain from particular jobs. Whether sitting at a computer or doing heavy lifting, low back exercises might be a strong focus for a workout.

- Rewards or points may be given for achieving measurable results, winning contests, or simply for participating in programs. Participation rewards can be based on the honor system, having employees sign in on having participated, or can be substantiated by a third-party observer (health club employee or team coordinator).

- Some activities that may earn wellness points or bonuses include completing a health risk assessment, blood pressure checks, walking, running, biking, tennis, weight lifting; maintaining low medical claims or sick days; participating in weight loss or smoking cessation programs; competing in marathons; playing team sports; or attending wellness lectures.

- Rewards for following a wellness program or achieving wellness objectives may include a reduction in (or cutting out) health-care co-pays, increasing employer payments for health insurance, or offering health insurance rebates. Other health-related rewards may include time off for well behavior or fitness-related rewards such as t-shirts, gym bags, relaxation CDs, exercise DVDs, videos, or gift certificates to sporting goods stores.

- Organizations are available to coordinate a comprehensive program.

- Points systems can be run a number of ways. One way is to allow employees to accumulate points that can be cashed in any time with the value of prizes increasing as new plateaus are reached.

- Another system would be to make a list of 10 criteria and reward employees who meet a specified number over a determined period of time. You can offer one reward for an employee who meets 5 out of 10 and a greater reward for employees who meet 6 out of 10 and so on.

Motivational Phrases

- "We are offering chair massages in the cafeteria this week."

- "A number of people have requested early morning Tai Chi classes. I'm pleased to announce that they will begin next month on Tuesdays at 7 A.M."

- "Our insurance carrier offers reduced rates for nonsmokers. Anyone looking to save on your insurance contribution may want to attend our 'Smoke Free At Last' program."
- "Our entire department participated in the in-house weight loss program. We lost weight and gained energy. Congratulations everyone!"
- "Since you stopped smoking, your work is consistently accurate. Perhaps those frequent breaks broke your concentration. I know you stopped for your own reasons, but I appreciate the benefits to the department."
- "The breath work course will help reduce stress and improve overall health."
- "We can all use some stress reduction techniques. Please come to this week's seminar."
- "Please feel free to borrow from the fitness library."
- "We are all aware of the rising costs of health care. If you can help us and yourselves by participating in the new wellness program, we can help you with lower rates and co-pays."
- "We are offering one day off (or 1/2 day) to anyone who successfully completes one of our wellness programs."
- "The weight management meetings will now take place during work hours, from 1:00 P.M. to 1:30 P.M. on Mondays and Thursdays."
- "Human Resources e-mailed everyone an invitation to attend the presentation and kickoff of our new wellness program. We offer several ways to participate and a great rewards program. Please don't miss this opportunity to hear the coordinator's comprehensive overview."
- "Attendance at the nutrition Webinar will earn 10 points toward your wellness program goals."

Retirement Plans

The Motivational Mindset

- Ask your broker to give a free seminar to educate employees about the plans and equity incentives you offer. The most effective plans will have little effect on motivation if employees don't fully understand the benefits.

- A strong retirement plan attracts strong employees. The 401(k) plan (or 403(b) for nonprofit corporations or schools) provides a sense of security, which is a strong motivator for many.

- The small business alternative to 401(k) plans is the Simple IRA. The Simple IRA allows employers to set up long-term savings plans for employees without high fees and overwhelming paperwork.

- Corporate matching of 401(k) funds shows a strong interest in the individual employee's future well-being.

- 401(k) plans have tax advantages for both employer and employee. When considering a 401(k), evaluate cost, investment of time, setup effort, and investment options.

- If your 401(k) allows employees to select investment options, educate employees about the risks and opportunities of investing. Keep employees informed about how their investments are doing.

- If your company is publicly traded, stock options are an inexpensive way to offer a big payoff, create an employee-ownership culture, and encourage buy-in in the company's success.

- Profit sharing plans give employees a sense of ownership, which adds greatly to incentive and to feeling like part of the larger picture.

➡

- Educate employees on the market. Provide materials and links.
- Educate employees about retirement planning.

Motivational Phrases

- "Those of you under 40 may think it's too early to plan for retirement. The earlier you plan, the more financially comfortable and personally rewarding your retirement will be."
- "Our Succession Planning Program not only brings new talent up the ranks, but ensures that those who have contributed consistently to the organization leave well compensated."
- "For a small company, we offer a variety of options for retirement savings."
- "Every new employee orientation includes a segment on retirement planning options. Anyone can check the calendar and register for that component. We encourage that."
- "Because many people keep looking for a 'better way,' we regularly bring in speakers for a variety of investment areas—stocks, bonds, real estate investments—for our lunchtime learning series."
- "In today's economic climate, you can't just close your eyes and hope your money is 'working smart.' Either you watch it carefully or pay someone else to watch it."
- "We offer strong retirement incentives to continue to create room at the top."
- "There was some confusion about the 401(k) plan. These are your benefits and you have a right to understand them fully. If you have any questions about the plan,

please see the 401(k) link from the Web site or call extension 201."

- "We are running a Webinar on retirement investing. Attendance is optional, but I hope everyone will attend and feel free to post questions."
- "Stock options are a way for you to invest in yourselves."
- "This is your choice and any stock, even one that we firmly believe in, is always a gamble."
- "We offer stock options because we want you to share in our success. We encourage you to follow the corporation's stock. It's your company, too."
- "Every day you're working toward our future. We'd like to help you work toward yours."

Personal Days, Sick Days, and Vacation Days

The Motivational Mindset

- Rather than the standard allotment of a number of vacation, sick, and personal days, each a separate category, many companies offer a package of days. This allows, appropriately, for the extended vacations or the unexpected personal event.

- A strict policy of a set number of days that expires annually forces employees to "use them up." Less rigid personal day policies benefit both employee and employer.

- Separating sick days, personal days, and vacation impedes flexibility.

- Packages allow employees with minimal health problems to be available for ailing parents or sick children. Packages simplify tracking and paperwork.

- Packages eliminate the employee's need to justify the time out.

- Allowing personal and vacation days to rollover from one year to the next is a small thing that can make a big difference for someone who would like to plan for an extended holiday or a reasonable length of time to visit distant relatives.

- Rollovers and packages work well for employees who would be penalized by losing days off when the year ends. Not everyone works the system.

- Rollover eliminates a sudden employee shortage during the month of December.

Motivational Phrases

- "We offer personal day packages to give you the freedom to use your days whenever and however you'd like."

- "If you're planning to go to Europe again next year, you might want to save up some vacation days to allow you a longer stay."

- "We offer _____ days per year and they roll over for one year. These may be used for illness, personal days, and additional vacation time. Everyone's needs are different."

- "Congratulations on your excellent no absentee record. I'm sure those extra days will make your trip home more convenient."

- "We don't want to penalize employees for being healthy and dedicated. Our package plan works like a bank account with days in it ready to use when needed."

- "How exciting that your niece is getting married in India! I'm glad the package plan will give you the time you need."

- "What a shame that you had to cancel your December cruise plans. The good news is that your vacation time rolls over to next year."

- "You spent your day off working from home to help us out in a crunch. Of course, that doesn't count as a personal day. You get a do-over."

Flextime

The Motivational Mindset

- Flextime has become an important consideration for many in the workforce.
- Employees value—even demand—attention to work/life balance or, as it is now called, *work/life effectiveness*.
- Flextime attracts talented employees who might otherwise not be able to bring their skills and abilities to the workplace.
- Flextime reduces requests for time off and/or late arrivals/early departures to attend to family and personal matters that a nine-to-five schedule cannot accommodate.
- Employees who have the freedom of flexibility are willing to come through in a crunch. Many service jobs don't require a nine-to-five presence. Often, flexible employee hours benefit customers and clients as well as employees.
- Flextime does not mean a free-for-all.
- The more flexible you are, the more important structured scheduling becomes.
- Flextime provides for a routine that keeps work flowing smoothly.
- Don't arbitrarily suggest flextime when other solutions are more viable.
- Flextime can be a lifesaver for anyone with young children.

Motivational Phrases

- "Hit or miss scheduling doesn't work, but tell me which time frame is best and I'll try to work with you."
- "I realize that our eight-to-four schedule has been a problem for you. I appreciate your trying to make it work. What flextime hours would work best?"

➥

- "What would your ideal working hours be? Let's see how close we can come to that."

- "Would shifting your workday to start one hour earlier help you with your afternoon childcare issues?"

- "I don't want to lose you. Let's see what we can work out."

- "As long as the work gets done on time, it doesn't matter what time you're working on it."

- "I'm sorry I can't give you exactly what you're looking for in flextime. I wish I could. Would this alternative work for you?"

- "Congratulations on the adoption. I'm sure we can adjust your schedule for the next few weeks."

- "Flextime benefits all of us; however, the system works best when we establish a schedule and, barring emergencies, stick to it."

- "We all want to accommodate one another, but last-minute schedule changes disrupt workflow and productivity. Let's work out best times and stay with them."

- "Julio, your work is 95 percent communicating with clients by phone and PC. During your wife's recuperation period, I have no problem with your working from home."

- "Naomi, I understand that a full-time office schedule no longer works for you. Would you be interested in continuing to handle e-mail inquiries from home and coming in once a week to update us?"

- "The traffic from and to your area during A.M. and P.M. rush hours is horrendous. You can save at least one hour each way if you start at 10 A.M. and stay until 6 P.M. What do you think?"

"While your car is in the shop, you can have some latitude to conform with your temporary car pool."

Chapter 10

Perfect Perks and Rewards

"Nine-tenths of wisdom is appreciation."

—Dale Dauten

Our emphasis throughout this book has been motivation through communicating your expectations, satisfaction, and recommendations. Feedback—honest, timely, and concrete—motivates. Chapter 9 addresses tangible motivators and programs that show employees that you care about their health, well-being, families, and futures. Chapter 10 goes to the next level: What more can you do to encourage and reward excellence? How can you spur, excite, and entice your employees to reach for the brass ring?

Denise Rounds, owner of Bellezza Salons at three Atlantic City casino/hotels—the Hilton, Caesar's, and Bally's Park Place—has developed a dedicated corps of full- and part-time workers. "I run contests regularly, always with an educational benefit. The winner of our recent hair color contest will travel to Italy with me—some education, mostly fun. Our staff takes great pride in the salons and their work. I encourage ownership, letting people make decisions about their customers, getting as much input as possible from the people who do the work."

Public Recognition and Awards

The Motivational Mindset

■ Not all public recognition requires formal awards and certificates. Public recognition can come in the form of announcements at company events, bulletin boards, press releases, company newsletters, and Web site.

■ A certificate, plaque, or trophy is a lasting symbol of gratitude for excellence. Certificates are low-cost ways to show your appreciation or acknowledge accomplishments, but don't give them out so liberally that they lose meaning.

■ If you or your department is the recipient of an honor or reward, share the limelight.

■ Committee appointments within the company and without say that you have confidence that someone will represent you and your company well.

■ Groom employees to present information, findings, or ideas at company meetings.

■ Delegate key responsibilities that involve others—internally and externally.

■ Pass customer/client letters of praise up the chain of command. Don't keep your shining stars under a cloud.

■ Use your company Web site to acknowledge outstanding achievements.

Motivational Phrases

■ "We present this customer service award to honor your customer care skills and the smile our customers mention on so many of our customer care surveys."

■ "These certificates represent completion of _____ hours of training. This was no small achievement. You each worked hard and pulled through a tough course. Congratulations! You are now _____ (name, new title, or level of achievement)."

- "Congratulations to _____! This month's customer service award goes to _____, for her ongoing commitment to customer care."

- "As you know, I have received this year's outstanding manager's award. I share that honor with you. I know how lucky I am to have each and every one of my department members working with me. This award is for all of us. Congratulations to you, and thank you."

- "The company has been named one of the top 10 in our industry. Each one of you contributes to that success and deserves to feel very proud. Thank you all."

- "I received a letter from Customer X praising your handling of a difficult situation. I'm going to copy our VP with a note that this is typical of your work. You make us all look good."

- "I've noticed how diplomatically you handle the turf skirmishes around here. The company is creating an Internal Public Relations Committee and I'd like to suggest that you be on it."

- "Your ongoing research and recommendations for improving production have been outstanding. A Best Practices Committee is forming to study company-wide processes and related processes in similar companies. You would be an asset. May I submit your name?"

- "I've been asked to represent the company on a statewide Supplier Diversity Council. I'd like you to attend with me and serve as my alternate."

- "Our company Web site is starting a section, Kudos of the Month. I've submitted your recent turnaround project for inclusion."
- "Our department is responsible for the fiscal report at the quarterly meeting. I'd like you to work with me on my presentation and attend the next meeting with me. Eventually, I'd like you to take over."
- "When you draft the information for the press release about our company's participation in the charity event, remember to include your role. It was critical."
- "So many in our department have contributed creative ideas to the strategic planning process that we've been acknowledged in the company newsletter. Thank you all!"
- "So many customers comment regularly about how gracious and helpful you are that I've submitted your name and accomplishments for Employee of the Month. Good luck!"

The Motivational Mindset

- When people go above and beyond or their work on a particular job brings in a substantial amount of money for the company, share the wealth with a bonus.

- Bonuses show appreciation, create a sense of buy-in to the company's success, and inspire higher levels of work and dedication in the future.

- People expect holiday bonuses and those who say "bah humbug" will forever be known as Scrooge. Whatever your faith, whatever you feel personally about holidays, commercialization, or religion, you live and work in a culture where this is a time for giving. See what is reasonable within your budget and join in the joys of holiday giving.

- While cash is a great motivator, products and experiences are long-lasting and long-remembered, making them more lasting ways of feeling the company's appreciation and generosity.

- Companies specializing in incentive programs offer every solution from scratch-off cards with a variety of possible perks to comprehensive online points systems, including specialized catalogues and phone support.

- A points system allows employees to enjoy immediate rewards or earn bigger rewards over time. You might let employees choose from among a variety of rewards: golf, hot air balloon ride, cruises, show tickets, restaurant gift certificates, spa packages, or gift cards from leading retailers.

➡

- Computer-based incentive programs can track and record performance markers and points earned.
- Your company logo is not always appropriate on employee incentives and rewards. Items without logos may feel more like gifts and less like advertising.
- Encourage growth and foster skills that will allow you to promote from within the company. Tuition reimbursement may be applicable to college courses, degrees, external seminars, or online courses. Investing in employees promotes a high return on investment.

Motivational Phrases

- "Thank you for your hard work and dedication. Your input made the difference."
- "Because you went so far above and beyond the call of duty, you deserve to share in the wealth of this latest success. Thank you."
- "It was a great year! Thank you for all of your hard work."
- "Our company management wants everyone to understand the incentive program so you will be sure to enjoy the rewards. Human Resources e-mailed the promotions site and logon information to each of you with an explanation of ways to obtain points. I know we have a department of winners. I'd like you to be rewarded."
- "If you have any questions regarding the new incentive program, please call extension 208. I want everyone to understand the system so you will be able to enjoy the rewards of your hard work."
- "Congratulations, Jack! I signed onto the system and saw the number of points you've accumulated this month. Great work! Do you know what reward you'll choose?"

- "Brian, you will receive a cash bonus at our customer care meeting this month. Customer comments, supervisor observations, and coworker comments show that your caring dedication keeps customers returning and makes coworkers appreciative."
- "Ricardo, your saving that contract that everyone else gave up on was masterful. You will find a well-earned bonus in your paycheck."
- "I'm delighted that you want to move up to a paralegal position. Of course, tuition reimbursement is available."
- "I understand that you're interested in earning a degree. Let's discuss what tuition reimbursement options are available to you."
- "We cannot provide full tuition reimbursement, but we can help you in other ways. For example, every employee has a maximum education allowance and we can work out flexible scheduling while you're in school."
- "While your support services are outstanding and I'd hate to lose you, your math skills make you a natural for the accounting department. Would you like to take some courses to build your confidence in that area?"
- "Having that degree would certainly put you in a better position for promotion and I believe you would be an asset at that level. Would you be interested in discussing a tuition reimbursement program?"

Contests and Competitions

The Motivational Mindset

- Contests may be centered around sales numbers, customer service ratings, or any other measurable result you want to inspire.

- Beware of running a contest that defeats its own purpose. A sales contest that inspires pushy tactics in an atmosphere where a soft sell is most appropriate may inspire your customers to go elsewhere.

- Contests and competitions, if promoted in good spirit, can be motivational, but do not promote a cutthroat atmosphere; ensure that everyone has a fair chance.

- Establish and reinforce customer care standards. Then reward those who surpass your benchmark.

- Stipulate how many times in a row or in a year one person can win contests. If one salesperson is more seasoned than the others and has a long-established client base, others may not even come close enough to feel motivated to strive.

- Let the top performer know your appreciation publicly and privately, but have an honest conversation about trying to motivate those who are struggling to make the numbers. You may find this top performer willing to let go of or divide the perk.

- If you have people working in two leagues of success, offer two rewards. Offer the "Grand Prize" and "First Place" or "Salesperson of the Month" and "Star Seller."

- Devise a system that works, keeping in mind that motivation is the goal.

➡

Motivational Phrases

- "This is a friendly competition. Let's maintain the supportive environment that I know this team creates."
- "Each month the winner will receive a gift certificate to dinner at Chez Shishi. Rules are posted on the board and on the Web site. Good luck!"
- "This year's winner will receive _____."
- "Monthly top performers will receive _____."
- "Contest winners will be posted on the board/Web site."
- "Dave and Hanna decided to remove themselves from the monthly competition to give our next generation of salespeople a chance. As you know, with their long histories here and well-established client cases, they have been our two consistent winners. In addition to monthly contests, the first person to break Dave or Hanna's numbers will win an additional prize." (name the prize)
- "This month, we are looking for the best team. Choose a partner for the month. Any support you can provide each other will strengthen your team."
- "The shift that gets the most positive customer comment cards this month earns 25 bonus dollars for each employee."
- "We know that customers are more outspoken about negative than positive events. The company created a simple one-minute feedback card to ensure that more employees get the praise they deserve."
- "Whoever can list the most names of our regular patrons will win our *We Care* Award this month."
- "In addition to exceptional service, we honor outstanding acts. This year's honoree is Ricky."

- "Our *Teacher of the Year* Award goes to Shu Chou, whose personal, caring approach has helped countless underachlevers become successful college students."
- "Congratulations to Sashi, our Employee of the Month for the third time this year. Enjoy the day, Sashi."
- "Amos, you regularly win a Star Award for customer service. We're going to try something new—a partner award."

Gifts and Special Occasions

The Motivational Mindset

- After an especially taxing day, a small surprise waiting on the desk (even a candy bar or piece of fruit) in the morning with a note shows your appreciation. Any small, unexpected gift to say "Thanks" or "You're doing a great job!" can make someone's day.

- If you have a formal incentive program, do not give small gifts in lieu of points. Someone who is working toward a catalogue item will most likely wish you showed your gratitude in points (if it is up to your discretion).

- A hand-written note becomes even more caring as the custom fades.

- You might want to bring back a small gift from the islands for the person who picked up your slack or took care of a difficult problem while you were gone. Don't bring back gifts for some and not others with the exception of the person who took care of things for you when you were gone.

- If you choose to give a personal gift for birthdays or holidays (holiday gifts do not replace bonuses), choose something appropriate. A gag gift you would give to a friend might not be appropriate in the office. Giving a gift of a sexual nature constitutes sexual harassment.

- Birthdays are personal holidays and many companies include birthdays off in their packages. If you cannot give a birthday off, a lunchtime or short office celebration shows that you believe the person and the day are special.

- If someone is sensitive about a birthday, respect that person's wishes and privacy. You can still celebrate the people who enjoy it without making the ones who don't uncomfortable.

- Weddings, commitment ceremonies, births, and adoptions are important events and should be acknowledged and cheered. Depending on time, budget, policy, and often size of your staff, choose an appropriate level of celebration. Be sure to treat all like events the same.
- While acknowledging occasions makes people feel good and gives everyone a chance to celebrate, it's important not to burden people with gift-giving obligations, especially in a large department.

Motivational Phrases

- "Remember our policy of birthdays off. Put in for the day early and ensure coverage."
- "With our flexible scheduling it's hard to pull a group together for occasions. I'd like to take you out for a birthday lunch."
- "Go home a little early today and enjoy the rest of your birthday."
- "Let's take an afternoon break to celebrate Kim's engagement."
- "We all signed a card for Katelyn's birthday. Let's be sure to do the same for Larry's next week."
- At the end of an e-mail update, on a calendar or bulletin board: "Happy Birthday to Leona!"
- "You mentioned that you're sensitive about your birthday. We love to celebrate birthdays, but we don't want to make anyone uncomfortable. Are you okay with your birthday _____ (being announced, being celebrated over lunch, being celebrated on an afternoon break)?"

- "Congratulations on the adoption! I know how long you've been waiting. Several of us would like to celebrate with you over lunch."
- "I appreciate all the late nights you've put in lately. Enclosed is a gift certificate to the Brick Oven for you and your wife to make up for one of those dinners you missed at home. Enjoy!"
- "I found this beautiful handcrafted box on my vacation. I hope you like it. I was able to totally relax knowing you had things under control. Thank you."
- "I picked up a bag full of fun stuff from the trade show. Everyone, feel free to dig in and take something you like."
- "I won these specialty chocolates in a raffle. I'd like you to have them."
- "I hope these flowers brighten your morning. Thanks for working so late."
- "I know how you enjoy your mid-day chocolate charge. With all the pressure of the last few weeks, I thought you could use some Godiva. Enjoy it!"

Conclusion

We mentioned self-motivation in the beginning of this book and would like to close with a friendly reminder. Whether you are a supervisor or a business owner, it's a struggle to fire people up when your own fires are barely burning because of overwork, lack of sleep, or no time left in the day, week, or month to enjoy the rewards of your hard work. Many of the most put-upon employees are those who are *self*-employed or dynamic entrepreneurs.

As you focus on motivating employees, think, as well, about your own motivators. If you started this venture to afford a beautiful house you hardly see, a boat you never seem to get to, or vacations that your schedule won't allow, it may be time to think about your own perks and rewards. It's never easy finding time, but even small rewards keep us inspired: a hot bath at the end of a long day, quality family time, relaxing with friends, a weekend getaway without the laptop, or that class you've always wanted to take.

Airplane safety instructions tell us to put on our oxygen masks first so we can assist others. That theory helps with motivation, too. Be inspired and you cannot help but to inspire others.

About the Authors

Douglas Max is Managing Director, LR Communication Systems, Berkeley Heights, New Jersey. He is responsible for all marketing and sales, selection, training, and supervision of a staff of 15. His firm designs and conducts onsite seminars in writing and presentation skills. He was formerly moderator of TRDEV, the largest training-oriented e-mail discussion group on the Web. He has an MA in Industrial/Organizational Psychology from the University of Missouri at St. Louis. Visit his Web site at www.lrcom.com.

Robert Bacal is an accomplished consultant, book author, trainer, and public speaker. He is the author of *Performance Management* and *The Manager's Guide to Performance Reviews*, titles in the Briefcase Books series (McGraw-Hill). He is also author of *The Complete Idiot's Guide to Dealing with Difficult Employees* and *The Complete Idiot's Guide to Consulting* (Alpha Books). Under the imprint of Bacal & Associates, Bacal has also published the *Defusing Hostile Customers Workbook* and *Conflict Prevention in the Workplace*. Visit his popular Web site at www.work911.com.

About the Authors

Harriet Diamond recently sold Diamond Associates, Multi-Faceted Training and Consulting, a firm she created in 1985. She designed and delivered a full spectrum of programs and services that spanned all areas of oral and written communication, personal development, and management skills. Through those programs, she and her team have motivated and informed staff members, supervisors, and senior executives throughout a broad range of businesses and industries.

The author of six books, Harriet has addressed a variety of audiences on topics related to communication, management, and motivation and served as consultant to two work-related educational series. Her credits include a number of published magazine articles. She received three NJ Author's Awards and several honors, including The New Jersey Business Woman of the Year, Salute to Women Leaders Award, and a NJ Senate Citation for Outstanding Contributions to Adult Education. Harriet currently serves on the Advisory Board of *Enterprising Women*, a national magazine for established women business owners for which she writes regularly.

Linda Eve Diamond has been in the corporate training business for over a decade, writing, customizing, and designing training materials in all areas of communication. Additionally, she is a contributing author and editor to *Executive Writing*, *Writing the Easy Way*, and *Grammar in Plain English* and has written a number of technical manuals for several industries.

In addition to writing, Linda has been an adjunct professor of writing and reading at Middlesex County College in New Jersey. She has also given talks regarding her work in communication in her role as advisory board member for an organization that helps transition talented lower-income teens into successful college careers.

Linda's writing and design of print materials for Diamond Associates earned her an award from the New Jersey Association for Lifelong Learning, and her poetry, which has been published in literary journals, won a small press award.

Currently, she serves on the board of the International Listening Association (ILA) for which she is the editor of *The Listening Post*, an ILA newsletter publication.

The authors, a mother-and-daughter team, have collaborated on several writing projects. The two have shared a uniquely strong working relationship either due to or in spite of their family bond.

The Right Phrase for Every Situation…Every Time.

Perfect Phrases for Building Strong Teams
Perfect Phrases for Business Letters
Perfect Phrases for Business Proposals and Business Plans
Perfect Phrases for Business School Acceptance
Perfect Phrases for College Application Essays
Perfect Phrases for Cover Letters
Perfect Phrases for Customer Service
Perfect Phrases for Dealing with Difficult People
Perfect Phrases for Dealing with Difficult Situations at Work
Perfect Phrases for Documenting Employee Performance Problems
Perfect Phrases for Executive Presentations
Perfect Phrases for Landlords and Property Managers
Perfect Phrases for Law School Acceptance
Perfect Phrases for Lead Generation
Perfect Phrases for Managers and Supervisors
Perfect Phrases for Medical School Acceptance
Perfect Phrases for Meetings
Perfect Phrases for Motivating and Rewarding Employees
Perfect Phrases for Negotiating Salary & Job Offers
Perfect Phrases for Perfect Hiring
Perfect Phrases for the Perfect Interview
Perfect Phrases for Performance Reviews
Perfect Phrases for Real Estate Agents & Brokers
Perfect Phrases for Resumes
Perfect Phrases for Sales and Marketing Copy
Perfect Phrases for the Sales Call
Perfect Phrases for Setting Performance Goals
Perfect Phrases for Small Business Owners
Perfect Phrases for the TOEFL Speaking and Writing Sections
Perfect Phrases for Writing Grant Proposals
Perfect Phrases in American Sign Language for Beginners
Perfect Phrases in French for Confident Travel
Perfect Phrases in German for Confident Travel
Perfect Phrases in Italian for Confident Travel
Perfect Phrases in Mexican Spanish for Confident Travel
Perfect Phrases in Spanish for Construction
Perfect Phrases in Spanish for Gardening and Landscaping
Perfect Phrases in Spanish for Household Maintenance and Childcare
Perfect Phrases in Spanish for Restaurant and Hotel Industries

Visit mhprofessional.com/perfectphrases for a complete product listing.

Learn more. Do more.